Adventures of the O Ioway Indians ir France, and Belgium

(Vol. 2)

being Notes of Eight Years' Travels and Residence in Europe with his North American Indian Collection

George Catlin

Alpha Editions

This edition published in 2024

ISBN : 9789366385341

Design and Setting By
Alpha Editions
www.alphaedis.com
Email - info@alphaedis.com

As per information held with us this book is in Public Domain. This book is a reproduction of an important historical work. Alpha Editions uses the best technology to reproduce historical work in the same manner it was first published to preserve its original nature. Any marks or number seen are left intentionally to preserve its true form.

(VOL. 2)

CHAPTER XVII.

Arrival of fourteen Ioway Indians in London—Their lodgings in St. James's Street—The Author visits them—Their portraits and names—Mr. Melody, their conductor—Jeffrey Doraway, their interpreter—Landlady's alarm—Indians visit the Author's Collection in the Egyptian Hall—Arrangement to dance in the Collection—The Doctor (Medicine or Mystery man) on top of the Hall—Their first drive in a bus—Doctor's appearance outside—Indians' first impressions of London—Lascars sweeping the streets—Man with a big nose—The Doctor lost, and found on the housetop—Their first exhibition in Egyptian Hall—Eagle-dance—The Doctor's speech—Great amusement of the ladies—His description of the railroad from Liverpool to London—War-dance, great applause—The "jolly fat dame"—She presents a gold bracelet to the Doctor by mistake—Her admiration of the *Roman-nose*—War-whoop—Description of—Approaching-dance—Wolf-song, and description of—Great amusement of the audience—Shaking hands—Mistake with the bracelet.

The event which I spoke of at the close of my last chapter—the arrival of another party of Indians—was one which called upon me at once for a new enterprise, and I suddenly entered upon it, again deferring the time of my return to my native land.

The "fourteen Ioway Indians," as report had said, had arrived, and were in apartments at No. 7, St. James's Street, with their interpreter. This party was in charge of Mr. G. H. C. Melody, who had accompanied them from their own country, with a permission gained from the Secretary at War to bring them to Europe, which permission was granted in the following words:—

War Department, Washington City, Sept. 14th, 1843.

DEAR SIR,

In answer to your application relative to Mr. Melody's making a tour to Europe with a party of Ioway Indians, as well as to a similar one on his behalf from the Rev. Wm. P. Cochran, of Marian County, Missouri, I beg leave to say, that it has not been usual to grant any permissions of the kind, and the verbal instructions to the Agents, Superintendents, &c. have been against permitting such tours, for the reason, I presume, that the persons having them in charge are usually men who merely wish to make money out of them by exhibitions, without taking any care of their habits or morals, or inducing them to profit by what they see and hear upon their route.

In the present case, however, I do not think that the evils usually to be apprehended will occur, from the character of Mr. Melody, and the mode in which the Indians are proposed to be selected. This I understand is to be done by the Chief, White Cloud, with the full assent of the individuals thus selected, and their continuance on the tour to be their own act.

Under all the circumstances, I suppose all the Department can do, is to allow Mr. Melody and the Chiefs of the tribe to do as they please, without imposing the usual or any prohibition.

I am, yours, very truly,
J. M. PORTER,
Secretary at War.

Vespasian Ellis, Esq.

Washington City, Sept. 1843.

DEAR SIR,

Under this letter you are authorised to make any arrangement with the Chief of the tribe of Indians that you and he may please to make; and the War Department agrees, in consideration of your well-known integrity of character, not to interfere with the arrangement which you and the Chief or the Indians may make.

Your obedient Servant,
VESPASIAN ELLIS.

Mr. Melody.

Mr. Melody called upon me immediately on his arrival in London, and I went with him to see his party, several of whom I at once recognized as I entered their rooms. On seeing me they all rose upon their feet and offered me their hands, saluting me by their accustomed word, "How! how! how! *Chip-pe-ho-la!*" and evidently were prepared for great pleasure on meeting me. *White Cloud*, the head chief of the tribe, was of the party, and also the war-chief *Neu-mon-ya* (the Walking Rain). These two chiefs, whose portraits were then hanging in my collection, had stood before me for their pictures several years previous in their own village, and also one of the warriors now present, whose name was *Wash-ka-mon-ya* (the Fast Dancer). These facts being known, one can easily imagine how anxious these good fellows had been, during a journey of 2000 miles from their country to New York, and then during their voyage across the ocean, to meet me in a foreign land, who had several years before shared the hospitality of their village, and, to their knowledge, had done so much to collect and perpetuate the history of their race. They had come also, as I soon learned, in the full expectation to dance in my collection, which they were now impatient to see.

This first interview was during the evening of their arrival, and was necessarily brief, that they might get their night's rest, and be prepared to visit my rooms in the morning. A few pipes were smoked out as we were all seated on the floor, in a "talk" upon the state of affairs in their country and incidents of their long and tedious journey, at the end of which they now required rest, and I left them.

By entering the city at night, they had created little excitement or alarm, except with the landlady and her servants, where they had been taken in. Their rooms had been engaged before their arrival, but the good woman "had no idea they were going to look so savage and wild; she was very much afraid that their red paint would destroy her beds," not yet knowing that they were to wash the paint all off before they retired to rest, and that then they were to spread their buffalo robes upon the floor and sleep by the side of, and under her beds, instead of getting into them. These facts, when they became known, amused her very much; and Mr. Melody's representations of the harmlessness and honesty of the Indians, put her at rest with respect to the safety of her person and her property about her house.

The objects of these being the same as those of the former party, of seeing the country and making money by their exhibitions, I entered into a similar arrangement with Mr. Melody, joining with my collection, conducting their exhibitions, and sharing the expenses and receipts of the same, on condition that such an arrangement should be agreeable to the Indians.

Their first night's rest in London being finished, they were all up at an early hour, full of curiosity to see what was around them; and their fourteen red heads out of their front windows soon raised a crowd and a novel excitement in St. James's. Every body knew that the "Indians had gone," and the conjectures amongst the crowd were various and curious as to this strange arrival. Some said it was "the wedding party returned;" others, more sagacious, discovered the difference in their appearance, and pronounced them "the real cannibals from New Zealand;" and others said "their heads were too red, and they could be nothing else than the real *red*-heads—the man-eaters—that they had read of somewhere, but had forgotten the place."

The morning papers, however, which are the keys for all such mysteries, soon solved the difficulty, but without diminishing the crowd, by the announcement that a party of fourteen Ioway Indians, from the base of the Rocky Mountains, had arrived during the night and taken up their lodgings in St. James's Street.

After taking their breakfasts and finishing their toilets, they stepped into carriages and paid their first visit to my collection, then open in the Egyptian Hall. Instead of yelling and shouting as the Ojibbeways did on first entering it, they all walked silently and slowly to the middle of the room, with their hands over their mouths, denoting surprise and silence. In this position, for some minutes (wrapped in their pictured robes, which were mostly drawn over their heads or up to their eyes), they stood and rolled their eyes about the room in all directions, taking a general survey of what was around them, before a word was spoken. There was an occasional "she-e" in a lengthened whisper, and nothing more for some time, when at length a gradual and almost imperceptible conversation commenced about portraits and things which they recognized around the room. They had been in a moment transferred into the midst of hundreds of their friends and their enemies, who were gazing at them from the walls—amongst wig-wams and thousands of Indian costumes and arms, and views of the prairies they live in—altogether opening to their view, and to be seen at a glance, what it would take them years to see in their own country. They met the portraits of their chiefs and other friends, upon the walls, and extended their hands towards them; and they gathered in groups in front of their enemies, whom the warriors had met in battle, and now recognized before them. They looked with great pleasure on a picture of their own village, and examined with the closest scrutiny the arms and weapons of their enemies. One may easily imagine how much there was in this collection to entertain these rude people, and how much to command their attachment to me, with whom they had already resolved to unite.

A council was held and the pipe lit under the Crow wig-wam, which was standing in the middle of my room, when Mr. Melody explained to the Indians that he had now got them safe across the ocean as he had promised, and into the midst of the greatest city in the world, where they would see many curious things, and make many good and valuable friends, if they conducted themselves properly, which he was confident they would do.

"You have met," said he, "your old friend *Chip-pe-ho-la*, whom you have talked so much about on the way; you are now in his wonderful collection, and he is by the side of you, and you will hear what he has to say." (*"How! how! how!"*)

I reminded the White-cloud of the time that I was in his village, and lived under his father's tent, where I had been kindly treated, and for which I should always feel grateful. That in meeting them here, I did not meet them as strangers, but as friends. (*"How! how! how!"*) That they had come a great way, and with a view to make something to carry home to their wives and little children; that Mr. Melody and I had entered into an arrangement by which I was in hopes that my efforts might aid in enabling them to do so. (*"How! how! how!"*) That I was willing to devote all my time, and do all that was in my power, but the continuation of my exertions would depend entirely upon their own conduct, and their efforts to gain respect, by aiding in every way they could, and keeping themselves entirely sober, and free from the use of spirituous liquors. (*"How! how! how!"*)

Mr. Melody here remarked that they had pledged their words to him and their Great Father (as the condition on which they were allowed to come), that they would drink no ardent spirits while absent, and that he was glad to say they had thus far kept their promise strictly. (*"How! how! how!"*)

I told them I was glad to hear this, and I had no doubt but they would keep their word with me on that point, for every thing depended on it. We were amongst a people who look upon drunkenness as low and beastly, and also as a crime; and as I had found that most white people were of opinion that all Indians were drunkards, if they would show by their conduct that such was not the case, they would gain many warm and kind friends wherever they went. (*"How! how! how!"*) I told them that the Ojibbeways whom I had had with me, and who had recently gone home, gave me a solemn promise when they arrived that they would keep entirely sober and use no spirituous liquors,—that they kept that promise awhile, but I had been grieved to hear that before they left the country they had taken up the wicked habit of drinking whiskey, and getting drunk, by which they had lost all the respect that white people had for them when they first came over. (A great laugh, and *"How! how! how!"*)

Neu-mon-ya (the war-chief) replied to me, that they were thankful that the Great Spirit had kept them safe across the ocean and allowed them to see me, and to smoke the pipe again with me, and to hear my wise counsel, which they had all determined to keep (*"How! how! how!"*). He said that they had been very foolish to learn to drink *"fire-water"* in their country, which was very destructive to them, and they had promised their Great Father, the President, that they would drink none of it whilst they were abroad. He said he hoped I would not judge them by the Ojibbeways who had been here, "for," said he, "they are all a set of drunkards and thieves, and always keep their promises just about as well as they kept them with you." (A laugh, and *"How! how! how!"*)[1]

This *talk*, which was short, was ended here, to the satisfaction of all parties, and the Indians were again amusing themselves around the room, leaving the wig-wam and further conversations to Mr. Melody, the interpreter, and myself. Mr. Melody, though a stranger to me, bearing the high recommendations contained in the letter of the Secretary at War, already published, at once had my confidence (which I am pleased to say his conduct has kept up) as an excellent and honest man.

Their interpreter, Jeffrey Doraway (a mulatto), and who had been one of the first to recognize and hail me when I entered their rooms, had been an old and attached acquaintance of mine while travelling in that country, and that acquaintance had several times been renewed in St. Louis, and New York, and other places where I had subsequently met him. He had been raised from childhood in the tribe, and the chiefs and all the party were very much attached to him, and his interest seemed to be wholly identified with that of the tribe. He was of a most forbearing and patient disposition, and of temperate habits, and as he was loved by the chiefs, had great influence with them, and control over the party.

I related to Mr. Melody and Jeffrey the difficulties that laid before us; the prejudices raised in the public, mind by the conduct of Mr. Rankin with his party of Ojibbeways, and the unfortunate season of the year at which they had arrived in London. That the middle of July was the very worst season in which to open an exhibition, and that it might be difficult to raise a second excitement sufficiently strong to pay the very heavy expenses we must incur; but that I had resolved to unite my whole efforts to theirs, to bring their party into notice; which formed so much more complete and just a representation of the modes and appearance of the wild Indians of America than the Ojibbeways had given.

Finishing our conversation here, we found the Indians adjusting their plumes, and their robes, and their weapons, preparing to step into their "omnibus and four," to take their first rapid glance at the great City of London, in "a drive," which was to pass them through some of its principal thoroughfares for their amusement. At this moment of excitement it was suddenly announced that one of the party (and a very essential one), the *"Doctor"* (or *medicine man*), was missing! Search was everywhere making for him, and when it was quite certain that he could not have passed into the street, Jeffrey inquired of the curator of the Hall if there was any passage that led out upon the roof? to which the curator replied, "Yes." "Well then," said Jeffrey, "we may be sure that he is there, for *it is 'a way that he has*:' he always is uneasy until he gets as high as he can go, and then he will stay there all night if you will let him alone." I went immediately to the roof, and found him standing on one corner of the parapet, overlooking Piccadilly,—wrapped in his buffalo robe, and still as a statue, while thousands were assembling in the streets to look at him, and to warn him of the danger they supposed him in.

The readers who have not had the pleasure of seeing this eccentric character, will scarcely be able to appreciate the oddity of this freak until they become better acquainted with the Doctor in the following pages. I invited him down from his elevated position, which he seemed reluctant to leave, and he joined his party, who passed into their carriage at the door. In this moment of confusion, of escaping from the crowd and closing the door, heads were counted, and the old Doctor was missing again. A moment's observation showed, however, that his *ascending* propensity had gained him a position over their heads, as he had seated himself by the side of the driver, with his buffalo robe wrapped around him, the long and glistening blade of his spear passing out from underneath it, near to his left ear, and his vermilioned face surmounted by a huge pair of buffalo horns, rising out of a crest of eagle's quills and ermine skins. Thus loaded, and at the crack of the whip, and amidst the yelling multitude that had gathered around them, did the fourteen Ioways dash into the streets, to open their eyes to the sights and scenes of the great metropolis.

An hour or so in the streets, in a pleasant day, enabled them to see a great deal that was unlike the green prairies where they lived; and the "old Doctor," wrapped in his robe, and ogling the pretty girls, and everything else that he saw that was amusing as he passed along, raised a new excitement in the streets, and gave an extensive notification that "the wedding party had actually got back," or that another party of *red skins* had arrived. They returned to their lodgings in great glee, and amused us at least for an hour with their "first impressions" of London; the *leading, striking* feature of which, and the one that seemed to afford them the greatest satisfaction, was the *quantity of fresh meat* that they saw in every street hanging up at the doors and windows—pigs, and calves, and sheep, and deer, and prairie hens, in such profusion that they thought "there would be little doubt of their getting as much fresh meat as they could eat." Besides this, they had seen many things that amused them, and others that excited their pity. They laughed much about the "black fellows with white eyes" who were carrying bags of coal, and "every one of them had got their hats on the wrong side before." They had seen many people who seemed to be very poor, and looked as if they were hungry: for they held out their hands to people passing by, as if they were asking for something to eat. "They had passed two *Indians*, with brooms in their hands, sweeping the dirt in the streets!"

This occurrence had excited their greatest anxieties to know "what Indians they could be, that would be willing to take a broom in their hands and sweep the dirt from under white men's feet, and then hold out their hands to white people for money to buy food to eat." They all agreed "that *Ioways* would not do it, that *Sioux* would not, that *Pawnees* would not;" and when they were just deciding that their enemies, the *Ojibbeways*, *might* be *slaves* enough to do it, and that these were possibly a part of the Ojibbeway party that had been flourishing in London, I explained the mystery to them, by informing them that their conjectures were wrong—that it was true they were Indians, but not from North America. I agreed with them that no North American Indian would use that mode of getting his living, but that there were Indians in different parts of the world, and that these were from the East Indies, a country many thousands of miles from here; that these people were Indians from that country, and were of a tribe called *Lascars*; that many of them were employed by the captains of English ships to help to navigate their vessels from that country to this; and that in London they often come to want, and are glad to sweep the streets and beg, as the means of living, instead of starving to death. It seemed still a mystery to them, but partly solved, and they made many further remarks among themselves about them. The good landlady at this moment announced to Mr. Melody and Jeffrey that the dinner for the Indians was ready, and in a moment all were seated save the Doctor; he was missing. "That old fool," said Jeffrey, "there's no doubt but he has found his way to the top of the house." I was conducted by one of the servants through several unoccupied rooms and dark passages, and at last through a narrow and almost impassable labyrinth that brought me out upon the roof. The "Doctor" was *there*; and, wrapped in his buffalo robe, with his red face and his buffalo horns, was standing like a *Zealand penguin*, and smiling upon the crowds of gazers who were gathering in the streets, and at the windows, and upon the house-tops, in the vicinity.

For the several days succeeding this, while the Indians were lying still, and resting from their long and tedious voyage, and I was announcing in the usual way their arrival, and the time of the commencement of their exhibitions, I held many curious and amusing conversations with them about things they had already seen, and scenes and events that were yet in anticipation and before them. These are subjects, however, that must be passed over for events that were before us, and fuller of interest and excitement.

They had much amusement at this time also, about a man they said they had seen, with a remarkably big nose, which they said looked like a large potato (or *wapsapinnakan*), and one of the women sitting near the door of the omnibus declared "that it was actually a *wapsapinnakan*, for she could distinctly see the little holes where the sprouts grow out." The bus, they said, had passed on rather too quick for all to have a fair look, but they believed they would at some future time meet him again, and take a good look at him.

The evening for their first appearance before the public having arrived, the Ioways were prepared in all their rouge and fine dresses, and made their *début* before a fashionable, but not a crowded audience. Their very appearance, as they entered the room, was so wild and classic, that it called forth applause from every part of the hall. The audience was composed chiefly of my friends, and others who had been familiar with the other group, and who were able to decide as to the comparative interest of the two parties; and it was proclaimed in every part of the room, that they were altogether more primitive in their appearance and modes, and decidedly a finer body of men. I had accompanied them on to the platform, and when they had got seated, and were lighting their pipe, I introduced them by stating, that in the exhibition of this party of Indians, I felt satisfied that I was bringing before the eyes of the audience the most just and complete illustration of the native looks and modes of the red men of the American wilderness, that had ever been seen on this side of the Atlantic; and that I should take great pleasure in introducing them and their modes, as they so satisfactorily illustrated and proved what I had been for several years labouring to show to English people, by my numerous paintings and Indian manufactures which I had collected, as well as by my notes of travel amongst these people, which I had recently published: That the *Ioway* was one of the remote tribes, yet adhering to all their native customs and native looks; and that this party, composed, as it was, of the two principal men of the tribe, and several of its most distinguished warriors, not only conveyed to the eyes of people in this country the most accurate account of primitive modes, but was calculated to excite the deepest interest, and to claim the respect of the community. That the position of this tribe being upon the great plains between the Missouri and the Rocky Mountains, 1000 miles farther west than the country from which the Ojibbeways came, their modes and personal appearance were very different, having as yet received no changes from the proximity of civilization: That I had visited this tribe several years before, during my travels in the Indian countries, and that I had there formed my first acquaintance with the two chiefs who were now here, and which acquaintance, from the hospitable manner in which they had welcomed me in their humble wig-wams, I now felt great pleasure in renewing: (*"Hear, hear," and applause.*)

That these facts being known, with others which would be incidentally given, I felt fully assured that they would meet with a kind reception in this country, and that the audience were prepared for the introduction I was now to make of them and their modes.[2] (*Great applause.*)

I then pointed out and explained to the audience, the characteristic differences between the appearance and modes of this party and the Ojibbeways, whom they had seen, and which will be obvious to the reader in the annexed illustration (*Plate No. 9*). The Ioways, like three other tribes only, in North America, all adhere to their national mode of shaving and ornamenting their heads. This is a very curious mode, and presents an appearance at once that distinguishes them from the Ojibbeways and other tribes, who cultivate the hair to the greatest length they possibly can, and pride themselves on its jet and glossy black. Every man in the Ioway tribe adheres to the mode of cutting all the hair as close as he can, excepting a small tuft which is left upon the crown, and being that part which the enemy takes for the scalp, is very properly denominated the *"scalp-lock."* He then rouges with vermilion the whole crown of his head (and oftentimes his whole face), and surmounts his *scalp-lock* by a beautiful crest, made of the hair of the deer's tail, dyed of vermilion red.

The chief man of this party, the "*White Cloud,*" the son of a distinguished chief of the same name, who died a few years since, was 35 years of age, and hereditary chief of the tribe. By several humane and noble acts, after he received his office of chief, he gained the admiration and friendship of the officers of the United States Government, as well as of his tribe, and had therefore been countenanced by the Government (as has been shown) in the enterprise of going abroad.

Neu-mon-ya (the Walking Rain), and war-chief of the tribe, was 54 years of age, and nearly six feet and a half in height. A noble specimen of the manly grace and dignity that belong to the American wilderness, and also a man who had distinguished himself in the wars that he had led against his enemies.

Se-non-ti-yah (the Blistered Feet), the *Medicine* or *Mystery Man*, was a highly important personage of the party, and held a high and enviable position, as physician, soothsayer, and magician, in his tribe.

These personages are found in every tribe, and so much control have they over the superstitious minds of their people, that their influence and power in the tribe often transcend those of the chief. In all councils of war and peace they have a seat by the chiefs, and are as regularly consulted by the chiefs, as soothsayers were consulted in ancient days, and equal deference and respect is paid to their advice or opinions, rendering them *oracles* of the tribe in which they live.

Nº. 9.

A good illustration of this was given by this magician, while on their voyage to this country, a few weeks since, when near the land, off the English coast. The packet ship in which the Indians were passengers, was becalmed for several days, much to the annoyance of the Indians and numerous other passengers, when it was decided, by the Indian chief, that they must call upon the *Medicine Man*, to try the efficacy of his magical powers in the endeavour to raise a wind. For this purpose he very gradually went to work, with all due ceremony, according to the modes of the country, and after the usual ceremony of a mystery feast, and various invocations to the *spirit* of the *wind* and the *ocean*, both were conciliated by the sacrifice of many plugs of tobacco thrown into the sea; and in a little time the wind began to blow, the sails were filled, and the vessel soon wafted into port, to the amusement of the passengers, and much to the gratification of the Indians, who all believed, and ever will, that the vessel was set in motion by the potency of the Doctor's mysterious and supernatural powers.

Of the *Warriors*, *Shon-ta-yi-ga* (the Little Wolf) and *Nu-ho-mun-ya* (called the "Roman Nose") were the most distinguished, and I believe the world will agree with me, that it would be an act of injustice on my part, should I allow the poor fellows to carry through this country, without giving them publication, the subjoined documents,[3] by which it will be seen that they saved, in a humane manner, and worthy of warriors of better *caste*, the lives of ten unarmed and unoffending enemies.

Okee-wee-me (the wife of the Little Wolf) is the mother of the infant pappoose, called Corsair. This child is little more than three months old, and slung in the cradle on the mother's back, according to the general custom practised by all the American tribes, and furnishes one of the most interesting illustrations in the group.

All tribes in America practise the same mode of carrying their infant children for several months from their birth upon a flat board resting upon the mother's back, as she walks or rides, suspended by a broad strap passing over her forehead, or across her breast. By this mode of carrying their children, the mothers, who have to perform all the slavish duties of the camp, having the free use of their hands and arms, are enabled to work most of the time, and, in fact, exercise and labour nearly as well as if their children were not attached to their persons. These cradles are often, as in the present instance, most elaborately embroidered with porcupine quills, and loaded with little trinkets hanging within the child's reach, that it may amuse itself with them as it rides, with its face looking *from* that of its mother, while she is at work, so as not to draw upon her valuable time.

This rigid, and seemingly cruel mode of binding the child with its back to a straight board, seems to be one peculiarly adapted to Indian life, and, I believe, promotes straight limbs, sound lungs, and long life.

I having thus introduced the party to their first audience in England, and left other remarks upon them for their proper place, the Indians laid by their pipe, and commenced their evening's amusements by giving first their favourite, the *Eagle-Dance*. The *Drum* (and their "*Eagle-Whistles*," with which they imitate the chattering of the soaring eagle), with their voices, formed the music for this truly picturesque and exciting dance. At their first pause in the dance, the audience, who had witnessed nothing of this description in the amusements of the Ojibbeways, being excited to the highest degree, encouraged the strangers with rounds of applause. The song in this dance is addressed to their favourite bird the war-eagle, and each dancer carries a fan made of the eagle's tail, in his left hand, as he dances, and by his attitudes endeavours to imitate the motions of the soaring eagle. This, being a part of the war-dance, is a *boasting* dance; and at the end of each strain in the song some one of the warriors steps forth and, in an excited speech, describes the time and the manner in which he has slain his enemy in battle, or captured his horses, or performed some other achievement in war. After this the dance proceeds with increased spirit; and several in succession having thus excited their fellow-dancers, an indescribable thrill and effect are often produced before they get through.

In the midst of the noise and excitement of this dance the Doctor (or *mystery-man*) jumped forward to the edge of the platform, and making the most tremendous flourish of his spear which he held in his right hand, and his shield extended upon his left arm, recited the military deeds of his life—how he had slain his enemies in battle and taken their scalps; and with singular effect fitting the action to the word, acting them out as he described.

The thrilling effect produced by the Doctor's boast brought him showers of applause, which touched his vanity, and at the close of the dance he imagined all eyes in admiration fixed upon him, and no doubt felt himself called upon for the following brief but significant speech which he delivered, waving his right hand over the heads of the audience from the front of the platform where he stood, and from which he dropped his most humble and obsequious smiles upon the groups of ladies who were near him, and applauding at the end of every sentence:—

> "My Friends,—It makes me very happy to see so many smiling faces about me, for when people smile and laugh, I know they are not angry—"

Jeffrey, the *Interpreter*, now made *his* début; the Doctor had beckoned him up by his side to interpret his speech to the audience, and when he explained the above sentence, the "Doctor" received a round of applause, and particularly from the ladies, who could not but be pleased with the simple vanity of the speaker and the self-complacent smiles which he always lavished upon the fair sex who were around him. The Doctor, though advanced to the sound and efficient age of 45, had never taken to him a wife; and, like too many of his fraternity, had always lived upon the excessive vanity of believing that he was the *beau idéal* of his tribe, and admired too much by all to be a legitimate subject of exclusive appropriation to any particular one. And more than this (which may not have quite fallen to the happy lot of any of his brother bachelors in the polished world), from the sort of *charitable* habit he had of spreading his glowing smiles upon the crowds about him, one would almost be of opinion that, in his own community, under the aids and charms of his profession, he in a measure had existed upon the belief that his smiles were food and clothing for the crowds upon whom they were bestowed.

The Doctor yet stood, the concentration of smiles and anxious looks from every part of the room, and at length proceeded (*Plate No. 10*):—

"My Friends,—I see the ladies are pleased, and this pleases me—because I know, that if they are pleased, they will please the men."

It was quite impossible for the Doctor to proceed further until he had bowed to the burst of laughter and applause from all parts of the room, and particularly from the ladies. This several times ceased, but suddenly burst out again, and too quick for him to resume. He had evidently made a "hit" with the ladies, and he was braced strong in courage to make the best use of it, although the rest of his comrades, who were seated and passing the pipe around, were laughing at him and endeavouring to embarrass him. One of the party, by the name of *Wash-ka-mon-ya*, and a good deal of the *braggart*, had the cruelty to say to him, "You old fool, you had better sit down, the white squaws are all laughing at you." To which the Doctor, deliberately turning round, sarcastically replied, "You badger, go into your burrow backwards: I have said more in two sentences than you ever said in your life." He then turned round, and calling Jeffrey nearer to his side, proceeded—

"My Friends,"—[here was a burst of irresistible laughter from the ladies, which the drollness of his expression and his figure excited at the moment, and in which, having met it all in good humour, he was taking a part, but continued]—

"My Friends,—I believe that our dance was pleasing to you, and that our noise has not given you offence. (*Applause.*)

"My Friends,—We live a great way from here, and we have come over a great salt lake to see you, and to offer you our hands. The Great Spirit has been kind to us; we know that our lives are always in his hands, and we thank him for keeping us safe. (*How, how, how!* from the Indians, and applause, with *Hear, hear, hear!*)

"My Friends,—We have met our friend *Chip-pe-ho-la* here, and seen the medicine things that he has done, and which are hanging all around us, and this makes us happy. We have found our chiefs' faces on the walls, which the Great Spirit has allowed him to bring over safe, and we are thankful for this. (*How, how, how!*)

"My Friends,—This is a large village, and it has many fine wig-wams; we rode in a large carriage the other day and saw it all. (*A laugh,* and *Hear!*) We had heard a great deal about the people on this side of the water, but we did not think they were so rich; we believe that the *Saganoshes* know a great deal. (*How, how, how!*)

"My Friends,—We have come on your great *medicine road,* and it pleased us very much. When we landed from our ship, we came on your *medicine road,* and were told it would be very fine; but when we started, we were all very much alarmed; we went in the dark; we all went right down into the ground, under a high mountain; we had heard that a part of the white people go into the ground when they die, and some of them into the fire; we saw some fire; there was a great hissing, and a great deal of smoke coming out of this place,[4] and we could not get out; we were then somewhat afraid, my friends and I began to sing our '*death-song;*' but when we had commenced, our hearts were full of joy, we came out again in the open air, and the country was very beautiful around us. (*How, how, how!* and great applause.)

"My Friends,—After we got out from under the ground, we were much pleased all the way on the *medicine road* until we got to this village. There were many things to please us, and I think that before the trees were cut down, it was a very beautiful country. My friends, we think there were Indians and buffalos in this country then. (*How, how, how!*)

"My Friends,—We think we saw some of the *k'nick k'neck*[5] as we came along the *medicine road,* and some *quash-e-gon-eh-co,*[6] but we came so fast that we were not certain; we should like to know. My Friends, this is all I have to say." (*How, how, how!* and great applause.)

Nº. 10.

The Doctor's speech, which would have been terminated much sooner if he had been allowed to proceed unmolested, had a very pleasing effect upon the audience, and had allowed abundant time for the rest of the party to prepare for the next *dance*.

I now announced to the audience that the Indians were about to give the *Warrior's-dance*, as performed by their tribe. I explained the meaning of it, the circumstances under which it was given, and the respects in which it differed from the War-dance as given by the Ojibbeways. After which they were all upon their feet, and, with weapons in hand, proceeded to give it the most exciting, and even *alarming* effect.

They received great applause at the end of this dance, and also a number of presents, which were handed and thrown on to the platform. This created much excitement and good cheer among them, and I was not a little surprised, nor was I less amused and gratified, to discover at this moment, that the (so-called) "*jolly fat dame*," of Ojibbeway notoriety, was along side of the platform, at her old stand, and, in her wonted liberality, the first one to start the fashion of making the poor fellows occasional presents. I regretted, however, that I should have been the ignorant cause of her bestowing her first present upon a person for whom she did not intend it. The finest-looking man of the party, and one of the youngest, was *No-ho-mun-ya* (the *Roman-nose*), upon whom it seems this good lady's admiration had been fixed during the evening, notwithstanding the smiles that had been lavished by the

Doctor, and the eloquence which he had poured forth in his boastings and speeches.

The elegant limbs, Herculean frame, and graceful and terrible movements of this six foot and a-half young man, as she had gazed upon him in this last dance, had softened her heart into all its former kindness and liberality, and she had at this moment, when I first discovered her, unclasped a beautiful bracelet from one of her arms, and was just reaching over the platform to say to me as she did, "Wonderful! wonderful! Mr. Catlin; I think it one of the wonders of the world! Will you hand this to that splendid fellow, with my compliments—give him my compliments, will you—it's a bracelet for his arm (Cadotte has got the other, you know). Oh! but he is a splendid fellow—give him my compliments, will you. I think them a much finer party than the other—oh, far superior! I never saw the like; hand it to him, will you, and if he can't put it on, poor fellow, I will show him how."

All this had been run over so rapidly that I scarcely could recollect what she said, for several were speaking to me at the same time; and at that unfortunate moment it was that I committed the error, for which I was almost ready to break my own back when I found it out. I presented it by mistake to the Doctor, who, I supposed, had of course been winning all the laurels of the evening, and with them the good lady's compliments, which it would have been quite awkward on her part and mine also to have unpresented. The Doctor raised up the bracelet as high as he could reach, and made the house ring and almost tremble with the war-whoop, which he several times repeated.[7] What could be done? *She* was too gallant, and I did not yet know the mistake. The Doctor happened to know how to put it on—it fitted to his copper-coloured arm above his elbow—and his true politeness led him to bow and to smile a thousand thanks upon the fair dame as he bent over her from the platform.

The *Approaching-dance*[8] was now given, in which the Doctor took the lead in great glee, and of course with great effect. He tilted off with a light and elastic step, as he was "following the track of his enemy," and when he raised his brawny arm to beckon on his warriors to the attack, he took great pains to display the glistening trinket which he had accepted with such heartfelt satisfaction.

This dance finished, they all sat down upon the platform and passed the pipe around, whilst I was further explaining upon their appearance and modes, and the dance which they had just given. I asked them what amusement they proposed next, and they announced to me, that as the Doctor was taking all the honours and all the glory to himself on that night (and of whom they all seemed extremely jealous), they had decided that he should finish the amusements of the evening by singing the "*Wolf-song.*" He was so conscious of having engrossed the principal attention of the house that he at once complied with their request, though at other times it required a great effort to get him to sing it. I had not myself heard this song, which seemed, from their preparations, to promise some amusement, and which Jeffrey told me belonged exclusively to the Doctor, he having composed it. The Doctor was ready to commence, and wrapping his robe around him, having his right arm out, he shook a rattle (she-she-quoin) in his right hand, as he tilted about the platform, singing alone; at the end of a sentence he commenced to bark and howl like a wolf, when another jumped upon his feet and ran to him, and another, and another, and joined in the chorus, with their heads turned up like wolves when they are howling. He then sang another strain as he moved about the platform again, all following him, singing, and ready to join in the deafening chorus. This strange and comic song drew roars of laughter, and many rounds of applause for the Doctor, and left him, sure enough, the lion of the evening.[9]

After he had finished his song, he traversed the platform a few times, lavishing his self-complacent smiles upon the ladies around the room, and then desired me to say to the audience, that on the next evening they were going to give the *Pipe of Peace-dance, and the Scalp-dance*, which he wished all the ladies to see, and that *now* the chiefs and himself were ready to shake hands with all the people in the room.

This of course brought a rush of visitors to the platform, anxious to welcome the new comers by giving them their hands. A general shake of the hands took place, and a conversation that occupied half an hour or more, and much to the satisfaction of the Indians as well as to those who came to see them.

Much curiosity was kept up yet about the Doctor. The impression that his countenance and his wit had made upon the women had secured a knot of them about him, from whom it was difficult to disengage him: some complained that they were sick, and desired him to feel their pulse; he did so, and being asked as to the nature of their disease, he replied that "they were in love,"—and as to the remedy, he said, "Get husbands, and in a day and a night you will be well." All this they could have got from other quarters, but coming from an Indian, whose naked shoulders were glistening around the room, it seemed to come with the freshness and zest of something entirely new, and created much merriment.

The amusements of their first night being over, the Indians were withdrawn from the room, and the audience soon dispersed. Daniel, as usual, had been at his post, and his report of a few moments' chat with the "jolly fat dame" gave me the first intelligence of the awful error I had committed in giving her bracelet to the Doctor instead of the Roman-nose, for whom she had intended it. She had said to him, however, that "it was no matter, and the error must not be corrected; she would bring one on the following evening for the Roman-nose, and begged that the Doctor might never be apprised of the mistake which had resulted to his benefit." "They are a splendid set of men, Daniel—far superior to the others. It is the greatest treat I ever had—I shall be here every night. You'll think by and by that I am a pretty good customer; ha, Daniel? That *Roman-nose* is a magnificent fellow—he's got no wife, has he, Daniel?" "No, Madam, he is the youngest man of the party." "He is an *elegant* fellow—but then his *skin*, Daniel. Their skins are not so fine as the others—they are *too* black, or red, or what you call it; but Cadotte! what a beautiful colour he was, ha? But I dare say a little *washing* and living in a city would bring them nearly white? These people love Mr. Catlin—he's a curious man—he's a *wonderful* man; these are his old acquaintance, he has boarded with them; how they love him, don't they? Ah, well, good night, good night." She was the last of the visitors going out of the door, and did not know that I was so close behind her.

CHAPTER XVIII.

Character of the Doctor (*mystery* or *medicine man*)—An omnibus drive—The Doctor's admiration of the "jolly fat dame"—Jealousy—War-dress and war-paint of the *Roman-nose*—His appearance—He leads the War-dance—The Welcome-dance, and Bear-dance—Description of—Pipe-of-peace (or Calumet) dance, and Scalp-dance—*Chip-pe-ho-la (the Author)*—Speech of the War-chief—The "jolly fat dame"—She presents a gold bracelet to *Roman-nose*—Jealousy and distress of the Doctor—She converses with Daniel—Two reverend gentlemen converse with the Indians about religion—Reply of White-cloud and War-chief—Questions by the reverend gentlemen—Answers by the War-chief—Indians invited to breakfast with Mr. Disraeli, M.P., Park Lane—Indians' toilette and dress—The Doctor and Jim (Wash-ka-mon-ya) fasting for the occasion.

On paying a visit to the lodgings of the Indians, after they had returned from the exhibition, I found them in a merry mood, cracking their jokes upon the Doctor, who had put himself forward in so conspicuous a manner, to the great amusement of the ladies. During the exhibition, it would have appeared, from his looks and his actions, that he was to be perfectly happy for a twelvemonth at least; but he now appeared sad and dejected as he listened to their jokes, and turned his splendid bracelet around with his fingers. Several of the women had received brooches and other trinkets of value, and all had been highly pleased.

It seemed that the War-chief was looked upon by the rest of the party as their orator; and, on an occasion like that which had just passed by, it was usual, and was expected, that he would have arisen and made a speech; and it was as little expected that the Doctor, who, they said, was a very diffident and backward man on such occasions, should have had so much, or anything to say. But the Doctor was a man of talent and wit, and with an exorbitant share of vanity and self-conceit, which were excited to that degree by the irresistible smiles of the ladies, that he was nerved with courage and ambition to act the part that he did through the evening. Under the momentary excitement of his feelings, he had, to be sure, but innocently, stepped a little out of his sphere, and in the way of the chiefs, which had somewhat annoyed them at the time, but of which they were now rather making merry than otherwise. The Doctor was a good-natured and harmless man, and entirely the creature of impulse. He was always polite, though not always in good humour. The two leading traits in his character, one or the other of which was always conspicuous, were extreme buoyancy of spirits and good humour, when he smiled upon everybody and everything around him, or silent dejection, which bade defiance to every social effort. In either of these moods he had the peculiarities of being entirely harmless, and of remaining in them but a very short time; and *between* these moods, he was like a *spirit level*, exceedingly difficult to hold at a balance.

The jokes that had been concentrated on the Doctor had been rather pleasant and amusing than otherwise, though there had been so many of them from the chiefs, from the warriors, from the squaws, and also from Mr. Melody, and Jeffrey and Daniel, all of whom were laughing at his expense, that I found him, and left him, sitting in one corner of the room, with his robe wrapped around him, in stoic silence, occasionally casting his eyes on his gold bracelet, and then upon the smoking beef-steaks and coffee which were on the table for their suppers, and of which he partook not.

Whilst the rest were at the table, he silently spread his robe upon the floor, and wrapped himself in it. In the morning he washed, as usual, at the dawning of day, spent an hour or so in solitary meditation on the roof of the house, and afterwards joined with a pleasant face at the breakfast table, and through the amusements of the day and evening.

Mr. Melody had, with my cordial approbation, employed an omnibus with four horses, to drive them an hour each day for the benefit of their health; and, at the same time, to amuse and instruct them, by showing them everything that they could see in the civilized world to their advantage. The Doctor joined, in good spirits, in the "drive" of that day; and, as on the day before, was wrapped in his buffalo, and seated by the side of the driver, with the polished blade of his lance glistening above his head, as many Londoners who read this will forcibly recollect.

From their drive, in which they had seen many strange things, they returned in good spirits, and received in their chambers a private party of ladies and gentlemen, my esteemed friends, and several editors of the leading journals of London. A long and very interesting conversation was held with them on several subjects, and the clear and argumentative manner in which their replies were made, and the truly striking and primitive modes in which they were found, at once engaged the profound attention of all, and procured for them, besides some handsome presents at the time, the strongest recommendations from the editors of the press, as subjects of far greater interest than the party of Ojibbeways, whom they had before seen. Amongst these visiters they recognized with great pleasure, and shook hands with, my kind friend Dr. Thomas Hodgkin, at whose hospitable board they had, a few days before, with the author, partaken of an excellent dinner prepared for them. This was the first gentleman's table they were invited to in the kingdom, and probably the first place where they ever tried the use of the knife and fork in the English style.

Dr. Hodgkin being of the Society of Friends, they received much kind and friendly advice from him, which they never forgot; and from the unusual shape of his dress, they called him afterwards (not being able to recollect his name) *Tchon-a-wap-pa* (the straight coat).

At night they were in the Hall again, and around them, amidst a greatly increased audience, had the pleasure of beholding nearly all the faces they had seen the night before; and the Doctor, in particular, of seeing the smiling ladies whom he had invited to see the *scalp-dance* and the *scalps*, and, to his more identical satisfaction, of beholding, at the end of the platform where he had taken pains to spread his robe and seat himself, the fair dame of *gushing* charms, to whom he was occasionally gently turning his head on one side and smiling, as he presented to her view his copper-coloured arm, encompassed with the golden bracelet.

This kind lady's goodness was such that she could not but respond to the bows and the smiles of the Doctor, though (within herself) she felt a little annoyed at the position which he had taken, so immediately between her place, which the crowd prevented her from changing, and that of the splendid "*Roman Nose*," who was now much more an object of admiration than he had been the night before, and more peremptorily called for all her attention. He had been selected to lead in the *scalp-dance* which was to be given that night; and for this purpose, in pursuance of the custom of the country, he had left off his shirt and all his dress save his beautifully garnished leggings and mocassins, and his many-coloured sash and kilt of eagle's quills and ermine around his waist. His head was vermilioned red, and dressed with his helmet-like red crest, and surmounted with a white and a red eagle's quill, denoting his readiness for peace or for war. His shoulders and his arms were curiously streaked with red paint, and on his right and his left breast were the impresses, in black paint, of two hands, denoting the two victims he had struck, and whose scalps he then held attached to his painted tomahawk, which he was to wield in triumph as he had in the *scalp-dance*. Thus arrayed and ornamented, he appeared in his "war dress," as it is termed; and as he arose from his seat upon the platform, and drew his painted shield and quiver from his back, shouts of applause rung from every part of the hall, and, of course, trepidation increased in the veins of the fair dame, whose elbows were resting on the edge of the platform, while she was in rapture gazing upon him, and but partly concealing at times a beautiful trinket, the sparkling of which the sharp eyes of the Doctor had seen, as she endeavoured to conceal it in her right hand.

The Doctor could not speak to this fair lady except with his eyes, with the softest expressions of which he lost no time or opportunity; and (for several combined reasons, no doubt) he seemed quite unambitious to leave his seat to "*saw the air*," and strike for a repetition of the applause he had gained the night before.

Unfortunately in some respects, and as fortunately no doubt in others, the splendid "*Roman Nose*" held his position at the farther end of the platform during the greater part of the evening; and the Doctor, for the several reasons already imagined, remained in the close vicinity of the fair dame, whose over-timidity, he feared, held her in an unnecessary and painful suspense.

In this position of things and of parties, the amusements allotted for the evening had commenced, and were progressing, amidst the roars of applause that were ready at the close of each dance. They commenced by giving the *"Welcome Dance" and song*[10] peculiar to their tribe. The sentiment of this being explained by me, gave great pleasure to the audience, and prepared them for the dances and amusements which were to follow.

They next announced the *"Bear Dance"* and amused the audience very much in its execution. This curious dance is given when a party are preparing to hunt the *black bear*, for its delicious food; or to contend with the more ferocious and dangerous *"grizly bear*," when a similar appeal is made to the *bear-spirit*, and with similar results, (*i.e.*) all hands having strictly attended to the important and necessary form of conciliating in this way the good will and protection of the peculiar *spirit* presiding over the destinies of those animals, they start off upon their hunt with a confidence and prospect of success which they could not otherwise have ventured to count upon. In this grotesque and amusing mode, each dancer imitates with his hands, alternately, the habits of the bear when running, and when sitting up, upon its feet, its paws suspended from its breast.

It was customary with them to be seated a few minutes after each dance, and to pass around the pipe; and in the interval they were thus filling up after this dance, the Indians, as well as the audience, were all surprised at the appearance of a large square parcel handed in, and on to the platform, by a servant in livery, as a present to the Indians from his anonymous mistress. "Curiosity was on tip-toe" to know what so bulky a parcel contained; and when it was opened, it was found to contain 14 beautifully bound Bibles—the number just equal to the number of Indians of the party; and a very kind letter addressed to them, and which was read, exhorting them to change the tenor of their lives, to learn to read, and to profit by the gifts enclosed to them.

The Bibles being distributed amongst them, the War-chief arose, and in the most respectful and appropriate manner returned his thanks for the liberal present and the kind wishes of the lady who gave them; he said he was sorry he did not know which lady to thank, but by thanking all in the room, he considered he was taking the surest way of conveying his thanks to her.

After this, the *ne plus ultra* (as the Doctor would undoubtedly call it), the frightful "*Scalp Dance*,"[11] was announced. All parties, the modest *squaws* (of whom they had four with them) as well as the men, were arranging their dresses and implements to take part in it. The drums struck up, and the "splendid *Roman Nose*" led off, waving his two scalps on the point of a lance, until he was once around the circle, when they were placed in the hands of a squaw to carry, whilst he wielded his tomahawk and scalping-knife, and showed the manner in which his unfortunate enemies had fallen before him. This was probably the first time that the Scalp Dance, in its original and *classic* form, was ever seen in the city of London, and embellished by the presence of real and *genuine scalps*.

This exciting scene, with its associations, had like to have been too much for the nerves and tastes of London people; but having evidently assembled here for the pleasure of receiving shocks and trying their nerves, they soon seemed reconciled, and all looked on with amazement and pleasure, whilst they were sure for once in their lives, at least, that they were drawing information from its true and native source. This dance was long and tedious, but when it was finished, it was followed by a deafening round of applause, not of approbation of the shocking and disgusting custom, but of the earnest and simple manner in which these ignorant and thoughtless people were endeavouring to instruct and to amuse the enlightened world by a strict and emphatic illustration of one of the barbarous, but valued, modes of their country.

The subject and mode of *scalping*, and of thus celebrating their victories, so little understood in the enlightened world, afforded me an interesting theme for remarks at this time; and when the Indians were again seated and "*taking a smoke*," I took the occasion of this complete illustration to explain it in all its parts and meanings, for which, when I had done, I received five times as much applause as I deserved for doing it.

The Pipe of Peace (or Calumet) *Dance*[12] was the next announced; and was danced with great spirit, and gained them much applause. At the close of this, their favourite dance, it became peculiarly the privilege of the War-chief to make his boast, as the dance is given only at the conclusion of a treaty of peace between hostile tribes, and at which treaty he is supposed to preside. For this purpose he rose, and straightening up his tall and veteran figure, with his buffalo robe thrown over his shoulder and around him, with his right arm extended over the heads of his fellow warriors, made a most animated speech to them for several minutes (with his back turned towards the audience), reminding them of the principal exploits of his military life, with which they were all familiar. He then called upon one of the younger men to light his pipe, which being done, and placed in his hand, he took several deliberate whiffs through its long and ornamented stem; this done, and his ideas all arranged, he deliberately turned around, and passing his pipe into his left hand, extended his right over the heads of the audience and commenced:—

"My Friends,—We believe that all our happiness in this life is given to us by the Great Spirit, and through this pipe I have thanked Him for enabling me to be here at this time, and to speak to you all who are around me. (*How, how, how!* and applause)

"My Friends,—We have had a long journey, and we are still very much fatigued. We prayed to the Great Spirit, and He has heard our prayers; we are all here, and all well. (*How, how, how!* and *Hear!*)

"My Friends,—We are poor and live in the woods, and though the Great Spirit is with us, yet He has not taught us how to weave the beautiful things that you make in this country; we have seen many of those things brought to us, and we are now happy to be where all these fine things are made. (*How, how, how!*)

"My Friends,—The Great Spirit has made us with red skins, and taught us how to live in the wilderness, but has not taught us to live as you do. Our dresses are made of skins and are very coarse, but they are warm; and in our dances we are in the habit of showing the skins of our shoulders and our arms, and we hope you will not be angry with us—it is our way. (*How, how, how!* and great applause.)

"My Friends,—We have heard that your chief is a woman, and we know that she must be a great chief, or your country would not be so rich and so happy. (Cheers and *Hear!*) We have been told that the Ojibbeways went to see your queen, and that she smiled upon them; this makes us the more anxious to see her face, as the Ojibbeways are our enemies. (*How, how, how!*)

"My Friends,—We hope to see the face of your queen, and then we shall be happy. Our friend *Chippehola*[13] has told us that he thinks we shall see her. My Friends, we do not know whether there are any of her relations now in the room. (*How, how, how!* and a laugh.)

"My Friends,—We shall be glad to shake your hands. This is all I have to say." (Great applause.)

At the close of his speech, and as he turned around to meet the approbation of his fellow-warriors, there was a sudden burst of laughter amongst the Indians, occasioned by the sarcastic and exulting manner in which the old Doctor told him he had better say something more before he sat down, "because," said he, "you have not made half as much laugh yet as I did last night." "I should be sorry if I had," said the War-chief; "the audience always laugh the moment they see your ugly face."

The Doctor's troubles commenced here, for just at that moment the "fair dame" had caught the eye of the "*Roman-nose*," and holding up a beautiful bracelet enclosing a brilliant stone, she tempted him up, while she clasped it upon his arm as it was extended immediately over the Doctor's head, whose unfailing politeness induced him to bow down his head to facilitate the operation.

When the "*Roman-nose*" had taken his seat, and the poor Doctor had raised up his head to meet the eyes and the taunts of his fellow-Indians, who were laughing at him, and the gaze of the visitors from every quarter of the room, there *was* a *smile*, but altogether a *new* one, and a *new word* should be coined for the sudden and singular distress of the dilemma he was in: it would not do to undervalue the beautiful present that was already upon his arm, and to save his life he could not smile as pleasantly upon the *fair hand* that gave it as he had been smiling a few minutes before. The trinket had instantly fallen fifty per cent. in its value—the *brilliant* prospect that had been before him had fled, and left him in the dread, not only that his beautiful commercial prospects were blighted, but that he was to have an enemy in the field.

The *Roman-nose* received his present in a respectful and thankful manner, but it was too late to be *affectionately* accepted, as it was the *second* one that was afloat, and taken by him, partly as an evidence of a kind heart, and partly as a foil to cover the true meaning of the first one that had been bestowed. However, he valued it very much, and the secret respecting the mistake that had been made in presenting the first, having been committed only to Daniel and myself, was thought best, for the peace of all parties, not to be divulged.

The amusements of the evening being finished, there commenced a general shake of the hands, and when it had been requested by some of the audience that the Indians should come on to the floor, the request was instantly complied with, which afforded the most gratifying opportunity for the visitors to get near to them, and scan them and their costumes and weapons more closely. There was a general outcry by the ladies for the wife of the Little-wolf to descend from the platform with her little pappoose slung on her back in its splendid cradle, ornamented with porcupine's quills and ermine skins. It was a beautiful illustration, and formed one of the most attractive features of the exhibition, for gentlemen as well as for ladies, as thousands will recollect.

The "jolly fat dame" had an opportunity of meeting the *Roman-nose* and of shaking his hand: but, "oh, the distress!" she could not speak to him as she had done to Cadotte,—it was impossible for her to explain to him the abominable mistake of the first night, and she feared he never would properly appreciate the present which she had just made him; nevertheless they were "a noble, fine set of fellows." The Doctor passed about in the crowd shaking hands, and shaking his fan also, which was made of the eagle's tail. He met the "fair dame," and (cruel that he could not speak to her) he dropped many smiles as he looked down upon and over her dimpled cheeks and round neck, as he raised and showed her his brawny arm with the golden bracelet.

The Indians soon withdrew, and after them the crowd; and after the crowd the "jolly fat dame," who said to Daniel as she passed, "I can't stop to-night, Daniel, I am in a great hurry; but I gave the bracelet to the *Roman-nose*—I got a good opportunity, Daniel—I buckled it on myself: oh, yes, I did—that I did—the good fellow, he stood it well—he never stirred. He'll recollect me, won't he, Daniel? I am going; but oh, look here—I can't, to save my life, make the poor fellow understand how the accident took place—it is so provoking!—it's awkward—it is very annoying to me. *You* can tell him, Daniel—I wish you would tell him—I want you to explain it to him. Come, will you, Daniel? that's a good fellow. Tell him I never intended to give a bracelet to the old Doctor. But stop, he won't tell the Doctor that, will he? I wouldn't for the world hurt the poor old man's feelings—no, Daniel, not for twenty bracelets—what shall we do?" "Oh, there is no danger, Madam, that the Doctor will ever hear of it." "You think so?" "Oh, I am sure, Madam." "Then it's all right—good night. I shall be here every night, you know."

The next morning after this, the Rev. Mr. —— and Mr. —— called upon me at my family residence, to ask if it would be consistent with my views and the views of the Indians for them to have some conversation with them in private on the subject of religion and education. I replied, that it was one of the greatest satisfactions I could have during their stay in England, to promote as far as in my power such well-meant efforts to enlighten their minds, and to enable them to benefit in that way by their visit to this country. I told them also, that I was very glad to say that this party was under the charge of Mr. Melody, a man who was high in the confidence of the American Government, and that I knew him to be a temperate and moral man: as he was interested in the missionary efforts being made in this very tribe, I felt quite certain that he would do all in his power to promote their object, and they had better call on him. They did so, and an appointment was made for them to visit the Indians in the afternoon, subsequent to their usual daily "drive."

Mr. Melody had had a conversation with the Indians on the subject, and although they felt some reluctance at first, on account of the little time they would have to reflect upon it, they had agreed to see the reverend gentlemen in the afternoon, and I was sent for to be present. I was there at the time, and when the reverend gentlemen called, I introduced them to the Indians in their rooms. The Indians were all seated on the floor, upon their robes and blankets, and passing around the pipe. After the usual time taken by strangers to examine their curious dresses, weapons, &c., one of the reverend gentlemen mentioned to the chiefs, in a very kind and friendly manner, the objects of their visit, and with their permission gave them a brief account of the life and death of our Saviour, and explained as well as he could to their simple minds the mode of Redemption. He urged upon them the necessity of their taking up this belief, and though it might be difficult for them to understand at first, yet he was sure it was the only way to salvation. This gentleman took full time to explain his views to them, which was done in the most suitable language for their understanding, and every sentence was carefully and correctly interpreted to them by Jeffrey, who seemed to be himself much interested in hearing his remarks.

After the reverend gentleman had finished, Mr. Melody stated to the Indians that he believed all that the gentleman said was true, and that he knew it to be worth their closest and most patient consideration. He then asked White-cloud if he had anything to answer; to which he said, "he had but a few words to say, as he did not feel very well, and *Neu-mon-ya* (the War-chief) was going to speak for him." He thought, however, that it was a subject which they might as well omit until they got home.

Neu-mon-ya during this time was hanging his head quite down, and puffing the smoke as fast as he could draw it through his pipe, in long breaths, and discharging it through his nostrils. He raised up after a moment more of pause, and passing the pipe into White-cloud's hand, folded his arms, with his elbows on his knees, when he drew a deep sigh, and followed it with the last discharge of smoke from his lungs, which was now passing in two white streams through his distended nostrils, as he said—

"My friends,[14]—The Great Spirit has sent you to us with kind words, and he has opened our ears to hear them, which we have done. We are glad to see you and to hear you speak, for we know that you are our friends. What you have said relative to our learning to read and to write, we are sure can do us no good—we are now too old; but for our children, we think it would be well for them to learn; and they are now going to schools in our village, and learning to read and to write. As to the white man's religion which you have explained, we have heard it told to us in the same way, many times, in our own country, and there are white men and women there now, trying to teach it to our people. We do not think your religion good, unless it is so for white people, and this we don't doubt. The Great Spirit has made our skins red, and the forests for us to live in. He has also given us our religion, which has taken our fathers to 'the beautiful hunting grounds,' where we wish to meet them. We don't believe that the Great Spirit made us to live with pale faces in this world, and we think He has intended we should live separate in the world to come.

"My friends,—We know that when white men come into our country we are unhappy—the Indians all die, or are driven away before the white men.

Our hope is to enjoy our hunting grounds in the world to come, which white men cannot take from us: we *know* that our fathers and our mothers have gone there, and we don't know why we should not go there too.

"My friends,—You have told us that the Son of the Great Spirit was on earth, and that he was killed by white men, and that the Great Spirit sent him here to get killed; now we cannot understand all this—this may be necessary for white people, but the red men, we think, have not yet got to be so wicked as to require that. If it was necessary that the Son of the Great Spirit should be killed for white people, it may be necessary for them to believe all this; but for us, we cannot understand it."

He here asked for the pipe, and having drawn a few whiffs, proceeded.

"My friends,—You speak of the '*good book*' that you have in your hand; we have many of these in our village; we are told that 'all your words about the Son of the Great Spirit are printed in that book, and if we learn to read it, it will make good people of us.' I would now ask why it don't make good people of the pale faces living all around us? They can all read the good book, and they can understand all that the '*black coats*'[15] say, and still we find they are not so honest and so good a people as ours: this we are sure of; such is the case in the country about us, but *here* we have no doubt but the white people who have so many to preach and so many books to read, are all honest and good. In *our* country the white people have two faces, and their tongues branch in different ways; we know that this displeases the Great Spirit, and we do not wish to teach it to our children."

He here took the pipe again, and while smoking, the reverend gentleman asked him if he thought the Indians did all to serve the Great Spirit that they ought to do—all that the Great Spirit required of them? to which he replied—

"My friends,—I don't know that we do all that the Great Spirit wishes us to do; there are some Indians, I know, who do not; there are some bad Indians as well as bad white people; I think it is very difficult to tell how much the Great Spirit wishes us to do."

The reverend gentleman said—

"That, my friends, is what we wish to teach you; and if you can learn to read this good book, it will explain all that."

The chief continued—

"We believe the Great Spirit requires us to pray to Him, which we do, and to thank Him for everything we have that is good. We know that He requires us to speak the truth, to feed the poor, and to love our friends.

We don't know of anything more that he demands; he may demand more of white people, but we don't know that."

The reverend gentleman inquired—

"Do you not think that the Great Spirit sometimes punishes the Indians in this world for their sins?"

War-chief.—"Yes, we do believe so."

Rev. Gentleman.—"Did it ever occur to you, that the small pox that swept off half of your tribe, and other tribes around you, a few years ago, might have been sent into your country by the Great Spirit to punish the Indians for their wickedness and their resistance to his word?"

War-chief.—"My Friends, we don't know that we have ever resisted the word of the Great Spirit. If the Great Spirit sent the small pox into our country to destroy us, we believe it was to punish us for listening to the false promises of white men. It is white man's disease, and no doubt it was sent amongst white people to punish *them* for their sins. It never came amongst the Indians until we began to listen to the promises of white men, and to follow their ways; it then came amongst us, and we are not sure but the Great Spirit then sent it to punish us for our foolishness. There is another disease sent by the Great Spirit to punish white men, and it punishes them in the right place—the place that offends. We know that disease has been sent to punish them; that disease was never amongst the Indians until white men came—they brought it, and we believe we shall never drive it out of our country."

The War-chief here reached for the pipe again for a minute, and then continued—

"My Friends,—I hope my talk does not offend you; we are children, and you will forgive us for our ignorance. The Great Spirit expects us to feed the poor; our wives and children at home are very poor; wicked white men kill so many of our hunters and warriors with *fire-water*, that they bring among us, and leave so many children among us for us to feed, when they go away, that it makes us very poor. Before they leave our country they destroy all the game also, and do not teach us to raise bread, and our nation is now in that way, and very poor; and we think that the way we can please the Great Spirit first, is to get our wives and children something to eat, and clothes to wear. It is for that we have come to this country, and still we are glad to hear your counsel, for it is good."

The reverend gentlemen, and several ladies who had accompanied them, here bestowed some very beautiful Bibles and other useful presents upon the Indians; and thanking them for their patience, were about to take leave of them, when Mr. Melody begged their attention for a few moments while he read to them several letters just received from reverend gentlemen conducting a missionary school in this tribe, giving a flattering account of its progress, and presented them a vocabulary and grammar, already printed in the Ioway language, by a printing-press belonging to the missionary school in their country. This surprised them very much, and seemed to afford them great satisfaction.

The comments of the press, as well as the remarks of the public who had seen them, now being made upon the superior interest of this party, they were receiving daily calls from distinguished persons, and also numerous invitations to gentlemen's houses, which daily increased their consequence, and, of course, their enjoyment. Amongst the first of these kind invitations was one from Mr. Disraeli, M.P., for the whole party to partake of a breakfast at his house, in Park Lane.

This was for the next morning after the interview just described; and, not knowing or even being able to imagine what they were to see, or what sort of rules or etiquette they were to be subjected to, they were under the most restless excitement to prepare everything for it, and the greatest anxiety for the hour to approach. They were all up at an unusually early hour, preparing every trinket and every article of dress, and spent at least an hour at their toilets in putting the paint upon their faces. The Doctor had been told that he would sit down at the table amongst many very splendid ladies; and this, or some other embarrassment, had caused him to be dissatisfied with the appearance of the paint which he had put upon his face, and which he was carefully examining with his little looking-glass. He decided that it would not do, and some bear's grease and a piece of deer-skin soon removed it all. He spent another half hour with his different tints, carefully laying them on with the end of his forefinger; and, displeased again, *they* were all demolished as before. Alarm about time now vexed him, and caused him to plaster with a more rapid and consequently with a more "masterly touch." The effect was fine! He was ready, and so were all the party, from head to foot. All their finest was on, and all were prepared for the move, when I came in at about eight o'clock to advise them of the hour at which we were to go, and which I had forgotten to mention to them the evening before. I then referred to the note of invitation, and informed them that the hour appointed was twelve o'clock. The whole party, who were at that time upon their feet around me, wrapped in their robes, their shields and quivers slung, and the choice tints upon their faces almost too carefully arranged to be exposed to the breath of the dilapidating wind, expressed a decided shock when the hour of twelve was mentioned. They smiled, and evidently thought it strange, and that some mistake had been made. Their conjectures were many and curious: some thought it was *dinner* that was meant, instead of *breakfast*; and others thought so late an hour was fixed that they might get their own breakfasts out of the way, and then give the Indians theirs by themselves. I answered, "No, my good fellows, it is just the reverse of this; you are all wrong—it is to *breakfast* that you are invited, and lest their family, and their friends whom they have invited to meet you, should not have the honour of sitting down and eating with you, they have fixed the hour at twelve o'clock, the time that the great and fashionable people take their breakfasts. You must have your breakfasts at home at the usual hour, and take your usual *drive* before you go; so you will have plenty of time for all, and be in good humour when you go there, where you will see many fine ladies and be made very happy."

My remarks opened a new batch of difficulties to them that I had not apprehended, some of which were exceedingly embarrassing. To wait four hours, and to eat and to ride in the meantime, would be to derange the streaks of paint and also to soil many articles of dress which could not be put on excepting on very particular occasions. To take them off and put them on, and to go through the vexations of the toilet again, at eleven o'clock, was what several of the party could submit to, and others could not. As to the breakfast of huge beefsteaks and coffee which was just coming up, I had felt no apprehensions; but when it was on the table I learned that the *old Doctor* and *Wash-ka-mon-ya* and one or two others of the young men were adhering to a custom of their country, and which, in my rusticity (having been seven or eight years out of Indian life), I had at the moment lost sight of.

It is the habit in their country, when an Indian is invited to a feast, to go as hungry as he can, so as to be as fashionable as possible, by eating an enormous quantity, and for this purpose the invitations are generally extended some time beforehand, paying the valued compliment to the invited guest of allowing as much time as he can possibly require for starving himself and preparing his stomach by tonics taken in bitter decoctions of medicinal herbs. In this case the invitation had only been received the day before, and of course allowed them much less than the usual time to prepare to be *fashionable*. They had, however, received the information just in time for the *Doctor* and *Wash-ka-mon-ya* and the *Roman-nose* to avoid the annoyance of their dinners and suppers on that day, and they had now laid themselves aside in further preparation for the *feast* in which they were to be candidates for the mastery in emptying plates and handling the "knife and fork" (or "knife and fingers"), the custom of their country.

In this condition the *Doctor* particularly was a subject for the freshest amusement, or for the profoundest contemplation. With all his finery and his trinkets on, and his red and yellow paint—with his shield, and bow and quiver lying by his side, he was straightened upon his back, with his feet crossed, as he rested in a corner of the room upon his buffalo robe, which was spread upon the floor. His little looking glass, which was always suspended from his belt, he was holding in his hand, as he was still arranging his beautiful feathers, and contemplating the patches of red and yellow paint, and the *tout ensemble* of the pigments and *copper colour* with which he was to make a sensation where he was going to *feast* (as he had been told) with ladies, an occurrence not known in the annals of the Indian country. He had resolved, on hearing the hour was *twelve*, not to eat his breakfast (which he said might do for women and children), or to take his usual ride in the bus, that he might not injure his growing appetite, or disturb a line of paint or a feather, until the hour had arrived for the honours and the luxuries that awaited them.

I reasoned awhile with these three epicures of the land of *"buffaloes' tongues and beavers' tails,"* telling them that they were labouring under a misconception of the ideas of gentility as entertained in the civilized and fashionable world; that in London, the genteel people practised entirely the opposite mode from theirs; that light dinners and light breakfasts were all the fashion, and the less a lady or gentleman could be seen eating, the more sentimental he or she was considered, and consequently the more transcendently genteel: and that when they went to breakfast with their friends at 12, or to dine at 7 or 8, they were generally in the habit of promoting gentility by eating a little at home before they started.

My reasoning, however, had no other effect than to excite a smile from the Doctor, and the very philosophic reply, "that they should prefer to adhere to their own custom until they got to the lady's house, when they would try to conform to that of the white people of London." The drollness of these remarks from this droll old gentleman entirely prevented Mr. Melody and myself from intruding any further suggestions, until the hour arrived, and it was announced that the carriage was at the door.

CHAPTER XIX.

Kind reception at Mr. Disraeli's—View of Hyde Park from the top of his house—Review of troops, and sham fight—Breakfast-table—The Doctor missing—The Author finds him in the bathing-room—Champagne wine—Refused by the Indians—*Chickabobboo: Chippehola* tells the story of it—The Indians drink—Presents—The "big looking-glass"—The Doctor smiles in it—Speech of the War-chief—Shake of hands, and return—Exhibition-room, Egyptian Hall—Doctor presents a string of wampum and the "*White-feather*" to the "jolly fat dame"—Indians talk about *chickabobboo*—The Rev. Mr. G—— calls—A different religion (a Catholic)—Interview appointed—Two Methodist clergymen call—Indians refuse to see them—The giant and giantess visit the Indians—The Doctor measuring the giantess—The talk with the Catholic clergyman.

This chapter begins with the introduction of the Ioways into fashionable life, through the various phases of which they had the good or bad fortune to pass, in this and other countries, as will be seen, before they returned to resume the tomahawk and scalping-knife in their favourite prairies, and the Rocky Mountains in America.

Mr. Melody and myself accompanied the Indians, and all together were put down at the door, where we met a host of waiters in livery, ready to conduct us to the kind lady and gentleman, whom they instantly recollected to have seen and shaken hands with in the exhibition room. This gave them confidence, and all parties were made easy in a moment, by a general introduction which followed. Through the interpreter, the ladies complimented them for their dances and songs, which they had heard, and pronounced to be very wonderful. Their women and little children were kindly treated by the ladies, and seats were prepared for them to sit down. The men were also desired to be seated, but on looking around the room, upon the richness of its furniture, the splendid carpet on which they stood, and the crimson velvet of the cushioned chairs that were behind them, they smiled, and seemed reluctant to sit upon them, for fear of soiling them. They were at length prevailed upon to be seated, however, and after a little conversation, were conducted by Mr. Disraeli through the different apartments of his house, where he put in their hands, and explained to them, much to their gratification, many curious daggers, sabres, and other weapons and curiosities of antiquity. In passing through the dining saloon, they passed the table, groaning under the weight of its costly plate and the luxuries which were prepared for them; upon this the old Doctor smiled as he passed along, and he even turned his head to smile again upon it, as he left it.

After we had surveyed all below, the party were invited to the top of the house, and Mr. Disraeli led the way. The ladies, of whom there were a goodly number, all followed; and altogether, the pictured buffalo robes—the rouged heads and red feathers—the gaudy silks, and bonnets, and ribbons—glistening lances and tomahawks—and black coats, formed a novel group for the gaze of the multitude who were gathering from all directions, under the ever exciting cry of "Indians! Indians!"

Hyde Park was under our eye, and from our position we had the most lovely view of it that any point could afford; and also of the drilling of troops, and the sham-fight in the park, which was going on under our full view. This was exceedingly exciting and amusing to the Indians, and also the extensive look we had in turning our eyes in the other direction, over the city. The ladies had now descended, and we all followed to the saloon, where it was soon announced that the breakfast was ready; and in a few moments all were seated at the table, excepting the Doctor, who was not to be found. Jeffrey and I instantly thought of his *"propensity"* and went to the house-top for him, but to our amazement he was not there. In descending the stairs, however, and observing a smoke issuing out of one of the chambers, into which we had been led, on going up to examine the beautiful arrangement for vapour and shower baths, we stepped in, and found the Doctor seated in the middle of the room, where he had lit his pipe, and was taking a more deliberate look at this ingenious contrivance, which he told us pleased him very much, and which he has often said he thought would be a good mode to adopt in his practice in his own country. He was easily moved, however, when it was announced to him that the breakfast was on the table and ready, where he was soon seated in the chair reserved for him.

Great pains were taken by the ladies and gentlemen to help the Indians to the luxuries they might like best; and amongst others that were offered, their glasses were filled with sparkling champagne, in which their health was proposed. The poor fellows looked at it, and shaking their heads, declined it. This created some surprise, upon which Mr. Melody explained for them that they had pledged their words not to drink spirituous liquors while in this country. They were applauded by all the party for it, and at the same time it was urged that this was only a light *wine*, and could not hurt them: we were drinking it ourselves, and the ladies were drinking it, and it seemed cruel to deny them. Poor Melody!—he looked distressed: he had a good heart, and loved his Indians, but he felt afraid of the results. The *Doctor* and *Wash-ka-mon-ya* kept their hands upon their glasses, and their eyes upon Melody and myself, evidently understanding something of the debate that was going on, until it was agreed and carried, by the ladies and all, that taking a little champagne would not be a breach of their promise in the least, and that it would do them no harm. Their health and success were then proposed, and all their glasses were drained to the bottom at once.

The Doctor, after finding the bottom of his glass, turned round, and smacking his lips, dropped me a bow and a smile, seeming to say that "he was thankful, and that the wine was very good."

I told them that this was not "*fire-water*" as they could themselves judge, but that it was "*chickabobboo*." This word seeming to them to be an Indian word, excited their curiosity somewhat, and being called upon by the ladies to explain the meaning of it, as they did not recollect to have met such a word in Johnson's Dictionary or elsewhere, I related to them the story of *chickabobboo*, as told by the war-chief of the Ojibbeways, at Windsor Castle; and the manner in which those Indians partook of the Queen's wine, or "*chickabobboo*" as they called it, on that occasion.

This explanation afforded much amusement to the party, and to the Indians also, as Jeffrey interpreted it to them; and it was soon proposed that their glasses should be filled again with *chickabobboo*. The Doctor sat next to me at the table, and every time he emptied his glass of *chickabobboo* I was amused to hear him pronounce the word "good!"—the first word of English he had learned, and the first occasion on which I had heard him sound it. After the wine was first poured out, he had kept one hand around his glass or by the side of it, and had entirely stopped eating. He had minced but a little in the outset, and seeming to have a delicate stomach, was giving great pain to the ladies who were helping him and urging him to eat, in his irrevocable resolution to be *genteel*, as he had before suggested, and which they probably never understood.

The last dish that was passed around the table, and relished by the Indians quite as much as the *chickabobboo*, was a plate of trinkets of various kinds, of brooches, bracelets, chains, and other ornaments for their persons, which they received with expressions of great thankfulness as they were rising from the table. Thus ended the "feast," as they called it; and on entering the drawing-room the Doctor became a source of much amusement to the ladies, as his attention was arrested by the enormous size of a mirror that was before him, or by the striking effect of his own beautiful person, which he saw at full length in it. He affected to look only at the frame, as the ladies accused him of vanity; and he drew out from under his belt his little looking-glass, about an inch square, imbedded in a block of deal to protect it from breaking. The contrast was striking and amusing, but what followed was still more so. The ladies were anxious to examine his looking-glass (which was fastened to his person with a leathern thong), and in pulling it out, there necessarily came out with it, attached to the same thong, a little wallet carefully rolled up in a rattle-snake's skin; and which, on inquiry, was found to be his toilet of pigments of various colours, with which he painted his face. A small pair of scissors also formed a necessary appendage, and by the side of them hung a boar's tusk and a human finger shrivelled and dried. This he had taken from a victim he had slain in battle, and now wore as his *"medicine,"* or *talismanic charm*, that was to guard and protect him in all times of trouble or danger. This remarkable trophy was generally, on occasions when he was in full dress, suspended from his neck by a cord, and hung amongst the strings of wampum on his breast; but on this occasion he had so many other things to think of, that he had forgotten to display it there.

The War-chief at this time preparing his mind to make some remarks before leaving, and to thank the lady for her kindness, was asking "if he should give any offence by lighting his pipe;" to which they all answered at once, "No, oh no! we shall be glad to see the old chief smoke; get him some fire immediately." When the fire arrived, he had lighted his pipe with his flint and steel, and was arranging his ideas as he was drawing the smoke through its long stem. It amused the ladies very much to see him smoke, and when he was ready he passed the pipe into White Cloud's hand, and rising, and throwing his head and his shoulders back, he said to the lady that "he was authorized by the chief to return to her and her husband his thanks, and the thanks of all the party, for the kindness they had shown them." He said they were strangers in the country, and a great way from home, and this would make them more thankful for the kindness they had met this day.

> "My Friends (said he), the Great Spirit has caused your hearts to be thus kind to us, and we hope the Great Spirit will not allow us to forget it. We are thankful to all your friends whom we see around you also, and we hope the Great Spirit will be kind to you all.
>
> "My friend the chief wishes to shake hands with you all, and then we will bid you farewell."

The kindest wishes were expressed, in reply to the old man's remarks, for their health and happiness; and after a general shaking of hands we took leave, and our omnibus, for St. James's Street.

The usual dinner hour of the Indians was just at hand when they returned, which was a joyful occurrence for the Doctor, who had, at some inconvenience, been endeavouring to practise Indian and civilized gentility at one and the same time. He smiled when dinner came on, and others smiled to see him endeavouring to mend the breach that had been made.

The excitements of this day had put the Indians in remarkably good humour for their evening's amusements at the Hall, which they gave to a crowded house, and, as usual, with great applause. The "jolly fat dame" was there as she had promised, still admiring, and still "quite miserable that she could not speak to them in their own language, or something that they could understand." Daniel had taken a private opportunity to tell the Doctor the whole story of her attachment to Cadotte, and to assure him, at the same time, of her *extraordinary* admiration of him, the evidence of which was, that "she had made him the first present, after which all others were mere foils." The Doctor took a peculiar liking to Daniel from that moment, and little else than a lasting friendship could be expected to flow from such a foundation as was then so kindly laid. This most welcome information had been communicated to the Doctor's ear on the evening previous, and he had now come prepared to present her (with his own hand, and the most gracious smile, and at the end of the platform) a string of wampum from his own neck, and a *white feather* with two spots of red painted on it, to which he pointed with great energy, and some expression that she heard, but did not understand. The "*fair dame*" held her exciting present in her hand during the evening, with some little occasional trepidation, expecting to draw from Daniel some key to the meaning of the mysterious gift as she was leaving the rooms. This hope proved vain, however; for Daniel, it seems, was not yet deep enough in Indian mysteries to answer her question, and she carried the present home, with its mysterious meaning, to ruminate upon until the riddle could be solved.

Mr. Melody and I visited the Indians in their apartments that evening after their exhibition was over, and taking a beefsteak and a cup of coffee with them, we found them still in high glee, and in good humour for gossip, which ran chiefly upon the immense looking-glasses they had seen (and "forgot to measure"), and the *chickabobboo*, which they pronounced to be first-rate for a grand *feast*, which it would be their duty to get up in a few days to thank the Great Spirit for leading them all safe over the ocean, and to ensure their safe return when they should be ready to go. I then told them of the kind of *chickabobboo* that the Ojibbeways liked very much, and of which I had allowed each one glass every day at his dinner, and also at night after their dances were done, and which the physicians thought would be much better for them than the strong coffee they were in the habit of drinking; that I had talked with Mr. Melody on the subject, and he was quite willing, with me, that they should have it in the same way, provided they liked it.

"*How, how, how!*" they all responded; and while the servant was gone for a jug of ale, I explained to them that we did not consider that this was breaking their solemn promise made to us, "*not to drink spirituous liquors.*" I stated to them, also, that it was possible to get drunk by drinking *chickabobboo*; and if any of them drank so much of it as to produce that effect, we should consider it the same as if they had got drunk by drinking whiskey.

The ale came in foaming, and being passed round, they all decided that "it was good, but not quite so good as that the kind lady gave us at the *feast* to-day."

These evening gossips with these good-natured fellows in their own rooms, after their day's work and excitements were over, became extremely pleasing to me; so completely reviving the by-gone pleasures I had felt in whiling away the long evenings in their hospitable wigwams, when I was a guest in their remote country, amused with their never-ending fund of anecdotes and stories.

On the next morning, or the day after, at an early hour, Daniel announced to the Indians that there was a reverend gentleman in the sitting-room who wished to see them a little while, and to have some talk with them if possible. Daniel had taken this liberty, as he had heard Mr. Melody and myself say that we should feel disposed to promote, as far as we could, all such efforts. The Indians had not yet had their breakfasts, which were nearly ready, and felt a little annoyed; the War-chief observing "that they had had a long council with some clergymen, and had said to them all they had to say, and thought this gentleman had better go and see and talk with them; and another thing, as he believed that *Chippehola*[16] had written in a book all that he and the clergymen had said, he thought he might learn it all by going to him."

Daniel whispered to him, in an earnest manner, that "this was a *Catholic priest*, a different kind of religion altogether." This created some little surprise and conversation around the room, that the white people should have two kinds of religion; and it was at last agreed that the War-chief and Jeffrey should step into the other room a few minutes and see him, the White Cloud saying "he did not care about going in."

It seems that Jeffrey took some interest in this gentleman, as the little that his ancestors had learned of religion had been taught them by Roman Catholic clergymen, who have been the first to teach the Christian religion in most parts of the American wilderness. The conversation and manner of the priest also made some impression on the mind of the War-chief; and as they heard the others using their knives and forks in the adjoining room, they took leave of the reverend gentleman, agreeing to a council with him and a number of his friends in a few days. *White Cloud* and *Wash-ka-mon-ya* excited much laughter and amusement amongst the party, on learning that the War-chief had appointed another council, "when he was to make his talk all over again." They told him "they expected to take him home a preacher, to preach white man's religion when he got back;" and they thought he had better get a "black coat" at once, and be called "*Black-coat to the party of Ioway Indians.*"

The next day after the above interview, Daniel again announced to the chiefs and Jeffrey that there were two reverend gentlemen waiting to see them, who had seen Mr. Melody on the subject, and were to meet him there at that hour. White Cloud told the War-chief, that "as he had promised to meet them, he must do it; but as for himself, he would rather not see them, for he was not well." *Wash-ka-mon-ya* laughed at the old chief and Jeffrey as they went out. "Now," said he, "for your grand council!" The War-chief lit his long pipe, and he and Jeffrey entered the room; but finding they were not the persons whom they were expecting to meet, they had a few words of conversation with them, taking care not to approach near to the subject of religion, and left them, as they had some other engagements that took up their time.

There was much merriment going on in the meantime in the Indians' room, and many jokes ready for the War-chief and Jeffrey when they should get back, as Daniel had returned to their room, and told them that, by the cut of their clothes and their manners, he was quite sure that these two gentlemen were of a different religion still; he believed they were *Methodist preachers.*

The War-chief, who was always dignified and contemplative in his manners, and yet susceptible of good humour and jokes, returned to the Indians' room at this time, apparently quite insensible to the mirth and the remarks around him, as he learned from the Indians, and got the confirmation from Daniel, that this was the *third* kind of religion, and that there were the *Baptists*, the *Jews*, and several other kinds yet to come. He seated himself on his robe, which he spread upon the floor, and taking out of his pouch his flint and steel, and spunk, struck a light in the true Indian way (though there was fire within reach of his arm), and, lighting his pipe, commenced smoking. During this silent operation he seemed downcast, and in profound meditation. Mr. Melody and I entered the room at this moment, but seeing the mood he was in, did nothing to interrupt the train of his thoughts. When his pipe was smoked out, he charged it again with tobacco, but before lighting it he laid it aside, and straightening his long limbs upon the floor, and drawing another buffalo robe over his body and his head, he went to sleep.[17]

No. 11.

This was the day for "seeing the *Giants*," and they were soon after announced as having arrived, according to appointment. During one of the Indians' exhibitions there had been a great excitement produced amongst them by the appearance in the crowd, of two immense persons, a man and a woman, who stood nearly the whole length of their bodies above the heads of others about them! This had excited the amazement of the Indians so much, that for a while they stopped their dances, to sit down and smoke a pipe. They must necessarily make some sacrifice on such an occasion, and it was decided to be done with a piece of tobacco, which being duly consecrated by them, was carried by the Doctor (the medicine man) to an adjoining room, and burned in the fire.

There were no questions asked by the Indians about these unaccountable people, where they came from, &c., but they wished me to invite them to call at their lodgings at No. 7, St. James's-street, the next day at twelve o'clock, where they would be glad to see them a little while. This wish was communicated to them in a note which I wrote on my knee, and was passed to them over the heads of the audience; the *giant man* read it, and smiling, nodded his head, accepting of their invitation. This pleased the Indians, who all joined in sounding the war-whoop. These two extraordinary personages proved to be the well-known "Norfolk giants," who were brother and sister, and walking "arm-in-arm," so high that the eye of an ordinary man was just on a level with the apron string of the fair damsel; and the waist of the brother was, of course, yet some inches higher. I regret that I have not preserved the exact elevation of these two extraordinary persons, which I took pains to procure, but have somehow mislaid.

The invitation thus given brought them on their present visit to the Indians, who had great satisfaction in shaking their hands, and closely inspecting them: and not many minutes after their arrival a scene ensued that would have made a sick man laugh, or a rich subject for the pencil of Hogarth. The Indians had sent Daniel for a ball of twine, which they had unfolded upon the floor, and each one having cut off a piece of sufficient length, was taking for himself the measure of the *"giant man,"* from head to foot—from hand to hand, his arms extended—the span of his waist—his breast and his legs—the length of his feet, and his fingers; and tying knots in their cords to indicate each proportion. In the midst of all this, the Doctor presented the most queer and laughable point in the picture, as he had been applying his string to the back of the fair damsel, having taken her length, from the top of her head to the floor, and tied a knot in his cord at the place where the waist of her dress intersected it; he had then arrested the attention of all, and presented his singular dilemma, when he stood with both ends of his cord in his hands, contemplating the enormous waist and other proportions before him, which he coveted for other knots on his string, but which his strict notions of gallantry were evidently raising objections to his taking. I whispered to him, and relieved him from his distressing state of uncertainty, by saying I thought he had been particular enough, and he withdrew, but with a sigh of evident regret.

They insisted on the *giant* and *giantess* receiving from them some little keepsakes of trinkets, &c., as evidences of the pleasure they had afforded them by calling on them.

This extraordinary occurrence, like most others of an exciting or interesting nature which these jovial and funny fellows met with, made subject for much subsequent anecdote and amusement. *Wash-ka-mon-ya* (the fast dancer), a big-mouthed and waggish sort of fellow (who for brevity's sake was called, in English parlance, "Jim"), was continually teasing the Doctor about his gallantry amongst the ladies; and could rather easily and coolly do it, as he was a married man, and had his wife constantly by the side of him. He had naturally an abundant stock of wit and good humour, and being so much of a wag withal, he was rather a painful companion for the Doctor all the way, and was frequently passing jokes of a cruel as well as of a light and amusing kind upon him. It was known to the whole party that there was no record kept of the length and breadth of the *giant lady*, except the one that the Doctor had taken, and carefully rolled up and put away in a little box, amongst other precious things, at the head of his bed, and which he generally used as his pillow. It was known also that much stress would be laid upon this in his own country, when they returned home, as something which the rest of the party could not produce, and which for him, therefore, would be of great and peculiar interest there, and probably on other occasions, when it might be proper to refer to it as a thing he could swear to as a subject of interest in this country. Jim's best jokes (like most Indian jokes) were those which no one else takes a share in; and a piece of the twine that had caught his eye as it was lying upon the floor, probably first suggested the wicked idea of being cut about two feet longer than the Doctor's measure of the fair giantess, and with a knot about one foot higher than the one made for her waist, and of being rolled up in the same way, and slipped (in place of the other) into the same corner of the box, to which the Doctor had a key, but, according to all Indian practice, he never made use of it. The sequel to all this, and the fun it might have subsequently made for "Jim," with his "big mouth," the reader may as well imagine here, or patiently wait till we come to it.

In the afternoon the Catholic clergyman called with a couple of friends, for the interview which *Jeffrey* and the *War-chief* had promised. Mr. Melody sent me word when they called, and I came to the meeting, having taken a great interest in these interviews, which were eliciting opinions from the Indians which are exceedingly difficult to obtain in any other way, and which I was careful on all occasions to write down, as translated at the time. These opinions, however unimportant they may seem to be, I am sure many of my readers will find to be of curious interest; and I fully believe, if rightly appreciated, of much importance in directing future efforts to the right points in endeavouring to impress upon these ignorant and benighted people the importance of education, and a knowledge of the true Christian religion.

On this occasion *Wash-ka-mon-ya* (or "*Jim*" as I shall often call him) endeavoured to make himself conspicuous by teasing the War-chief and Jeffrey about "going to pray with the black-coats," and springing upon his feet, took his tomahawk in his hand, and throwing off his robe, jumped to the middle of the floor, where, naked down to the hips, he landed, in an attitude not unlike that of the colossal statue of Rhodes. He frowned a moment upon all around him, and then said, "Let me go in—I have said nothing yet; I want to make a speech to the black-coats."

White-cloud, who was at that moment taking up his robe to accompany Jeffrey and the War-chief to the "talk," very mildly said to *Jim*, that "he would look much more respectful if he would sit down again and hold his tongue, for these were very good people who were calling to talk with them, and must be treated with respect, however their opinions might differ from those of the Indians." This severe rebuke from the chief instantly silenced Jim, who quietly and respectfully joined the rest of the party, at White-cloud's request, who seated themselves in the room where the talk was to be held. The pipe was lit and passing around, while one of the reverend gentlemen stated the views with which they had come to visit them, and asked the Indians if it was perfectly convenient and agreeable for them to hear what they had to say, to which the chief replied in the affirmative. The reverend gentleman then proceeded with his remarks upon the importance of education and religion, the nature of which the reader can easily imagine, and save the time it would require to record them here. To these the chiefs and all the party (excepting Jim and the Doctor, who had fallen asleep) listened with patience and profound silence, as the pipe was passing around. The reverend gentleman having finished, the War-chief took a few deep-drawn breaths through the pipe, and passing it along, said—

> "My Friends,—I speak for the chief who is here, and not very well. My words are his words, and the words of all our party. We have heard what you had to say, because we had promised to do so.
>
> "My Friends,—We have talked many times on this subject, and some of our talks have been long; but at this time our words will be few, for we are weary, and as we have before said, we are poor, and our wives and children are hungry, and we have come over here to try to make some money to get them warm clothes and food to eat. (*How, how, how!*)
>
> "My Friends,—Many of our children are now in schools in our country, and the '*good book*' which is in your hands is in their hands at this time. We believe that the Great Spirit has made our religion good and sufficient for us if we do not in any way offend him. We see the religion of the white people dividing into many paths, and we cannot believe that it is pleasing to the Great Spirit. The Indians have but one road in their religion, and they all travel in that, and the Great Spirit has never told them that it was not right.
>
> "My Friends,—Our ears have been open since we came here, and the words we have heard are friendly and good; but we see so many kinds of religion, and so many people drunk and begging when we ride in the streets, that we are a little more afraid of white man's religion than we were before we came here.
>
> "My Friends,—The Indians occupied all the fine hunting grounds long before the white men came to them, but the white men own them nearly all now, and the Indians' hunting grounds are mostly all gone. The Indians never urge white men to take up their religion, they are satisfied to have them take a different road, for the Indians wish to enjoy their hunting grounds to themselves in the world to come. (*How, how, how!*)
>
> "My Friends,—We thank you, and shall wish the Great Spirit may be kind to you. I have no more to say."

Thus ended the conversation this time, and the Indians all rising (except the Doctor, who was still asleep) shook hands with the clergymen and retired to their own room.

These excellent gentlemen then expressed to Mr. Melody and myself their high admiration and respect for them as men, and said that they could make every allowance for them, travelling here only for the laudable objects which they had so clearly explained, and their patience taxed in so many instances as I had mentioned, of a similar nature. They agreed that it would be cruel to urge them to listen any further under their present circumstances, and that they had already exercised far greater patience than white men would in a similar condition. They said they should feel bound to call on another day (and did so), not to talk with them about religion, but to bring them some presents that would be serviceable to their wives and little children, and took leave.

CHAPTER XX.

The Doctor and Jim visit several churches—The Indians in St. Paul's—In Westminster Abbey—The exhibition at the Hall—The Doctor agrees to go in the carriage of the "jolly fat dame"—Mr. Melody objects—The Doctor's melancholy—Indians stop the bus to talk with Lascars—Make them presents of money—Indians discover *chickabobboo-ags* (gin-palaces)—and ladies lying down in their carriages reading books—*Chim-e-gotch-ees* (or fish)—Jim's story of "Fish"—Experiments in mesmerism—Wash-ka-mon-ya (Jim) mesmerized—The Doctor's opinions on mesmerism—Ioways in Lord's Cricket-ground—Archery and ball-playing—Encampment—Wigwams—Indians invited by Mrs. Lawrence to Ealing Park—Their kind reception—Their Royal Highnesses the Duke and Duchess of Cambridge—The Princess Mary—The Duchess of Gloucester—The Hereditary Grand Duke and Duchess, and other distinguished guests—Amusements—Beautiful grounds—Indians dine on the lawn—Roast beef and plum-pudding—*Chickabobboo*—Alarm of the parrots—Doctor's superstition—*Chickabobboo* explained—Speech of the War-chief—Taking leave—Fright of the poor birds—Handsome presents—Conservatory—The Doctor's ideas of it—Indians visit Surrey Zoological Gardens—Fright of the birds and animals—Indians sacrifice tobacco to the lion and the rattle-snakes.

Mr. Melody, feeling the high importance of the charge of these fourteen wild people intrusted to his hands by the Government while they were to see the sights of a foreign country, and feeling the strongest attachment to them personally, was stimulated to every exertion by which he could properly open their eyes to the benefits of civilization, and consequently was inquiring from day to day "what shall be shown them next?"

I had also, with feelings of the highest respect for the chiefs of the nation, knowing them to be of the party, enlisted my warmest exertions in their behalf, and resolved to render them, in all ways I could, the aid that was due from me for their hospitality which benefited me when I was in their country.

With these views we continued our omnibus in driving them about the City and country, and one or the other of us was almost daily accompanying them to some institution or public works from which they might derive some useful information. To these they generally went together and in their native dresses, but there were others where their costumes and their paint would render them too conspicuous, and for such purposes two or three suits of clothes, beaver hats and wigs, became necessary for such a number as wished at any time to look further (and unobserved) into the arcana and hidden mysteries of the great metropolis. And the reader will be ready to exclaim with me, that the field before us was a vast and boundless one.

The two most ambitious to profit by such adventures were "*Jim*" (as I have before denominated him) and the "*Doctor.*" the *first*, from a peculiar faculty he had of learning the English language (in which he was making daily progress), and a consequent insatiable desire to see and learn the modes, and everything he could, of white people, excepting their religion; and the *second*, from an indomitable desire to look in everywhere and upon everything, more for the pleasure of gratifying a momentary curiosity, and enjoying a temporary smile, than from any decided ambition to carry home and adopt anything, unless it might be a vapour-bath, or something of the kind, in the way of his profession.

In frock-coats and beaver hats, and boots, with a large stick or an umbrella under the arm, and the paint all washed off, there was not much in the looks of these two new-fangled gentlemen to attract the public gaze or remark; and consequently little in the way of the sights and treasures of London being opened to their view.

From the time that this expedient was adopted, our avocations became more diversified and difficult; our anxieties and cares increased, and with them our amusement: for with Melody the sights of London were as yet prospective; and with me, whether old or new, I met them with an equal relish with my unsophisticated brethren from the wilderness.

The amusement of "trying on" and "getting the hang" of the new dresses made merriment enough for the party for one day; and all but these two were quite willing to forego all the pleasures they could afford, rather than cover their cool and naked heads with beaver hats, their shoulders with frock-coats, and substitute for their soft and pliant mocassins and leggings of buckskin, woollen pantaloons and high-heeled boots. The two wiseacres, however, who had adopted them were philosophers, and knew that they were only for certain occasions, after which they were to be dropped off, and their limbs "at home again" in their light and easy native dresses. They were obliged, on such occasions (to be in keeping), to leave their long and ornamented pipes and tomahawks behind, and (not to lose the indispensable luxury of smoking) to carry a short and handy civilized pipe, with their tobacco, and a box of lucifers, in their pockets.

Reader, pray don't try to imagine what a figure these two copper-coloured "swells" cut, when they first sallied forth in their new attire, for it will be in vain: but behold them and me, in the future pages of this book, and when their dresses had got to work easy, profiting by gazing upon the wonders and glories of civilization, which we never otherwise could have beheld together.

As one of the first fruits of the new expedient (and while the subject was fresh and revolving in the minds of all), there was now a chance of gratifying the Doctor's desire to see the modes and places of worship of some of the different denominations of religion, of which he had heard so much, from Daniel and others, within the few days past. These visits were their first attempts in their assumed characters, and were mostly made in the company of Mr. Melody or Jeffrey, and without any amusing results either for the congregations or the Ioways, save an incident or two, such as must be expected in the first experiments with all great enterprises. The Doctor had been told that when he entered the Protestant Church, he must take his hat off at the door, and had practised it before he started; but, seeing such an immense number of ladies, he had unfortunately forgot it, and being reminded of it when he had been placed in his seat, his wig came off with it, exposing, but a moment however, his scalp-lock and the top of his head, where he had not deemed it necessary to wash off the red paint.

In the Methodist chapel, where these two queer fellows had ventured one day with Daniel, the sermon was long and tedious, and there was nothing observed curious excepting a blue smoke rolling up over the top of the pew, where the Doctor's pipe had been lit, and his head sunk down between his knees; and one other occurrence, that afterwards happened in the heat of the exhortation from the pulpit, and much to the amusement of the Doctor and Jim, of a young woman, in their immediate vicinity, who began to groan, then to sing, and at length tumbled down from her seat upon the floor. The Doctor thought at first she was very sick, and wondered there was no physician there to bleed her; but when Daniel told him what was the matter, the old man smiled, and often talked about it afterwards.

I took the whole party through Westminster Abbey and St. Paul's, where they stood and contemplated in amazement the works of human hands, so entirely beyond their comprehension that they returned in reserved and silent contemplation.

Returning again to the Exhibition-room at the Egyptian Hall, several evenings of which have passed by without mention, but much in the same way, we find the same excitement and applause, and the "jolly fat dame" at the end of the platform, nightly receiving the Doctor's impressive smiles, which are constantly ready for her; and which by this time, aided by the continued coldness of the *Roman-nose*, were making visible inroads upon her tender affections. She had had, it seemed, on this evening, some conversation with the Doctor, through the interpreter, who had heretofore studiously kept out of the way, and she had invited the Doctor to ride to her house in her carriage, after the exhibition was over, believing that he would be able to find in her garden, some roots which he was in great distress to find, and that she would bring him home again safe. Mr. Melody objected to this, which seemed to puzzle the fair dame, and to throw the Doctor into a profound melancholy and dejection.

This rebuff from Mr. Melody was so unexpected and so provoking, when she had so nearly accomplished her object, that the good lady passed out of the room earlier than usual, and tossed her head about with her ostrich plumes as she passed along in the crowd, without having the heart to stop and speak a few words to Daniel, as she had been in the habit of doing. Mr. Melody retired with the Indians, and I remained after the crowd had left, at the solicitation of a party of ladies, who had sent me their card and wished to see me after the exhibition was over. The room being nearly emptied, I saw a party of several fashionably-dressed ladies at the further end of the room, examining the paintings on the walls. In advancing towards them, the one who seemed to be the leader of the party turned around and exclaimed, "Oh, here comes Mr. Catlin, I believe?" "Yes, Madam, I am Mr. Catlin." "Oh, I am so happy to have the honour of seeing you, Sir, and of speaking to you—you have made all these paintings?" "Yes." "These Indians are curious fellows, and well worth seeing, but I consider you ten times more of a curiosity. Look here, ladies, here's Mr. Catlin, the very man that I have so often told you about. Dear me, what dangers and hardships you must have been through! Oh, I do think you are one of the wonders of the world—and not a grey hair in your head yet! My dear Sir, I know your whole history—you'd scarcely believe it—I know it 'like a book,' as they say. I recollect the very day when you started for India, and I have followed you the whole way—I have your book—I bought several copies to give to my friends; I have read every word of it over and over again—and, oh! it's wonderful—it's charming—one can't stop in it—there's no stopping place in it. By the way, I don't suppose you were down much in the neighbourhood of Chusan (I've got a nephew there—a fine fellow—he's a surgeon). I suppose you kept pretty much back in the mountains? You had no object in coming down about the coast; and they have had rather hot work there." "No, Madam, I had not the slightest object to take me near Chusan—I kept a great way back." "That was right; oh, how judicious! Oh, I have read your interesting work so often. By the way, these fellows are not from the coast—they are from a great way back, I dare say?" "Yes, Madam, they are a great way in the interior." "I thought so, I knew so—I can tell, d' ye see—I can always tell a coaster. These are fine men—they grow tea, I suppose, though?" "No, these people don't grow tea." "Ah, well, it's late, we won't take up your time; but I have been so happy to have seen you—glad, glad to see you home alive to your native soil, and out of that plagued India. Good night." "Good night, ladies."

As they left me, I turned round, and met a poor fellow approaching me on one leg and a pair of crutches, and his wife holding on to his arm. He said he had been waiting some time to have the honour of speaking to me before he left, having heard my name pronounced. He told me he lived at Woolwich, where he held some situation for life, as he had lost his leg in the service of his country, and it was a good living for him, luckily, though he had been so unfortunate as to lose his leg.

"My wife and I (said he) ave long eard of this extro'nary hexibition, and she as often hax'd me to come to see it; and though we ave been off and hon about it a great many times, we never got off together until this hafternoon—it's a wonderful sight, sir, hand we are appy to ave seen you halso."

I thanked the poor fellow, and asked him how he lost his leg.

"It was done by the kick of a orse, Sir."

"But your leg has been taken off above your knee."

"Yes, Sir, the bone was broken, hand it ad to be hamputated."

"It must have been very painful!"

"Ah, hit urt a little; though as for the pain of hamputation, I wouldn't give a penny for it: but the loss of my leg is worth a great deal to me; it's hall ealed up now, Sir, though it's very hunandy."

This simple and unfortunate man and his very pretty little wife left me, and I repaired to the Indians' rooms in St. James's Street, where I found them finishing their suppers and taking their *chickabobboo*. Here was in readiness a long catalogue of the adventures of the day—of things they had seen in their drive, &c., to be talked over, as well as the cruel jokes to be listened to, which they were all passing upon the poor Doctor, for the sudden failure of his prospects of digging roots in the fair dame's garden.

There were many subjects of an amusing nature talked over by these droll fellows during the pipes of this evening, and one of the themes for their comments was the drive which we had given them in two open carriages through Hyde Park, at the fashionable hour. They decided that "the Park, along the banks of the Serpentine, reminded them of the prairies on the shores of the Skunk and the Cedar rivers in their own country; and in fact, that some parts of it were almost exactly the same." They were amused to see many of the ladies lying down as they rode in their carriages; and also, that many of the great chiefs, pointed out to them riding on horseback, "didn't know how to ride—that they were obliged to have a man riding a little behind them to pick them up if they should fall off."

Jim, who was in an unusual good humour this evening, either from the effects of his *chickabobboo* or from some fine present he might have received in the room, seemed to be the chief "spokesman" for the evening, and for the purpose of assisting his imagination or aiding his voice had laid himself flat upon his back upon his robe, which was spread upon the floor. His loquacity was such, that there was little else for any of us to do than sit still and excessively laugh at the dryness of his jokes, and his amusing remarks upon the things they had seen as they were taking their ride on this and past mornings. He had now got, as has been said, a facility of using occasional words of English, and he brought them in once in a while with the most amusing effect.

He said they had found another place where there were two more Ojibbeway Indians (as he called them), Lascars. sweeping the streets; and it seems that after passing them they had ordered their bus to stop, and called them up and shook hands, and tried to talk with them. They could speak a few words in English, and so could *Jim*: he was enabled to ask them if they were Ojibbeways, and they to answer, "No, they were Mussulmen." "Where you live?" "Bombay." "You sweep dirt in the road?" "Yes," "Dam fool!" *Jim* gathered a handful of pennies and gave them, and they drove off.

It seemed that in their drive this day, Jim and the Doctor had both rode outside, which had afforded to Jim the opportunity of seeing to advantage, for the first time. the immense number of "gin palaces," as they passed along the streets; and into which they could look from the top of the bus, and distinctly see the great number of large kegs, and what was going on inside. The Doctor had first discovered them in his numerous outside rides, and as he was not quite sure that he had rightly understood them, hearing that the English people detested drunkards so much, he had not ventured to say much about them. He had been anxious for the corroboration of *Jim's* sharper eyes, and during this morning they had fully decided that the hundreds of such places they were in all directions passing, were places where people went to drink *chickabobboo*, and they were called *chickabobbooags*. The conversation of Jim and the Doctor enlarged very much on this grand discovery, and the probable effects they had upon the London people. They had seen many women, and some of them with little babies in their arms, standing and lying around them, and they were quite sure that some of those women were drunk. Jim said that he and the Doctor had counted two or three hundred in one hour. Some of the party told him he had made his story too big, so he said he and the Doctor next day would mark them down on a stick. Jim said there was one street they came through, where he hoped they would never drive them again, for it made their hearts sore to see so many women and little children all in dirty rags: they had never seen any Indians in the wilderness half so poor, and looking so sick. He was sure they had not half enough to eat. He said he thought it was wrong to send missionaries from this to the Indian country, when there were so many poor creatures here who want their help, and so many thousands as they saw going into the *chickabobbooags* to drink fire-water.

He said they came through a very grand street, where every thing looked so fine and splendid in the windows, and where the ladies looked so beautiful in their carriages, many of them lying quite down, and seemed as if they were very rich and happy; and some of them lay in their carriages, that were standing still, so as to let them read their books. And in this same grand street they saw a great many fine-looking ladies walking along the sides of the roads, and looking back at the gentlemen as they passed by them. These ladies, he and the Doctor observed, looked young, and all looked very smiling, and they thought they wanted husbands. A great deal, Jim said, they had seen of these ladies as they were every day looking out of their own windows in St. James's Street. A great many of these women, he said, behave very curious; he said he didn't know for certain but some of these might be *chimegotches*. This excited a tremendous laugh with the Doctor and several of the young men, and made some of the women smile, though it was rather hushed by the chiefs as an imprudent word for Jim to apply in the present case. This did little, however, to arrest the effects of Jim's joke, and he continued with some further ingenious embellishments, which set the chiefs into a roar, and Jim then kept the field. Melody and myself laughed also, not at the joke, for we did not understand it, but at their amusement, which seemed to be very great, and led us to inquire the meaning of *chimegotches*. "Fish," said Jim, "fish!" We were still at a loss for the meaning of his joke; and our ignorance being discovered, as well as our anxiety to know, they proposed that Jim should relate the story of *Chimegotches*, or "Fish." Some one was charging and lighting the pipe in the mean time, which was handed to him, as he rose and took a whiff or two, and then, resuming his former position, flat upon his back, he commenced—

> "When the great Mississippi river was a young and beautiful stream, and its waters were blue and clear, and the Ioways lived on its banks, more than a thousand snows since, *Net-no-qua*, a young man of great beauty, and son of a great chief, complained that he was sick. His appetite left him, and his sleep was not good. His eyes, which had been like those of the war-eagle, grew soft and dim, and sunk deep in his head. His lips, that had been the music for all about him, had become silent; his breast, that had always been calm, was beating, and deep sighs showed that something was wrong within. *O-za-pa*, whose medicine was great, and to whom all the plants and roots of the prairies were known, was quite lost; he tried all, and all was in vain; the fair son of the chief was wasting away, as each sweet breath that he breathed went off upon the winds, and never came back to him. Thus did *Net-no-qua*, the son of *Ti-ah-ka*, pine away. The medicine man told him at last that there was but one thing that could cure him, and that was attended with great danger. In his dream a small prairie snake had got upon a bush, and its light, which was that of the sun, opened his eyes to its brightness, and his ears to its words: 'The son of *Ti-ah-ka* grieves—this must not be—his breast must be quiet, and his thoughts like the quiet waters of the gliding brook; the son of *Ti-ah-ka* will grow like the

firm rocks of the mountain, and the chiefs and warriors, who will descend from him, will grow like the branches of the spreading oak.' The medicine man said to the son of *Ti-ah-ka* that he must now take a small piece of the flesh from his side for his bait, and in a certain cove on the bank of the river, the first fish that he caught was to be brought to his wigwam alone, under his robe, and she, whose blood would become warm, would be to him like the vine that clings around and through the branches of the oak: that then his eyes would soon shine again like those of the eagle; the music of his lips would soon return, and his troubled breast would again become calm, his appetite would be good, and his sleep would be sweet and quiet like that of a babe.

"*Net-no-qua* stood upon a rock, and when the hook, with a piece of his side, lay upon the water, the parting hair of *Lin-ta* (the river-born) was seen floating on the water, and its black and oily tresses were glistening in the sun as the water glided off from them; and her lips were opening to enclose the fatal hook that raised her beautiful breasts above the water. Her round and delicate arms shone bright with their beauty as she extended them to the shore, and the river shed its tears over her skin as her beautiful waist glided through its surface, above which the strong and manly arm of *Net-no-qua* was gently raising her. The weeping waves in sparkling circles clung around her swelling hips and pressing knees, until the folding robe of the son of *Ti-ah-ka* was over the wave and around her bending form. One hand still held her slim and tapering fingers, and with the other he encompassed her trembling form, as their equal steps took them from the shore and brought them to the wig-wam of *Net-no-qua*. His silent house was closed from the footsteps of the world; her delicate arms clung around the neck of the son of the chief, and her black and glossy tresses fell over and around his naked shoulders and mingled with his own. The same robe embraced them both, and her breath was purer than the blue waves from which she came. Their sleep was like the dreams of the antelope, and they awoke as the wild rose-buds open amidst the morning dew; the breast of *Net-no-qua* was calm, his eyes were again like the eyes of the eagle, his appetite was keen, and his lips sounded their music in the ears of Lin-ta. She was lovely, she was the wife of the son of the chief, and like the vine that clings around and through the branches of the oak, did she cling to *Net-no-qua*. They were happy, and many have been the descendants that have sprung from the dreams of the son of *Ti-ah-ka* and the beautiful *Lin-ta* (the river-born).

"*O-ne-ak'n* was the brother of *Net-no-qua*, and *Di-ag-gon* was his cousin: and *they* were sick; and they sat upon the rock in the cove in the river: and the two sisters of Lin-ta shone as they lifted their graceful forms above the wave, and their beautiful locks spread as they floated on the surface. The two young warriors sighed as they gazed upon them. The two sisters embraced each other as they glided through and above the waves. They rose to full view, and had no shame. The river 'shed no tears, nor did the sparkling waves hang in circles about their swelling hips and pressing knees;' and as they sank, they beckoned the two young warriors, who followed them to their water-bound caves. They stole back in the morning, and were ashamed and sick. Their tongues were not silent, and others went. The two sisters again showed their lovely forms as they glided above the water, and they beckoned all who came to their hidden caves, and all came home in the morning sick and sad, while every morning saw the son of the chief and his river-born Lin-ta calm and bright as the rising sun. Shame and fear they knew not, but all was love and happiness with them; very different were the sisters of Lin-ta, who at length ventured from their caves at night, and strolled through the village; they were hidden again at the return of the light. Their caves were the resorts of the young men, but the fair daughters of Lin-ta knew them not.

"Such was the story of Lin-ta (the river-born); she was the loved of her husband, and the virtuous mother of her children. Her beautiful sisters were the loved of all men, but had no offspring. They live in their hidden caves to this day, and sometimes in the day as well as in the night are seen walking through the village, though all the Indians call them *Chim-ee-gotch-es*, that is, *Cold-bloods*, or *Fish*."

Jim got a round of applause for his story, though the Doctor thought he had left out some of the most essential and funny parts of it. Jim, however, seemed well content with the manner in which it was received, and continued to remark that he and the Doctor had come to the conclusion that those beautiful young women, that they saw looking back at the gentlemen in the streets, as well as those who were standing in front of their windows, and bowing to them, and kissing their hands every day, must be "fish;" and that in the great village of London, where so much *chickabobboo* is drunk, there must be a great number of "fish." And they thought also that some of these they had seen in the Egyptian Hall when they were giving their dances.

The above and other critiques of Jim upon London modes seemed to the chiefs to be rather too bold, and an impolitic position for Jim to take; and whilst their reprimands were being passed upon him, the train of humour he had happened to get into on that night turned all their remarks into jokes, and they were obliged to join in the irresistible merriment he produced on this occasion, merely from his having taken (as his wife had refused it on this evening as it was just now discovered) the additional mug of his wife's *chickabobboo*.

Much merriment was produced amongst the Indians about this time by an appointment that had been made to see some experiments in mesmerism, to be performed by a Dr. M—— at the Indians' rooms. The Doctor was received at the appointed hour, and brought with him a feeble and pale-looking girl of 14 or 15 years of age to operate upon. This had taken the Indians rather by surprise, as no one had fully explained the nature of the operations to them. I got Jeffrey, however, to translate to them, as near as he could, the nature of this extraordinary discovery, and the effects it was to produce; and the doors being closed, and the young woman placed in a chair, the mesmeriser commenced his mysterious operations. I had instructed the Indians to remain perfectly still and not to laugh, lest they might hinder the operator, and prevent the desired effect. With one knee upon the floor, in front of her, and placing both of his extended thumbs (with his hands clenched) just in front of her two eyebrows, he looked her steadily in the face. This eccentric position and expression disposed Jim to laugh, and though he covered his huge mouth with his hand, and made no noise, still the irresistible convulsions in his fat sides shook the floor we were standing on; and the old Doctor at the same time, equally amused, was liable to do less harm, for all his smiles and laughter, however excessive, were produced by the curious machinery of his face, and never extended further down than the chin or clavicles. The little patient, however, was seen in a few minutes to be going to sleep, and at length fell back in the chair, in the desired state of somnambulism. The operator then, by mesmeric influences, opened her eyes, without touching them, and without waking her, and by the same influence closed them again. In the same way he caused her hand to close, and none of us could open it. Here our Doctor, who tried it, was quite at a stand. He saw the fingers of the operator pass several times in front of it, and its muscles relaxed—it opened of itself. He then brought, by the same influence, her left arm to her breast, and then the right, and challenged the strength of any one in the room to unbend them. This was tried by several of us, but in vain; and when his fingers were passed a few times lightly over them, they were relaxed and returned to their former positions. By this time the Indian women, with their hands over their mouths, began to groan, and soon left the room in great distress of mind. The chiefs, however, and the Doctor and Jim, remained until the experiments were all tried, and with unaccountable success. The operator then, by passing his fingers a few times over the forehead of his patient, brought her gradually to her senses, and the exhibition ended. The convulsions of Jim's broad sides were now all tempered down into cool quiet, and the knowing smiles of the old Doctor had all run entirely off from, and out of, the furrows of his face, and a sort of painful study seemed to be contracting the rigid muscles that were gathering over them.

Nº. 12.

The chiefs pronounced the unaccountable operation to be the greatest of medicine, and themselves quite satisfied, as they retired; but the old Doctor, not yet quite sure, and most likely thinking it a good thing for his adoption among the mysteries of his profession in his own country, was disposed to remain, with his untiring companion Jim, until some clue could be got to this mystery of mysteries. With this view he had the curiosity of feeling the little girl's pulse, of examining and smelling the operator's fingers, &c., and of inquiring whether this thing could be done by any others but himself; to which I replied, that it was now being done by hundreds all through the country, and was no secret. The charm had then fled—it had lost all its value to the old Doctor. The deep thoughts ceased to plough his wrinkled face, and his self-sufficient, happy smiles were again playing upon his front. His views were evidently changed. *Jim* caught the current of his feelings, and amusement was their next theme. The old Doctor "thought that *Jim* could easily be frightened," and would be a good subject. It was proposed that *Jim* should therefore take the chair, and it was soon announced to the squaws, and amongst them to his wife, that *Jim* had gone to sleep, and was *mesmerised*. They all flew to the room, which upset the gravity of his broad mouth, and, with its movements, as a matter of course, the whole bearing of his face; and the operator's fingers being withdrawn from his nose, he left the chair amidst a roar of laughter. It was then proposed that the old Doctor should sit down and be tried, but he resisted the invitation, on the grounds of the *dignity of his profession*, which he got me to explain to the medical man, whom he was now evidently disposed to treat rather sarcastically, and his wonderful performance as a piece of extraordinary juggling, or, at least, as divested of its supposed greatest interest, that of novelty. He told him "that there was nothing new or very wonderful in the operation, that he could discover; it was no more than the charm which the snakes used to catch birds; and the more frightful and ugly a man's face was, the better he could succeed in it. He had no doubt but many ill-looking men amongst white people would use it as a mode of catching pretty girls, which they could not otherwise do, and therefore it would be called amongst white people a very useful thing."

"All the *medicine-men* (said he) in the Indian country have known for many years how to do the same thing, and what the white people know of it at this time they have learned from the Indians; but I see that they don't yet half know how to do it; that he had brought a *medicine dress* all the way with him for the very purpose, and if the mesmeriser would come the next morning at 9 o'clock, he should see him with it on, and he would engage to frighten any white lady to sleep in five minutes who would take a good look at him without winking or laughing." The mesmeriser did not come, though the Doctor was on the spot and ready. (*Plate No. 12.*)

An event which they had long been looking for with great solicitude took place about this time—the prorogation of Parliament, which afforded the poor fellows their only opportunity of seeing the Queen. They were driven off in good season in their bus, and succeeded in getting the most favourable view of the Queen and the Prince as they were passing in the state-carriage; and, to use their own words for it, "The little Queen and the Prince both put their faces quite out of their carriage of gold to look at us and bow to us." There is no doubt but by the kindness of the police they were indulged in a favourable position and had a very satisfactory view of Her Majesty the Queen, and it is equally certain that they will never cease to speak of the splendour of the effect of the grand pageant as long as they live.

The nightly excitements and amusements going on at the Egyptian Hall were increasing the public anxiety to see these curious people more at large, and we resolved to procure some suitable ground for the purpose, where their active limbs could be seen in full motion in the open air, as they are seen on their native prairies with their ball-sticks, in their favourite game of the ball, and the use of their bows and arrows, all of which they had brought with them, but could not use in their amusements at the Hall. Their dances, &c., were, however, to be kept up as usual, at night; and for their afternoon exercises in the open air, an arrangement was made for the use of "Lord's Cricket Ground," and on that beautiful field (prairie, as they called it) they amused thousands, daily, by their dances, archery, and ball-playing.[18] For this purpose an area of an acre or two was enclosed by a rope, and protected for their amusements by the police. To this the visitors advanced on every side, and seemed delighted with their rude appearance and native sports. This arrangement afforded the Indians the opportunity of showing their games and amusements to the greatest advantage, and also of meeting again the acquaintances they had made at the Egyptian Hall, and shaking hands with all who felt disposed to do them that honour. They had also brought with them, to illustrate the whole of Indian life, no less than three tents (wigwams) made of buffalo hides, curiously but rudely painted, which the squaws daily erected on the ground, in presence of the spectators, forming by no means the least accurate and pleasing part of the exhibition.

The beautiful scenes presented there could be repeated but a few days, owing to other uses to be made of the grounds; but during that time they were visited by vast numbers of the nobility of London, and several members of the Royal Family. The incidents of those days, which were curious and many, must be passed over, excepting that the Doctor daily beheld in front of the crowd, and at full length, the "jolly fat dame," to whom he as often advanced, with a diffident smile, to receive a beautiful rose, which she handed to him over the rope.

These amusements in the open air in the daytime, with the dances, &c., at the Hall in the evenings, with their "drive" in the morning, and civil attentions to persons calling on them at their rooms, now engrossed completely all their time, and they were actually compelled to give offence to some parties who called on them, and to whom they could not devote the time. Amongst those were several deputations from public schools, of clergymen, and Sunday school teachers; and also three very excellent Christian ladies in a party, one of whom, Mrs. E——, I was well acquainted with, and knowing her extensive Christian and charitable labours, I had encouraged to call, as she had expressed a strong desire to talk with them on the subject of religion. They appealed to me, and I desired them to call at another hour, which they did, and I said to the chief that there was another proposition for a talk on the subject of religion. This seemed to annoy them somewhat, and after smoking a pipe, they decided not to see them. I then told them that they were three ladies; this seemed to startle them for a few moments, but they smoked on, and finally the War-chief said "it was a subject on which, if they had anything more to say, they would rather say it to the men than to women—they can talk with our women if they like." I then invited the Indian women into the room, and Jeffrey interpreted for the ladies, who had a long conversation with them, but, as the ladies afterwards told me, few words on the subject of religion: as to the first questions on that subject, the squaws answered that they left that mostly to their husbands, and they thought that if they loved their husbands, and took good care of their children, the Great Spirit would be kind to them. These kind ladies called the next day and left them fourteen Bibles and some other very useful presents, and their prayers for their happiness, feeling convinced that this was the most effectual and best way of making lasting and beneficial impressions on their minds.

One of the very high compliments paid them from the fashionable world was now before them, and this being the day for it, all parties were dressing and painting for the occasion. I had received a very kind note from Mrs. Lawrence, inviting me to bring them to pay her a visit in her lovely grounds at Ealing Park, a few miles from the city of London. The omnibus was ready, and being seated, we were there with an hour's drive, and received on the fine lawn in the rear of her house. Here was presented the most beautiful scene which the Ioways helped to embellish whilst they were in the kingdom—for nothing more sweet can be seen than this little paradise, hemmed in with the richness and wildness of its surrounding foliage, and its velvet carpet of green on which the Indians were standing and reclining, and the kind lady and her Royal and noble guests, collected in groups, to witness their dances and other amusements. Their Royal Highnesses the Duke and Duchess of Cambridge, with the lovely Princess Mary, the Hereditary Grand Duke and Duchess of Mecklenburgh Strelitz, the Duchess of Gloucester, and many of the nobility, formed the party of her friends whom this lady had invited, and who soon entered the lawn to meet these sons of the forest, and witness their wild sports.

At the approach of the lady and her Royal party, the Indians all arose, and the chiefs having been introduced, half an hour or more was passed in a conversation with them, through Jeffrey and myself, and an examination of their costumes, weapons, &c., when they seated themselves in a circle, and passing the pipe around, were preparing for a dance. The first they selected was their favourite, the eagle-dance, which they gave with great spirit, and my explanation of the meaning of it seemed to add much to its interest. (*Plate No. 13.*) After the dance they strung their bows and practised at the target, and at length Mr. Melody tossed up the ball, when they snatched up their ballsticks, which they had brought for the purpose, and darted over and about the grounds in the exciting game of the ball. This proved more amusing to the spectators than either of the former exercises, but it was short, for they soon lost their ball, and the game being completed, they seated themselves again, and with the pipe were preparing for the *war-dance*, in which, when they gave it, the beautiful lawn, and the forests around it, resounded with the shrill notes of the *war-whoop*, which the frightened parroquets and cockatoos saucily echoed back with a laughable effect, and a tolerable exactness. The pipe of peace (or calumet) dance was also given, with the pipes of peace in their hands, which they had brought out for the purpose.

While these exciting scenes were going on, the butler was busy spreading a white cloth over a long table arranged on the lawn, near the house, and on it the luxuries that had been preparing in the kitchen, for their dinners. This arrangement was so timed that the roast beef was on and smoking just when their amusements were finished, and when the announcement was made that their "dinner was up," all parties moved in that direction, but in two divisions, the one to partake, and the other to look on and see how wild people could handle the knife and fork. This was to be the *last*, though (as I could see by the anxiety of the spectators) not the *least amusing* of their amusements, and it was in the event rendered peculiarly so to some of us, from the various parts which the kind and illustrious spectators were enabled to take in it, when in all their former amusements there was no possible way in which they could "lend a hand." Every one could here assist in placing a chair or handing a plate, and the Indians being seated, all were ready and emulous, standing around the table and at their elbows, to perform some little office of the kind, to assist them to eat, and to make them comfortable. His Royal Highness proposed that I should take my stand at the head of the table, before a huge sirloin of roast beef, and ply the carving knife, which I did; whilst he travelled, plates in hand, until they all were helped. The young Princess Mary, and the two little daughters of the kind lady, like the three Graces, were bending about under loads of bread and vegetables they were helping the Indians to, and the kind lady herself was filling their glasses from the generous pitcher of foaming ale, and ordering the butler to uncork the bottles of champagne which were ready and hissing at the delay.

Nº. 13.

This unusual scene was taking place in the nearer vicinity of the poor parroquets and cockatoos, who seemed, thus far, awed into a discretionary silence, but were dancing to the right and the left, and busily swinging their heads to and fro, with their eyes and their ears open to all that was said and done. When the cork flew from the first bottle of champagne, the parrots squalled out, "There! there!! there!!!" and the Indians as suddenly, "*Chickabobboo! chickabobboo!*" Both laughed, and all the party *had* to laugh, at the simultaneous excitement of the parrots and the Indians; and most of them were as ignorant of the language (and of course of the wit of) the one as of the other. *Chickabobboo*, however, was understood, at least by the Indians; and their glasses being filled with champagne, the moment they were raising it to their lips, and some had commenced drinking, the cockatoos suddenly squalled out again, "*There! there!! there!!!*" The old Doctor, and his superstitious friend Jim, who had not got their glasses quite to their mouths, slowly lowered them upon the table, and turned, with the most beseeching looks, upon Mr. Melody and myself, to know whether they were breaking their vow to us. They said nothing, but the question was sufficiently plain in their *looks* for an answer, and I replied, "No, my good fellows, the parrots are fools, they don't know what they are talking about; they, no doubt, thought this was whiskey, but we know better; it's some of the '*Queen's chickabobboo*,' and you need not fear to drink it." This curious affair had been seen but by a part of the company, and only by the Indians at our end of the table, and therefore lost its general effect until I related it. The queer-sounding word "*chickabobboo*" seemed to amuse, and to excite the curiosity of many, and there was no understanding it without my going over the whole ground, and explaining how and where it originated, which, when finished, created much

- 62 -

amusement. While I was relating this story the plates were being changed, and just at the end of it the parrots sang out again, *"There! there!! there!!!"* as before; but it was discovered that, at that instant, one of the waiters was passing near them with a huge and smoking plum-pudding, and so high that we could but just see his face over the top of it. This was placed before me, and as I divided and served it, the same hands, Royal and fair, conveyed it to the different parts of the table. This was a glorious pudding, and I had helped each one abundantly, expecting, as all did, that they would devour it without mincing; but, to the surprise of all, they tasted a little, and left the rest upon their plates. Fears were entertained that the pudding did not suit them, and I was constrained to ask why they did not eat more. The reply was reluctant, but very significant and satisfactory when it came. Jim spoke for all. He said, "They all agreed that it was good—very good; but that the beef was also very good, and the only fault of the pudding was, that it had come too late."

The War-chief at this time was charging his long pipe with *k'nick k'neck*, and some fire being brought to light it, it was soon passed from his into the chiefs hands, when he arose from the table, and offering his hand to His Royal Highness, stepped a little back, and addressed him thus:—

"My Great Father,—Your face to-day has made us all very happy. The Great Spirit has done this for us, and we are thankful for it. The Great Spirit inclined your heart to let us see your face, and to shake your hand, and we are very happy that it has been so. (*How, how, how!*)

"My Father,—We have been told that you are the uncle of the Queen, and that your brother was the King of this rich country. We fear we shall go home without seeing the face of your Queen, except as we saw it in her carriage; but if so, we shall be happy to say that we have seen the great chief who is next to the Queen. (*How, how, how!*)

"My Father,—We are poor and ignorant people from the wilderness, whose eyes are not yet open, and we did not think that we should be treated so kindly as we have to-day. Our skins are red, and our ways are not so pleasing as those of the white people, and we therefore feel the more proud that so great a chief should come so far to see us, and to help to feed us; this we shall never forget. (*How, how, how!*)

"My Father,—We feel thankful to the lady who has this fine house and these fine fields, and who has invited us here to-day, and to all the ladies and gentlemen who are here to see us. We shall pray for you all in our prayers to the Great Spirit, and now we shall be obliged to shake hands with you and go home. (*How, how, how!*)"

His Royal Highness replied to him,—

"That he and all his friends present had been highly pleased with their appearance and amusements to-day, and most of all with the reverential manner in which he had just spoken of the Great Spirit, before whom we must all, whether red or white, soon appear. He thanked the chiefs for the efforts they had made to entertain them, and trusted that the Great Spirit would be kind to them in restoring them safe home to their friends again."

At this moment, when all were rising and wrapping their robes around them preparing to start, the lady appeared among them, with a large plate in her hands, bearing on it a variety of beautiful trinkets, which she dispensed among them according to their various tastes; and with a general shake of the hand, they retired from the grounds to take their carriage for town. The parrots and cockatoos all bowed their heads in silence as they passed by them; but as the old Doctor (who always lingers behind to bestow and catch the last smile, and take the second shake of the hand where there are ladies in question) extended his hand to the kind lady, to thank her the second and last time, there was a tremendous cry of *"There! there!! there!!!"* and *"Cockatoo! cockatoo!"*—the last of which the poor Doctor, in his confusion, had mistaken for *"Chickabobboo! chickabobboo!"* He, however, kept a steady gait between the din of *"There! there!! there!!!"* and *"Cockatoo!"* that was behind him, and the inconceivable laughter of his party in the carriage, who now insisted on it (and almost made him believe), that his ugly face had been the sole cause of the alarm of the birds and monkeys since the Indians entered the ground.[19]

This was theme enough, to ensure them a merry ride home, where they arrived in time, and in the very best of humour, for their accustomed evening amusements at the Hall; and after that, of taking their suppers and *chickabobboo* in their own apartments, which resounded with songs and with encomiums on the kind lady and her *chickabobboo*, until they got to sleep.

The next morning we had an appointment to visit the Surrey Zoological Gardens, and having the greatest curiosity to witness the mutual surprise there might be exhibited at the meeting of wild men and wild animals, I was one of the party. The interview, in order to avoid the annoyance of a crowd, had been arranged as a private one: we were, therefore, on the spot at an early hour; and as we were entering (the Doctor, with his jingling dress and red face, being in advance of the party, as he was sure to be in *entering* any curious place, though the last to *leave* if there were ladies behind), we were assailed with the most tremendous din of *"There! there!! there!!!"* *"Cockatoo! cockatoo!"* and *"God dam!"* and fluttering of wings of the poor affrighted parrots, that were pitching down from their perches in all directions. I thought it best that we should retreat a few moments, until Mr. Cross could arrange the front ranks of his aviary a little, which he did by moving back some of their outposts to let us pass. We had been shown into a little office in the meantime, where Mr. Melody had very prudently suggested that they had better discharge as many of their rattling gewgaws as possible, and try to carry into the ground as little of the frightful as they could. Amusing jokes were here heaped upon the Doctor for his extreme ugliness, which, as Jim told him, had terrified the poor birds almost to death. The Doctor bore it all patiently, however, and with a smile; and partially turned the laugh upon Jim with the big mouth, by replying that it was lucky for the gentleman owning the parrots that Jim did not enter first; for if he had, the poor man would have found them all dead, instead of being a little alarmed, as they then were.

We were now entering upon the greatest field for the speculations and amusement (as well as astonishment) of the Indians that they were to meet in the great metropolis. My note-book was in my hand and my pencil constantly employed; and the notes that I then and in subsequent visits made, can be allowed very little space in this work. All were ready, and we followed Mr. Cross; the Indians, fourteen in number, with their red faces and red crests, marching in single file. The squalling of parrots and barking of dogs seemed to have announced to the whole neighbourhood that some extraordinary visitation was at hand; and when we were in front of the lions' cage, their tremendous bolts against its sides, and unusual roar, announced to the stupidest animal and reptile that an enemy was in the field. The terrible voice of the king of beasts was heard in every part, and echoed back in affrighted notes of a hundred kinds. Men as well as beasts were alarmed, for the men employed within the grounds were retreating, and at every turn they made amidst its bewildering mazes, they imagined a roaring lion was to spring upon their backs. The horrid roaring of the lions was answered by lions from another part of the garden. Hyenas and panthers hissed, wolves were howling, the Indians (catching the loved inspiration of nature's wildness) sounded their native war-whoop, the buffaloes bellowed, the wild geese stretched their necks and screamed; the deer, the elk, and the antelopes were trembling, the otters and beavers dived to the bottom of their pools, the monkeys were chattering from the tops of their wire cages, the bears were all at the summit of their poles, and the ducks and the geese whose wings were not cropped, were hoisting themselves out of their element into quieter regions.

The whole establishment was thus in an instant "brushed up," and in their excitement, prepared to be seen to the greatest possible advantage; all upon their feet, and walking their cages to and fro, seemingly as impatient to see what they seemed to know was coming, as the visiting party was impatient to see them.

I explained to the Indians that the lion was the king of beasts—and they threw tobacco before him as a sacrifice. The hyenas attracted their attention very much, and the leopards and tigers, of the nature of all of which I promised to give them some fuller account after we got home. They met the panther, which they instantly recognized, and the recognition would seem to have been mutual, from its evident alarm, evinced by its hissing and showing its teeth. *Jim* called for the Doctor "to see his brother," the wolf. The Doctor's *totem* or *arms* was the wolf—it was therefore *medicine* to him. The Doctor advanced with a smile, and offering it his hand, with a smirk of recognition, he began, in a low and soft tone, to howl like a wolf. All were quiet a moment, when the poor animal was led away by the Doctor's "*distant howlings*," until it raised up its nose, with the most pitiable looks of imploration for its liberty, and joined him in the chorus. He turned to us with an exulting smile, but to his "poor imprisoned brother," as he called it, with a tear in his eye, and a plug of tobacco in his hand, which he left by the side of its cage as a *peace-offering*.

The ostrich (of which there was a noble specimen there) and the kangaroo excited the admiration and lively remarks of the Indians; but when they met the poor distressed and ragged prisoner, the buffalo from their own wild and free prairies, their spirits were overshadowed with an instant gloom; forebodings, perhaps, of their own approaching destiny. They sighed, and even wept, for this worn veteran, and walked on. With the bears they would have shaken hands, if they could have done it, "and embraced them too," said the Little-wolf, "for he had hugged many a one." They threw tobacco to the rattlesnake, which is *medicine* with them, and not to be killed. The joker, *Jim*, made us white men take off our hats as we passed the beaver, for it was his relation; and as he had learned a little English, when he heard the ducks cry "quack," he pointed to them and told the Doctor to go there—he was called for.

Thus rapid were the transitions from surprise to pity, and to mirth, as we passed along, and yet to wonder and astonishment, which had been reserved for the remotest and the last. Before the massive *elephant* little or nothing was said; all hands were over their mouths; their tobacco was forgotten, they walked quietly away, and all of us being seated under an arbour, to which we were conducted, our kind guide said to Jeffrey, "Tell the Indians that the immense arch they see now over their heads is made of the jaw-bones of a whale, and they may now imagine themselves and the whole party sitting in its mouth." "Well, now," said Jeffrey, "you don't say so?" "Yes, it's even so." "Well, I declare! why, the elephant would be a mere baby to it." Jeffrey explained it to the Indians, and having risen from their seats, and being satisfied, by feeling it, that it was actually bone, they wished to go home, and "see the rest at a future time." We were then near the gate, where we soon took our carriage, and returned to their quarters in St. James's Street.

CHAPTER XXI.

Indians' remarks on the Zoological Gardens—Their pity for the poor buffalo and other animals imprisoned—Jim's talk with a clergyman about Hell and the hyænas—Indians' ideas of astronomy—Jim and the Doctor hear of the hells of London—Desire to go into them—Promised to go—Indians counting the gin-palaces (*chickabobboo-ags*)in a ride to Blackwall and back—The result—Exhibition in the Egyptian Hall—A sudden excitement—The War-chief recognises in the crowd his old friend "Bobasheela"—Their former lives on the Mississippi and Missouri—Bobasheela an Englishman—His travels in the "Far West" of America—Story of their first acquaintance—The doomed wedding-party—Lieut. Pike—Daniel Boone and Son—Indians visit a great brewery—Kind reception by the proprietors—Great surprise of the Indians—Immense quantities of *chickabobboo*—War-dance in an empty vat—Daniel commences Jim's book of the statistics of England—Indians visit the Tunnel—Visit to the Tower—The Horse Armoury—The Royal Regalia—Indians' ideas of the crowns and jewels—"*Totems*" (arms) on the fronts of noblemen's houses—Royal arms over the shops—Strange notions of the Doctor—They see the "man with the big nose" again—And the "great white War-chief (the Duke of Wellington) on horseback, near his wig-wam."

Three or four of my particular friends had joined us in our visit to the Zoological Gardens this morning, and amongst them a reverend gentleman, whose professional character was not made known to the Indians. He kept close to Jeffrey and the Indians all the way, and his ears were open to the translation of everything they said. He was not only highly amused at their remarks, but told me he heard enough to convince him that lessons of morality, of devotion, and religion, as well as of philosophy, might be learned from those poor people, although they were the savages of the wilderness, and often despised as such. Mr. Melody and I accompanied them to their rooms, and as we came in when their dinner was coming up, we sat down and partook of it with them. The Indian's mode is to *eat exclusively* while he eats, and to talk afterwards. We adhered to their rule on this occasion, and after the dinner was over, and a pipe was lit, there were remarks and comments enough ready, upon the strange things they had just seen.

As usual, the first thing was, to have a laugh at the Doctor for having frightened the parrots; and then to reflect and to comment upon the cruelty of keeping all those poor and unoffending animals prisoners in such a place, merely to be looked at. They spoke of the doleful looks they all wore in their imprisoned cells, walking to and fro, and looking through the iron bars at every person who came along, as if they wished them to let them out. I was forcibly struck with the truth and fitness of their remarks, having never passed through a menagerie without coming out impressed, even to fatigue, with the sympathy I had felt for the distressed looks and actions of these poor creatures, imprisoned for life, for man's amusement only.

Jim asked, "What have all those poor animals and birds done that they should be shut up to die? They never have murdered anybody—they have not been guilty of stealing, and they owe no money; why should they be kept so, and there to die?" He said it would afford him more pleasure to see one of them let loose and run away over the fields, than to see a hundred imprisoned as they were. The Doctor took up the gauntlet and reasoned the other way. He said they were altogether the happiest wild animals he ever saw; they were perfectly prevented from destroying each other, and had enough to eat as long as they lived, and plenty of white men to wait upon them. He did not see why they should not live as long there as anywhere else, and as happy. He admitted, however, that his heart was sad at the desolate look of the old buffalo bull, which he would like to have seen turned loose on the prairies.

The Roman-nose said he heard one of the parrots say "God dam." "So he did," said Jim; "and who could say otherwise, when the Doctor poked his ugly face so suddenly in amongst them? They know how to speak English, and I don't wonder they say God dam."[20]

I here diverted their attention from the jokes they were beginning upon the Doctor, by asking them how they liked the *chickabobboo* they got in the gardens, which they recollected with great pleasure, and which they pronounced to have been very good. Mr. Cross had invited the whole party to a private view, and after showing us, with great politeness, what he had curious, invited us into one of his delightful little refreshment rooms, and treated all to cold chickens, pork pies, pastries, and champagne, which the Indians called *chickabobboo*; and as he did not know the meaning of the word, I related the story of it, which pleased him very much.

The Doctor made some laugh, by saying that "he was going over there again in a few days, if he could find some strings long enough, to measure the elephant and the bones of the whale, as he had got the dimensions of the giant man." Jim told him "he had not got the measure of the *giant man*—he had only measured the *giant woman*, and getting scared, he only half measured her; and he was so much afraid of women, that he didn't believe he could ever take the measure of one of them correct, if a hundred should stand ever so still for him." The Doctor smiled, and looked at me as if to know if I was going to ask some question again. He was fortunately relieved at that moment, however, by Mr. Melody's question to Jim, "how he liked the looks of the hyenas, and whether he would like him to buy one to carry home with him?" Jim rolled over on to his back, and drew his knees up (the only position in which he could "think fast," as he expressed it; evidently a peculiarity with him, and a position, ungraceful as it was, which it was absolutely necessary for him to assume, if he was going to tell a story well, or to make a speech); and after thinking much more profoundly than it required to answer so simple a question, replied, "Very well, very well," and kept thinking on. The Little Wolf, who was lying by his side, asked him "what he was troubled about?—he seemed to be thinking very strong." Jim replied to this, that "he was thinking a great way, and he had to think hard." He said, that when he was looking at the hyenas, he said to Jeffrey that he thought they were the wickedest looking animals he ever saw, and that he believed they would go to hell; but that the gentleman who came to the garden with Mr. Melody[21] said to him, "No, my friend, none but the animals that laugh and cry can go to heaven or to hell." He said that this gentleman then wanted to know how he had heard of hell, and what idea he had of it. He said, he told Jeffrey to say to him that some white men (*black coats*) had told amongst his people, that there was such a place as hell, very low under the earth, where the wicked would all go, and for ever be in the fire. He said, the gentleman asked him if he believed it? and that he told him he thought there might be such a place for white people—he couldn't tell—but he didn't think the Indians would go to it. He said, the gentleman then asked him why he thought those poor ignorant animals the hyenas would go there? And he replied to him that *Chippehola*[22] said "the hyenas live by digging up the bodies of people after they are buried;" and he therefore thought they were as wicked as the white people, who also dig up the Indians' graves, and scatter their bones about, all along our country;[23] and he thought such white people would go to hell, and ought to go there. He said he also told the gentleman he had heard there were some hells under the city of London, and that he had been invited to go and see them: this, he said, made the gentleman laugh, and there was no more said: that he had begun to think that this gentleman was a *black coat*, but when he saw him laugh, he found out that he was not. "Just the time you were mistaken," said Mr. Melody; "for that gentleman *was* a clergyman, and you have made a very great fool of yourself." "I will risk all that," said Jim; "I have wanted all the time to make a speech to some of them, but the chiefs wouldn't let me."

The pipe, during these conversations, was being handed around, and Jim's prolific mind, while he was "thinking fast" (as he had called it), was now running upon the elephant, and he was anxious to know where it came from. I told him it was from the opposite side of the globe: he could not understand me, and to be more explicit, I told him that the ground we stood upon was part of the surface of the earth, which was round like a ball, and many thousands of miles around; and that these huge animals came from the side exactly opposite to us. I never could exactly believe that Jim, at the moment, doubted my word; but in the richness of his imagination (particularly in his thinking position) he so clearly saw elephants walking underside of the globe, with their backs downwards, without falling, that he broke out into such a flood of laughter, that he was obliged to shut out his thoughts, and roll over upon his hands and knees until the spasms went gradually off. The rest of the group were as incredulous as Jim, but laughed less vehemently; and as it was not a time to lecture further on astronomy, I thought it best to omit it until a better opportunity: merely waiting for Jim's pencil sketch (and no doubt according to his first impression), which he was then drawing, with considerable tact; and with equal wit, proposed I should adopt as my "arms" or *totem*, the globe with an inverted elephant.

Melody and I strolled off together, leaving the Indians in this amusing mood, while we were agreeing that they were a good-natured and well-disposed set of men, determining to take everything in the happiest way; and that they were well entitled to our protection, and our best energies to promote their welfare. We saw that they enjoyed every thing that we showed them, with a high relish; and in hopes that they might profit by it, and feel a stronger attachment to us, we resolved to spare no pains in showing them whatever we could, that they might wish to see, and which would be likely, in any way, to render them a benefit.

The reader will have seen, by this time, that they were a close observing and an amusing set of fellows: and knowing also that at this time nearly all the curious sights of London were still before us, he will be prepared to meet the most exciting and amusing parts of this book as he reads on.

We continued to give these curious and good fellows their daily drives in their bus, and by an hour spent in this way each day, for several months, they were enabled to form a tolerably correct idea of the general shapes and appearance of the city, and its modes, as seen in the streets. In these drives, as well as in institutions of various kinds, which they visited, they saw many curious things which amused them, and others which astonished them very much; but their private room was the place for their amusing debates, and remarks upon them, when they returned: and to that I generally repaired every night before they went to bed, to hear what they had to say and to think, of the sights they had seen during the day.

Chickabobboo, though an Ojibbeway word, had now become a frequent and favourite theme with them, inasmuch as it was at this time an essential part of their dinners and suppers, and as, in all their drives about town, they were looking into the "gin palaces" which they were every moment passing, and at the pretty maids who were hopping about, and across the streets, in all directions, both night and day, with pitchers of ale in their hands. The elevated positions of the Doctor and Jim, as they were alongside of the driver of the bus, enabling them, in the narrow streets, to peep into the splendid interior of many of these, as they were brilliantly illumined, and generally gay with bonnets and ribbons, and imagining a great deal of happiness and fun to reign in them, they had several times ventured, very modestly, to suggest to me a wish to look into some of them—"not to drink," as they said, "for they could get enough to drink at home, but to see how they looked, and how the people acted there."

I had told them that if they had the least curiosity, there should be no objection to their going with me on some proper occasion, when they again got on their frock coats and beaver hats; and also that if there were any other curious places they wished to see in London, Mr. Melody or I would take them there. Upon hearing this the big-mouthed and quizzical Jim at once took me at my word, and told me that "some gentleman with Daniel had been telling him and the Doctor that there were several *'hells'* under the city of London, and that they ought some time to go down and see them." He didn't think from what Daniel and that man said that they were hells of "fire," but he thought as Daniel had been to them, there could not be much danger, and he thought they would be very curious to see; he knew these were not the hells which the *black coats* spoke of, for Daniel told him there were many beautiful ladies, and fine music, and *chickabobboo* there; that they did not wish to drink the *chickabobboo*, but merely to look and see, and then come away; and they had no objections to put on the black coats for that purpose; he said, in fact, that Daniel had invited them to go, and that Jeffrey had agreed to go with them. Jim had me thus "upon the hip" for this enterprise, and when I mentioned it to poor Melody, he smiled as he seemed to shrink from it, and said, "Ah, Catlin, that never will do: we are going to spoil these Indians, as sure as the world; there will be in a little time nothing but what they will want to see, and we shall have no peace of our lives with them. They have all gone now, and Daniel and Jeffrey with them, in their bus, all the way to Blackwall, merely to see how many *chickabobbooags* (gin palaces) they can count in the way, going by one route and returning by another. Their minds are running on *chickabobboo* and such things already, and they are in the midst of such a scene of gin-drinking and drunkenness as they see every day, that I am almost sorry we ever undertook to drive them out at all. I am daily more and more afraid that they will all become drunkards, in spite of all I can do, and I sometimes wish I had them safe home, where we started from. You have no idea what a charge I have on my hands, and the annoyance I have about the front of their apartments every night, from women who are beckoning them down from their windows to the door, and even into the passages and streets. They seem daily to be losing their respect for me, and I find it every day more and more difficult to control them." "And so you will continue to find it," said I, "unless privileges and freedom to a reasonable extent are granted to them, while they are strictly adhering to the solemn promises and restraints we have laid them under. These people have come here under your promises to show them everything you can, and to teach them how the civilized world live and act. They have reposed the highest confidence in you to take care of and protect them, and in return they have solemnly promised to conduct themselves properly and soberly; and as long as they adhere to that, you should not let them doubt your confidence in them, by fearing to show them some parts of the shades as well as the lights of civilization. They are here to learn the ways of civilization, and I should deem it wrong to deny them the privilege, if they ask for it, of seeing such parts of it as you and myself would go to see. I have been to see the 'hells of London' myself, and would much sooner take my son there, and there give him the most impressive lesson in morality, than forbid him to go, expressing to him my fears of his contamination. These people are like children in some respects, and they are men in others; and while I fully appreciate all your noble attachment to them, and your anxieties for them, with the knowledge I have gained of the Indian character, I feel assured that as they are brought here to be shown everything of civilization, to restrict them in seeing the parts of it they desire to see, will be to exhibit to them a want of confidence which would be apt to lead to worse and more injurious results before you get home with them. I should have been very far from mentioning such places to them, or the many other dens of iniquity which exist in the great city of London and the cities of our own country, and which I hope they may remain strangers to; but they having heard of the hells of London, and expressed a desire to see them, I should feel no hesitation in giving Jim and the Doctor a peep into them, instead of representing them (as the means of keeping them away from them) as being a much greater degradation of human nature than they actually are."

Good, kind Melody looked so much distressed, that I finished my arguments here, and told him to "rest quite easy; there was a way by which we could get over it, and I not break my promise with Jim and the Doctor. That a friend of mine who had been into them recently and narrowly escaped with his life, would have a talk with them on the subject in a few days, and all would be right.[24] As for the joke they are on to-day, about the *gin-shops*, I don't see the least harm in it. They must have something to laugh at, and while they are getting their usual daily ride in the open air, they are passing one of the best comments that ever was made upon one of the greatest vices of the greatest city in the world."

The simple old Doctor, in his curious cogitations amidst the din of civilised excitements, while he had been ogling the thousands of ladies and gin-palaces, and other curious things all together, from the pinnacle of his bus, had brought home one day in round numbers the total amount of *chickabobbooags* that he had seen during the hour's drive on one morning. The enormous amount of these, when added up, seemed too great for the most credulous; and Jim, seeming to think that the Doctor had counted the ladies instead of the grog-shops, disputed the correctness of his report, which had led to the result that was being carried out to-day, by some pretty spirited betting between the Doctor, Jim, Daniel, and Jeffrey, as to the number of *gin palaces (chickabobbooags)* they should pass on their way from St. James's Street to Blackwall (where they had curiosity to taste "white bait"), and back again by a different route, taking *Euston Station* in their way as they returned. For this purpose it was arranged that the Doctor and Jim should take their customary seats with the driver; and *Roman Nose* and the *Little Wolf* inside of the bus, where there was less to attract their attention, should each take his side of the street, counting as they passed them, while the old War-chief should notch them on a stick which they had prepared for the purpose, having Daniel and Jeffrey by their sides to see that there was no mistake.

The amusements of this gigantic undertaking were not to be even anticipated until they got back, nor its difficulties exactly appreciated until they appeared in the prosecution of the design. At starting off, the *Roman Nose* and *Little Wolf* took their positions on opposite seats, each one appropriating a pane of glass for his observations, and the old War-chief with his deal stick in one hand and a knife in the other; and in this way they were ready for, and commenced operations. Each one as he passed a gin-shop, called out "*chickabobbooag!*" and the old chief cut a notch. This at first seemed to be quite an easy thing, and even allowed the old man an occasional moment to look around and observe the direction in which they were going, while the two amusing chubs who were outside could pass an occasional remark or two upon the ladies as they were commencing to keep an oral account, to corroborate or correct the records that were making inside. As they gradually receded from the temperate region of St. James's (having by an ignorant oversight overlooked the numerous *club-houses*), their labours began to increase, and the old War-chief had to ply his knife with precision and quickness; the two companions outside stopped all further conversation, holding on to their fingers for tens, hundreds, &c. The word *chickabobbooag* was now so rapidly repeated at times inside (and oftentimes by both parties at once), that the old chief found the greatest difficulty in keeping his record correct. The parties all kept at their posts, and attended strictly to their reckonings, until they arrived at Blackwall. They cast up none of their accounts there, but the old chief's record was full—there was no room for another notch. He procured another stick for the returning memorandums, and the route back, being much more prolific and much longer, filled each of the four corners of his new stick, and when it was full he set down the rest of his sum in black marks, with a pencil and paper which Daniel took from his pocket.

The reckoning, when they got back, and their curious remarks upon the incidents of their ride, were altogether very amusing, and so numerous and discordant were their accounts, that there was no final decision agreed upon as to the bets.

Their results were brought in thus:

War-chief	notches	446		
Jim	oral	432	doubtful	60
Doctor	oral	754	doubtful	0
	Average	544.		

What route they took I never was able to learn, but such were their accounts as they brought them in; and as it was ascertained that the Doctor had been adding to his account all the shops where he saw bottles in the windows, it was decided to be a reasonable calculation that he had brought into the account erroneously:

| Apothecaries and confectioners—say | 300 |
| Leaving the average of all together (which was no doubt very near the thing) Chickabobbooags | 450 |

So ended (after the half-hour's jokes they had about it) this novel enterprise, which had been carried out with great pains and much fatigue, and in which, it was suggested by them, and admitted by me, they had well earned a jug of *chickabobboo*.

The settlement of this important affair was not calculated by any means to lessen the Doctor's curiosity in another respect, and which has been alluded to before—his desire to visit some of those places, to see the manner in which the *chickabobboo* was made. I put him at rest on that subject, however, by telling him that there was none of it made at those shops where it was sold, but that I had procured an order to admit the whole party to one of the greatest breweries in the city, where the *chickabobboo* was made, and that we were all to go the next day and see the manner in which it was done. This information seemed to give great pleasure to all, and to finish for the present the subject of *chickabobboo*.

The night of this memorable day I had announced as the last night of the Indians at the Egyptian Hall, arrangements having been effected for their exhibitions to be made a few days in Vauxhall Gardens before leaving London for some of the provincial towns. This announcement, of course, brought a dense crowd into the Hall, and in it, as usual, the "jolly fat dame," and many of my old friends, to take their last gaze at the Indians.

The amusements were proceeding this evening, as on former occasions, when a sudden excitement was raised in the following manner. In the midst of one of their noisy dances, the War-chief threw himself, with a violent jump and a yell of the shrill war-whoop, to the corner of the platform, where he landed on his feet in a half-crouching position, with his eyes, and one of his forefingers, fixed upon something that attracted his whole attention in a distant part of the crowd. The dance stopped—the eyes of all the Indians, and of course those of most of the crowd, were attracted to the same point; the eyes of the old War-chief were standing open, and in a full blaze upon the object before him, which nobody could well imagine, from his expression, to be anything less exciting than a huge panther, or a grizly bear, in the act of springing upon him. After staring awhile, and then shifting his weight upon the other leg, and taking a moment to wink, for the relief of his eyes, he resumed the intensity of his gaze upon the object before him in the crowd, and was indulging during a minute or two in a dead silence, for the events of twenty or thirty years to run through his mind, when he slowly straightened up to a more confident position, with his eyes relaxed, but still fixed upon their object, when, in an emphatic and ejaculatory tone, he pronounced the bewildering word of *Bobasheela!* and repeated it, *Bobasheela?* "Yes, I'm *Bobasheela*, my good old fellow! I knew your voice as soon as you spoke (though you don't understand English yet)." *Chee-au-mung-ta-wangish-kee, Bobasheela.* "My friends, will you allow me to move along towards that good old fellow? he knows me;" at which the old chief (not of a *hundred*, but) of *many* battles, gave a yell, and a leap from the platform, and took his faithful friend *Bobasheela* in his arms, and after a lapse of thirty years, had the pleasure of warming his cheek against that of one of his oldest and dearest friends—one whose heart, we have since found, had been tried and trusted, and as often requited, in the midst of the dense and distant wildernesses of the banks of the Mississippi and Missouri. Whilst this extraordinary interview was proceeding, all ideas of the dance were for the time lost sight of, and whilst these veterans were rapidly and mutually reciting the evidences of their bygone days of attachment, there came a simultaneous demand from all parts of the room, for an interpretation of their conversation, which I gave as far as I could understand it, and as far as it had then progressed, thus:—The old Sachem, in leading off his favourite war-dance, suddenly fixed his eye upon a face in the crowd, which he instantly recognized, and gazing upon it a moment, decided that it was the well-known face of an old friend, with whom he had spent many happy days of his early life on the banks of the Mississippi and Missouri rivers in America. The old chief, by appealing to this gentleman's familiar Indian cognomen of *Bobasheela*, brought out an instant proof of the correctness of his recognition; and as he held him by both hands, to make proof doubly strong, he made much merriment amongst the party of Indians, by asking him if he ever "floated down any part of the great Mississippi river in the night, astride of two huge logs of wood, with his legs hanging in the water?" To which *Bobasheela* instantly replied in the affirmative. After which, and several *medicine* phrases, and masonic grips and signs had passed between them, the dance was resumed, and the rest of the story, as well as other anecdotes of the lives of these extraordinary personages postponed to the proper time and place, when and where the reader will be sure to hear them.

N°. 14.

The exhibition for the evening being over, Bobasheela was taken home with the Indians, to their lodgings, to smoke a pipe with them; and having had the curiosity to be of the party, I was enabled to gather the following further information. This *Bobasheela* (Mr. J. H., a native of Cornwall) (Plate No. 14), who is now spending the latter part of a very independent bachelor's life amongst his friends in London, left his native country as long ago as the year 1805, and making his way, like many other bold adventurers, across the Alleghany Mountains in America, descended into the great and almost boundless valley of the Mississippi, in hopes by his indefatigable industry, and daring enterprise, to share in the products that must find their way from that fertile wilderness valley to the civilized world.

In this arduous and most perilous pursuit, he repeatedly ascended and descended in his bark canoe—his pirogue or his Mackinaw boat, the Ohio, the Muskingham, the Cumberland, the Tennessee, the Arkansas, the Missouri, and Mississippi rivers; and amongst the thousand and one droll and amusing incidents of thirty years spent in such a sort of life, was the anecdote which the War-chief alluded to, in the unexpected meeting with his old friend in my exhibition-room, and which the two parties more fully related to me in this evening's interview. The good-natured Mr. H. told me that the tale was a true one, and the awkward predicament spoken of by the War-chief was one that he was actually placed in when his acquaintance first began with his good friend.

Though the exhibition had kept us to a late hour, the greetings and pleasing reminiscences to be gone over by these two reclaimed friends, and (as they called themselves) "brothers" of the "Far West," over repeatedly charged pipes of k'nick k'neck, were pleasing, and held us to a most unreasonable hour at night. When the chief, amongst his rapid interrogations to Bobasheela, asked him if he had preserved his *she-she-quoin*, he gave instant relief to the mind of his friend, from which the lapse of time and changes of society had erased the recollection of the chief's familiar name, *She-she-quoi-me-gon*, by which his friend had christened him, from the circumstance of his having presented him a *she-she-quoin* (or mystery rattle), the customary badge bestowed when any one is initiated into the degree of "doctor" or "brother."

From the forms and ceremonies which my good friend *Bobasheela* had gone through, it seems (as his name indicates) that he stood in the relationship of brother to the chief; and although the chief's interrogations had produced him pleasure in one respect, one can easily imagine him much pained in another, inasmuch as he was obliged to acknowledge that his sacred badge, his *she-she-quoin*, had been lost many years since, by the sinking of one of his boats on the Cumberland river. For his standing in the tribe, such an event might have been of an irretrievable character; but for the renewed and continued good fellowship of his friend in this country, the accident proved to be one of little moment, as will be learned from various incidents recited in the following pages.

In this first evening's interview over the pipe, my friend Mr. H., to the great amusement of the party of Indians, and of Daniel and the squaws, who had gathered around us, as well as several of my London friends, related the story of "floating down the Mississippi river on two logs of wood," &c., as follows:—

"This good old fellow and I formed our first acquaintance in a very curious way, and when you hear me relate the manner of it, I am quite sure you will know how to account for his recognizing me this evening, and for the pleasure we have both felt at thus unexpectedly meeting. In the year 1806 I happened to be on a visit to St. Louis, and thence proceeded up the Missouri to the mouth of the 'Femme Osage' to pay a visit to my old friend Daniel Boone, who had a short time before left his farm in Kentucky and settled on the banks of the Missouri, in the heart of an entire wilderness, to avoid the constant annoyance of the neighbours who had flocked into the country around him in Kentucky. The place for his future abode, which he had selected, was in a rich and fertile country, and forty or fifty miles from any white inhabitants, where he was determined to spend the remainder of his days, believing that for the rest of his life he would be no more annoyed by the familiarity of neighbours. I spent several weeks very pleasantly with the old pioneer, who had intentionally built his log cabin so small, with only one room and one bed for himself and his wife, that even his best friends should not break upon the sacred retirement of his house at night, but having shared his hospitable board during the day were referred to the cabin of his son, Nathan Boone, about four hundred yards distant, where an extra room and an extra bed afforded them the means of passing the night.

"The old hunter and his son were thus living very happily, and made me comfortable and happy whilst I was with them. The anecdotes of his extraordinary life, which were talked over for amusement during that time, were enough to fill a volume. The venerable old man, whose long and flowing locks were silvery white, was then in his 78th year, and still he almost daily took down his trusty rifle from its hooks in the morning, and in a little time would bring in a saddle of venison for our breakfast, and thus he chiefly supported his affectionate old lady and himself, and the few friends who found their way to his solitary abode, without concern or care for the future. The stump of a large cotton-wood tree, which had been cut down, was left standing in the ground, and being cut square off on the top, and his cabin being built around it, answered the purpose of a table in the centre of his cabin, from which our meals were eaten. When I made my visit to him, he had been living several years in this retired state and been perfectly happy in the undisturbed solitude of the wilderness, but told me several times that he was becoming very uneasy and distressed, as he found that his days of peace were nearly over, as two Yankee families had already found the way into the country, and one of them had actually settled within nine miles of him.

"Having finished my visit to this veteran and his son, I mounted my horse, and taking leave followed an Indian trail to the town of St. Charles, some thirty or forty miles below, on the north banks of the Missouri. I here visited some old friends with whom I had become acquainted on the lower Mississippi in former years, and intending to descend the river from that to St. Louis by a boat had sold my horse when I arrived there. Before I was ready to embark, however, an old friend of mine, Lieutenant Pike, who had just returned from his exploring expedition to the Rocky Mountains, had passed up from St. Louis to a small settlement formed on the east bank of the Mississippi, and a few miles below the mouth of the Missouri, to attend a wedding which was to take place on the very evening that I had received the information of it, and like himself, being intimately acquainted with the young man who was to be married, I resolved to be present if possible, though I had had no invitation to attend, it not being known to the parties that I was in that part of the country. The spot where the wedding was to take place being on the bank of the river, and on my route to St. Louis, I endeavoured to procure a canoe for the purpose, but not being able to get such a thing in St. Charles at that time for love or money, and still resolved to be at the wedding, I succeeded in rolling a couple of large logs into the stream, which laid upon the shore in front of the village, and lashing them firmly together, took a paddle from the first boat that I could meet, and seating myself astride of the two logs I pushed off into the muddy current of the Missouri, and was soon swept away out of sight of the town of St. Charles. My embarkation was a little before sundown, and having fifteen or twenty miles to float before I should be upon the waters of the Mississippi, I was in the midst of my journey overtaken by night, and had to navigate my floating logs as well as I could among the snags and sandbars that fell in my way. I was lucky, however, in escaping them all, though I sometimes grazed them as I passed, and within a few inches of being hurled to destruction. I at length entered the broad waters of the Mississippi, and a few miles below on the left bank saw the light in the cabins in which the merry circle of my friends were assembled, and with all my might was plying my paddle to propel my two logs to the shore. In the midst of my hard struggle I discovered several objects on my right and ahead of me, which seemed to be rapidly approaching me, and I concluded that I was drifting on to rocks or snags that were in a moment to destroy me. But in an instant one of these supposed snags silently shot along by the side of my logs, and being a canoe with four Indians in it, and all with their bows and war-clubs drawn upon me, they gave the signal for silence, as one of them, a tall, long-armed, and powerful man, seized me by the collar. Having partially learned several of the languages of the Indian tribes bordering on the Mississippi, I understood him as he said in the Ioway language, 'Not a word! if you speak you die!' At that moment a dozen or more canoes were all drawn close around my two logs of wood, astride of which I sat, with my legs in the water up to my knees. These canoes were all filled with warriors with their weapons in their hands, and no women being with them, I saw they were a war party, and preparing for some mischief. Finding that I understood their language and could speak a few words with them, the warrior who still held me by the collar made a sign to the other canoes to fall back a little while he addressed me in a low voice. 'Do you know the white chief who is visiting his friends this night on the bank yonder where we see the lights?' to which I replied 'Yes, he is an old friend of mine.' 'Well,' said he, 'he dies to-night, and all those wig-wams are to be laid in ashes. *Stet-e-no-ka* was a cousin of mine, and *Que-tun-ka* was a good man, and a friend to the white people. The pale faces hung them like two dogs by their necks, and the life of your friend, the white warrior, pays the forfeit this night, and many may be the women and children who will die by his side!' I explained to him as well as I could that my friend, Lieutenant Pike, had had no hand in the execution of the two Indians; that they were hung below St. Louis when Lieutenant Pike was on his way home from the Rocky Mountains. I told him also that Lieutenant Pike was a great friend of the Indians, and would do anything to aid or please them; that he had gone over the river that night to attend the wedding of a friend, and little dreamed that amongst the Indians he had any enemies who would raise their hands against him.

"'My friend,' said he, 'you have said enough: if you tell me that your friend, or the friend or the enemy of any man, takes the hand of a fair daughter on that ground to-night, an Ioway chief will not offend the Great Spirit by raising the war-cry there. No Ioway can spill the blood of an enemy on the ground where the hands and the hearts of man and woman are joined together. This is the command of the Great Spirit, and an Ioway warrior cannot break it. My friend, these warriors you see around me with myself had sworn to kill the first human being we met on our war excursion; we shall not harm you, so you see that I give you your life. You will therefore keep your lips shut, and we will return in peace to our village, which is far up the river, and we shall hereafter meet our friends, the white people, in the great city,[25] as we have heretofore done, and we have many friends there. We shall do no harm to any one. My face is now blackened, and the night is dark, therefore you cannot know me; but this arrow you will keep—it matches with all the others in my quiver, and by it you can always recognize me, but the meeting of this night is not to be known.' He gave me the arrow, and with these words turned his canoe, and joining his companions was in a moment out of sight. My arrow being passed under my hat-band, and finding that the current had by this time drifted me down a mile or two below the place where I designed to land, and beyond the power of reaching it with my two awkward logs of wood, I steered my course onward toward St. Louis, rapidly gliding over the surface of the broad river, and arrived safely at the shore in front of the town at a late hour in the night, having drifted a distance of more than thirty-five miles. My two logs were an ample price for a night's lodging, and breakfast and dinner the next day; and I continued my voyage in a Mackinaw boat on the same day to *Vide Pouche*, a small French town about twenty miles below, where my business required my presence. The wedding party proceeded undisturbed, and the danger they had been in was never made known to them, as I promised the War-chief, who gave me as the condition of my silence the solemn promise, that he would never carry his feelings of revenge upon innocent persons any farther.

"Thus ends the story of 'floating down the Mississippi River on the two logs of wood,' which the War-chief alluded to in the question he put to me this evening. On a subsequent occasion, some two or three years afterwards, while sitting in the office of Governor Clark, the superintendent of Indian affairs in St. Louis, where he was holding 'a talk' with a party of Indians, a fine-looking fellow, of six feet or more in stature, fixed his eyes intently upon me, and after scanning me closely for a few moments, advanced, and seating himself on the floor by the side of me, pronounced the word '*Bobasheela*,' and asked me if ever I had received an arrow from the quiver of an Indian warrior. The mutual recognition took place by my acknowledging the fact, and a shake of the hand, and an amusing conversation about the circumstances, and still the facts and the amusement all kept to ourselves. This step led to the future familiarities of our lives in the various places where the nature of my business led me into his society, and gained for me the regular adoption as Bobasheela (or Brother) and the badge (the *she-she-quoin*, or Mystery Rattle) alluded to in the previous remarks, and which, it has been already stated, was lost by the sinking of one of my boats on the Cumberland River."

There was a burst of laughter and mirth amongst the squaws and others of us who had listened to this curious tale, and, as the reader will easily decide, a great deal of pleasure produced by its relation. The supper-table by this time was ready, and Bobasheela took a seat by the side of his old friend. The author was also in the humour, and joined them at their beef-steak and *chickabobboo*, and so did Mr. Melody and Daniel, and all who had joined in the merriment of the occasion of *Bobasheela's* relation of the story of his going to the wedding astride of the two logs of wood. After the supper was over, and while the pipe was passing around, a number of other recitals of adventures in the "Far-West" continued the amusements of the evening to a late hour, when the author retired and left them to their own jokes and their night's rest.

The next morning after this was an exciting and bustling one, as all were preparing, at an early hour, to visit the great brewery on that day, as had been promised; and on their way back to see the Thames Tunnel, and the treasures of the Tower of London. One will easily see that here was a gigantic day's work struck out, and that material enough was at hand for my note-book. *Bobasheela* must be of this party, and therefore was not left behind: with all in (except the two bucks, who habitually went outside), the Indian bus, with four horses, was a travelling *music* box as it passed rapidly through the streets; and the clouds of smoke issuing from it at times often spread the alarm that "she was all on fire within" as she went by. At the brewery, where they had been invited by the proprietors, servants in abundance were in readiness to turn upon their giant hinges the great gates, and pass the carriage into the court; and at the entrance to the grand fountain of *chickabobboo* there were servants to receive them and announce their arrival, when they were met, and with the greatest politeness and kindness led by one of the proprietors, and an escort of ladies, through the vast labyrinths and mazes, through the immense halls and courts, and under and over the dry-land bridges and arches of this smoking, steeping, and steaming wonder of the world, as they were sure to call it when they got home. The vastness and completeness of this huge manufactory, or, in fact, village of manufactures, illustrated and explained in all its parts and all its mysterious modes of operation, formed a subject of amazement in our own as well as the Indians' minds—difficult to be described, and never to be forgotten.

When the poor untutored Indians, from the soft and simple prairies of the Missouri, seated themselves upon a beam, and were looking into and contemplating the immensity of a smoking steeping-vat, containing more than 3000 barrels, and were told that there were 130 others of various dimensions in the establishment—that the whole edifice covered twelve acres of ground, and that there were necessarily constantly on hand in their cellars 232,000 barrels of ale, and also that this was only one of a great number of breweries in London, and that similar manufactories were in every town in the kingdom, though on a less scale, they began, almost for the first time since their arrival, to evince profound astonishment; and the fermentation in their minds, as to the consistency of white man's teachings of temperance and manufacturing and selling ale, seemed not less than that which was going on in the vast abyss below them. The pipe was lit and passed around while they were in this contemplative mood, and as their ears were open, they got, in the meantime, further information of the wonderful modes and operations of this vast machine; and also, in round numbers, read from a report by one of the proprietors, the quantity of ale consumed in the kingdom annually. Upon hearing this, which seemed to cap the climax of all their astonishment, they threw down the pipe, and leaping into an empty vat, suddenly dissipated the pain of their mental calculations by joining in the Medicine (*or Mystery*) Dance. Their yells and screaming echoing through the vast and vapouring halls, soon brought some hundreds of maltsmen, grinders, firers, mashers, ostlers, painters, coopers, &c., peeping through and amongst the blackened timbers and casks, and curling and hissing fumes, completing the scene as the richest model for the infernal regions.

Every reader will paint (and *must* paint) this picture for himself, imagining the steeping vapour everywhere rising in curling clouds of white towards the blackened walls, and timbers, and wheels, and stairways, and arches, and bridges, and casks, and from amongst and between all of these, the blackened faces and glaring eyeballs piercing through the steam, upon the unusual, and to them as yet unaccountable, *fermentation* going on (to the admiration and amusement of those who were in the secret) in the empty vat! At the end of their dance, a foaming mug of the *delicious* was passed around, enabling them more easily and lightly to comprehend the wonders of this mighty scene; and after they had finished their round, and seen its varied mysteries, a huge and delicious beefsteak, and foaming mugs of the *cream of chickabobboo*, prepared for them by the kind lady of one of the proprietors of the establishment, soon smoothed off all the edges of their astonishment; and after the war-dance and the war-whoop, given to please the ladies, they again passed under the huge arches and gateways, and took their omnibus for a visit to the *Tower*.

The mood in which these good-natured fellows had left the brewery was a very merry one; they had got just ale enough for the present emergency, and seen an abundant and infallible source at the great fountain of *chickabobboo* to ensure them a constant supply, and seemed, as they passed along the streets, to be pleased with everything they saw. They met the man again with the "big nose," and succeeded in stopping the bus to take a good look at his wonderful proboscis. As the bus stopped, he, like many others, came up to catch a glimpse of the red skins, and they all declared, on close examination, that his nose at least must have been begot by a potato; for, as the women had before said, they could distinctly see the sprouts, and Jim and the Doctor both insisted, that "if it were planted it would sprout and grow."

They stopped the bus again to speak with some poor Lascars sweeping the streets; it was difficult to get any interpretation from them, though the Indians tried their own language on both sides, but in vain; they gave them fifteen shillings, and passed on.

The Tower, from its outward appearance, did not seem to excite in them any extravagant expectation of what they were to see within its gloomy walls. They remarked, when going in, that "they were going to prison;" and they were of opinion, no doubt, that it consisted of little else, as they had as yet heard no other description of it than that it was the *"Tower of London"* and they were going to see it. Poor fellows! they guessed right; they knew not of the illustrious prisoners who had pined within its gloomy walls, nor of the blood that had been shed within and around it. They went to *see*, and had enough to engage all their thoughts and attention without referring to the events of history. We were kindly conducted through the different rooms, and most of its curiosities explained to us. The "small-arms room," containing 200,000 muskets, had been burned. The "horse armoury" seemed to afford them much delight; the thousands of various spears and lances, they thought, presented some beautiful models for Indian warfare, and hunting the buffaloes. The *beheading block*, on which Lords Balmerino, Kilmarnock, and Lovat were beheaded in the Tower in 1746, attracted their attention, and the axe that severed the head of Anne Boleyn.

In the *Regalia Room*, the crown of her Majesty and four other crowns, the sceptres and staffs, and orbs, swords of justice, swords of mercy, royal spurs, salts, baptismal fonts, &c., in massive gold and brilliant stones, seemed rather to disappoint than to astonish them; and to us, who knew better than they did the meaning and value of these magnificent treasures, there seemed a striking incongruity in the public exhibition of them in so confined and humble an apartment.

The *Thames Tunnel* was our next object, and a drive of a quarter of an hour brought us to the dismal neighbourhood of its entrance. Paying our fees, and descending some hundred or more steps by a spiral staircase, we were ready to enter the tunnel. Walking through its gloomy halls, and spending a few shillings for toys protruded under our faces at every rod we advanced, by young women sitting at their little stalls under each of its arches, we at length ascended an equal number of steps, and came to the light of day on the opposite side of the Thames; and in the midst of one of the most unintelligible, forlorn, and forsaken districts of London or the world, we waited half an hour or more for our omnibus to make its circuit across the bridge and take us up. We sauntered and loitered our way through, and as long as we were passing this monster speculation of the world, we met, to the best of our recollection, but four or five persons passing through, who had paid their penny a-head for the privilege.

While waiting for the bus, some "on-the-spot" remarks were made by the Indians, which I thought had some sound sense in them. They thought it must have cost a great deal of money, and believed it was too far out of London ever to pay; and they did not see that it was any curiosity for them, as they had passed through several on the railway ten times as long. They did not think, however, that it need be time and money thrown away, as "they thought it might make a first-rate place to twist ropes." These and other remarks they were making about the great tunnel as we were jogging along towards home, and evidently somewhat surprised that we should have excited their curiosity so high about it.

On our return, after this fatiguing day's work was finished, their dinner was ready; and after that their pipe was smoked, a nap taken, and then their accustomed amusements in the Egyptian Hall. Their supper was the next thing, and with it their mug of *chickabobboo*, then their pipe, passing around as they all reclined on their buffalo robes on the floor, and then began the gossip about the sights they had seen and incidents they had witnessed during the day.

This extraordinary day's rambling had taken them across more bridges and through a greater number of crooked and narrow streets than they had passed on any former occasion, which brought the Doctor to one of the first and shrewdest remarks of the evening. He said "he thought from all that he had seen, sitting on top of the bus all day, that the English people had the best way in the world for crossing rivers, but he thought their *paths* were many of them too narrow and much too crooked."

"The poor people, and those who seemed to be drunk, were much more numerous than they had seen them in any other of their drives;" and they were counting the money left in their pouches to see how much they had thrown out to the poor. They soon agreed that "they had given away something more than thirty shillings, which they thought would do a great deal of good, and the Great Spirit would reward them for it."

The *Doctor* and *Jim*, the everlasting cronies, on the outside, were comparing their estimates of the numbers they had counted of the "*Kon-to-too-ags* (fighters with one horn)[26] that they had seen over the doors and shops as they had passed along, which they had been looking at every day since they came to London, but had never yet been able quite to learn the meaning of," and also "the *totems* (arms, as they supposed) of great chiefs, so beautifully painted and put out between their chamber windows."

The Doctor said "he believed the white people had got this custom from the Indians, as it was the habit of the great chiefs and warriors to put their '*totems*' over their wig-wam doors, but when they did so, they always put out scalps on certain days, to show what they had done. He had watched these totems in London as he had been riding, in all sorts of weather, and as he had seen no scalps or anything hung out by the side of them, he couldn't exactly see how all these people were entitled to them; still, it might all be right." Daniel put the Doctor's inquiries all at rest on the subject of totems and the "one-horn fighters," by telling him that if he would wait a little until Mr. Catlin and Mr. Melody had gone, he would give him the whole history of white men's totems, how they got them and the use they made of them; and he would also tell him all about the "Lion and the Unicorn fighting for the Crown," &c.

The Doctor here made some comments on the great white war-chief (the Duke of Wellington) who had been pointed out to them on horseback as they passed him in the street, and his wig-wam was also shown to them (*i.e.* to the Doctor and Jim as they sat outside with the driver). He was disposed to learn something more of him, and Daniel silenced him by saying, "Let that alone too for awhile, and I will tell you all about him."

Daniel and Jim I found at this time very busily engaged in a corner of the room, with a candle on the floor; whilst Daniel was entering in a little book the astonishing estimates given us at the brewery, of the quantity of ale on hand, the size and number of the vats, and the almost incredible quantity consumed in the kingdom each year. Jim, as I have before said, was the only one of the party who seemed ambitious to civilize; and as he was daily labouring to learn something of the English language, he had this day conceived the importance of instituting a little book of entries in which he could carry home, to enlighten his people, something like a brief statistical account of the marvellous things he was seeing, and was to see, amongst the white people.

Daniel had at this moment finished entering into it the estimates of the brewery and *chickabobboo*, which had opened their eyes wider, perhaps, than anything else they had seen; and he had very wisely left a few blank pages in the beginning of the book for other retrospective notes and estimates of things they had already seen since the day they left home. Jim's Journal was thus established, and he was, with Daniel's aid, to become a sort of historian to the party; and as the sequel will show, he became stimulated thereby to greater exertions to see and to understand what was curious and interesting, and to get estimates of the beauties and blessings of civilization to carry home. He laboured from that moment indefatigably, not to write or to read, but to speak; and made rapid progress, as will be seen hereafter, having known, as he said, but two English sentences when he came to England, which were, "How do do?" and "God dam."

CHAPTER XXII.

The Ioways in Vauxhall Gardens—Surrey Theatre—Carter in the lions' cage—Astonishment of the Indians—Indians in the Diving Bell, at the Polytechnic Institution—Indians riding—Shooting at target on horseback—Ball-play—"Jolly fat dame"—Ladies converse with the Doctor—His reasons for not marrying—Curious questions—Plurality of wives—Amusing scene—The Author in Indian costume—A cruel experiment—Ioways arrive in Birmingham—The Author's arrival there—Society of Friends—Indians all breakfast with Mr. Joseph Sturge—Kind treatment—Conversation after breakfast about religion and education—Reply of the War-chief—The button-factory of Turner and Sons—Generous presents to the Indians—*Bobasheela* arrives—Indians dividing their buttons—Doctor found on top of the Shakespeare Buildings—Indians' kindness to a beggar-woman—Poor-houses—Many Friends visit the Indians—Indians' visit to Miss Catherine Hutton—Her great age—Her kindness—Dinner—Her presents to them in money—Parting scene—The War-chief's speech to her—Her letters to the Author—Indians present to the two hospitals 370 dollars—Address read by the Presidents to the Indians—Doctor's reply—Indians start for York—A fox-hunt—Curious notions of Indians about it—Visit to York Minster—Ascend the grand tower—Visit to the castle and prison—Museum of the instruments of murder—Alarm of the Doctor—Kindness of the governor of the castle and his lady—Indians' ideas of imprisonment for debt, and punishment for murder.

The scene of the Indians' amusements was now changed from the Egyptian Hall to the open air in Vauxhall Gardens, and their dances and other exercises were given in the afternoon. Their lodgings were also changed at the same time to the buildings within the enclosure of the gardens. This arrangement was one of very great pleasure to the Indians, as it allowed a free space to exercise in during their leisure hours, amongst trees and shrubbery, affording them almost a complete resumption of Indian life in the wilderness, as they had the uninterrupted range of the gardens during the hours that the public were not there to witness their amusements. This arrangement was pleasing to them in another respect, and to us also, as there were many things they were yet anxious to see in London, and which, as they could only be seen at night, our former arrangements had entirely precluded them from seeing. Under these new arrangements they still had their omnibus drives, and at night attended the parties of numerous friends who had been desirous to show them some attentions, and also were taken to several instructive exhibitions, and to two or three of the principal theatres.

We were then in the vicinity of the Surrey Theatre, where Mr. Carter, "the lion-tamer," invited them several times to witness his wonderful feat of going into the lion's cage. This scene was one of the most impressive and exciting nature to them, and will probably be as long recollected by them as the wonders opened to their minds at the *fountain of chickabobboo*.

The Polytechnic Institution was one I took great pleasure in accompanying them to; and a scene of much amusement for a numerous audience as well as amusing and astonishing to themselves, was that of their descending in the diving-bell. They were at first afraid of it, but after the Doctor had made a descent with me, and come out unhurt and unwet, several others went down with Mr. Melody, others with Jeffrey—the old War-chief with his old friend *Bobasheela*, and so on, until every one of the party, men, women, and children, went down and experienced the curious sensation of that (to them) greatest of *medicine affairs*.

In Vauxhall Gardens the Indians erected their four wig-wams of buffalo hides, and in darting into and about them during their various games and amusements, whilst the blue smoke was curling out of their tops, presented one of the most complete and perfect illustrations of an Indian encampment that could possibly have been designed. It was *the thing itself*, and the very men, women, and children living and acting on a similar green turf, as they do on the prairies of the Missouri.

In the amusements as there given, there was an addition to those which had been made in *Lord's Cricket-ground* some weeks before, having in Vauxhall brought horses in to add, with equestrian exercises, to the completion of all the modes practised by this tribe. The Ioways, like most of the Indians of the prairies of America, subsist upon the food of the buffalo, and kill them from their horses' backs, with their bows and arrows, while running at full speed. In the same manner they meet their enemies in battle, in which they carry their shield and lance. Thus fully equipped, with their own native shields and lances, and bows, and even the saddles and trappings for their horses, they all mounted upon their backs, in the midst of their amusements, and dashing off at full speed, illustrated their modes of drawing the bow as they drove their arrows into the target, or made their warlike feints at it with their long lances as they passed.

This formed the most attractive part of their exhibition, and thousands flocked there to witness their powers of horsemanship and skill in prairie warfare. This exciting exhibition which pleased the visitors, I could have wished might have been less fatiguing, and even dangerous, to the limbs of the Indians than it actually was from the awkwardness and perverseness and fright of the horses, not trained to Indian modes. With all these difficulties to contend with, however, they played their parts cheerfully and well, and the spectators seemed highly pleased. Amidst the throngs who visited them here, we could discover most of their old standard friends and admirers, who came to see them on horseback, and in the beautiful game of ball, in the open grounds of Vauxhall, where they could more easily approach and converse with them; and amongst such, the "jolly fat dame" was present, and more pleased than ever, when she could catch the Doctor's smile as he passed by her at full speed, and raising his shield of buffalo's hide upon his arm, he darted his long lance in feints at her breast, and sounded the piercing warcry. The vanity of the Doctor was so well suited in this mode of the exhibition, where he could dash by ranks and files, and even phalanxes of ladies, with the endless flourishes of his shield and lance, that he soon began to exhibit convincing evidences that his ambition and his vanity were too much for his bodily resources, which it became necessary to replenish occasionally by refusing him his horse, on which occasions he made good use of his time, by placing himself, wrapped in his robe, with his fan in his hand, by the side of the ladies, with whom he could exchange by this time a few words, and many significant looks and gestures, which never failed to amuse, and seldom failed to operate upon their generous feelings, which were constantly adding to the contents of his tobacco pouch, which was now known to be a reservoir for money and trinkets of various kinds, instead of tobacco.

I happened to be by the side of the Doctor on one of these occasions, when I became so much amused with the questions and answers, that I immediately after retired and committed them to my note book. A number of jolly fat dames, of middle and knowing age, had drawn themselves around the Doctor, and looking over their shoulders and under their arms, a number of delicate and coy little girls. And having called Jeffrey to translate, they were enabled to get the gist of all he said, without loss from modesty or evasion, which seemed to be exactly what they most desired. His friend Jim having seen him thus enveloped, turned *his* horse loose and came to his aid (or countenance), and as the old man hesitated, Jim gave him the nod and the wink to be plain in his replies. They had first asked him if he was married? to which he replied "No." They then asked him why he did not get him a wife? he said "He had always been very particular about giving offence to the women, and he had feared that if he selected one in preference to the others, that the others would all be offended." This queer reply raised a great laugh amongst the crowd, and encouraged the Doctor to go on. Some one of the ladies then told him she feared he did not admire the ladies enough? he said, "he had always believed that the reason he did not get married was, that he admired them too much; he saw so many that he wanted, that he had never decided which to take, and so had taken none." Melody came up at this time, and seemed a little vexed, and said, "Catlin, you had better call that old fool away, those people will spoil him, he is quite vain enough now." "Oh, no," said I, "let him alone, he is gratifying the ladies, and we shall see, in a few moments, which is the fool, he or the ladies who are questioning him." Melody smiled, and looked on.

"I have been told," said one of the ladies, "that some of the Indians have a number of wives: is that so?"

"Yes," the Doctor replied in English, "sometimes have a heap." (The ladies all laughed.) Two or three inquired what a "*heap*" was? Jeffrey said, "Why, ma'am, it is what in our country means a '*lot*:' you know what they call a '*lot*' here?" "Oh, yes! it means a great many." "Yes, a number." "Well, tell the Doctor I want to know what they do with so many?"

Here the poor Doctor was quite at a loss to know what to say; one thing he was sure to do—he smiled—and it seemed as if he wished that to go for an answer: and it might have done so with most of her sex, but in this instance it was not quite satisfactory, and the question was again put: to which the big-mouthed Jim, who I said had come to the relief of his friend, and who had a wife of his own, put in an instant reply, which relieved the Doctor, and seemed very much to embarrass the lady, for she instantly added, (as all were bursting with laughter,) "That isn't what I mean: I want to know how a chief can get along with so many, how he can manage them all, and keep them in good humour and satisfied; for," said she, "in this country, one is quite as much as a man can manage."

This seemed to afford the Doctor a little relief, and he was evidently able to go on again, as he smilingly said, "It was quite easy, as Indian women were much more peaceable and quiet than white women, it was much more easy he thought to manage them; they drank no *chickabobboo*, and therefore did not require so much watching as white women."

The lady seemed quite balked in the debate she was about entering on with the Doctor, from her ignorance of the meaning of *chickabobboo*, and asked for an explanation of it, as if for all the company about; to which Jim put in (again in plain English), "Gin!" "Oh! Doctor," said she, "I hope you don't accuse the ladies of London of drinking gin?" The Doctor replied, that "he had not seen them do it, but that he had been told that they did, and that it was the reason why the ladies here grew so large and so fat." He said, "that they could always look out of the windows, where he lived, and just before going to bed they could see any night a hundred women going home with pitchers full of it, to drink after they got into bed, so as to sleep sound: and that one night, coming home in their carriage at a late hour, from a distance, where they had been to see a show, he and Jim had counted more than three hundred women running along in the street, with pitchers filled with it in their hands, to drink as they were going to bed."

The lady's explanation of this, that "It was only harmless ale that these women were carrying in for their masters and mistresses," excited the Doctor's smiles, but no reply.

She seemed not satisfied yet about the first subject that she had started, and reverting to it again, said, "Well, Doctor, I can't excuse the Indians for having so many wives. I like the Indians very much, but I don't like that custom they have; I think it is very cruel and very wicked. Don't you think it is wrong?"

The Doctor studied a moment, and replied, "that it might be wrong, but if it was, he didn't see that it was any worse than for white women to have a number of husbands." "But what, Doctor, what do you mean? I hope you have not so bad an opinion of white women as that?" To this he very coolly replied, "that when they drank a great deal of gin, he believed, from what he had seen in his practice, that a woman would require more than one husband; and that since he had been in London he had seen many walking in the streets, and some riding in fine carriages, whom he thought, from their looks, must have more than one husband: and from what he had been told, he believed that many women in London had a *heap*!" "That's a *lot*!" (cried out a very pretty little girl, who had been listening, and, frightened at her own unintentional interpretation, started to run.)

"Come, come, Catlin," said Melody, "pull the old fellow out, and take him away;" and so the debate ended, amidst a roar of laughter from all sides.

One more of the hundred little reminiscences of Vauxhall, and we will leave it. I have already said, that in the spacious apartments of Vauxhall, unoccupied, the Indians were quartered, and took their meals; and during the forepart of the day, between their breakfast and the hour of their afternoon exhibitions, their time was mostly spent in strolling around the grounds, or at their varied amusements. Many of my personal friends finding this a pleasing opportunity to see them, were in the habit of coming in, and amusing themselves with them. I had accidentally heard of a party of ladies preparing to come on a certain morning, some of them my esteemed friends, and others strangers to me: and from a wish to get relieved from a fatiguing conversation, as well as from a still stronger desire for amusement, I selected from my wardrobe a very splendid dress, head-gear and all complete, and fully arranged myself in Indian costume, "cap-à-pied," with face fully painted, and weapons in hand; and at the hour of their arrival in the house, took care to be strolling about in the grounds with Wash-ka-mon-ya (Jim). Whilst the ladies were amused with the party in the house, where there were constant inquiries for me, two of them observing us two beaus sauntering about in the garden, came out to keep us company, and to talk to us, and with themselves, in the English language, which of course we Indians knew nothing of: when we shook our heads to their inquiries, "Do you speak English, good

Indians?" I saw they did not recognize me, yet I trembled for fear, for they were lovely women, and every sentence almost which they uttered would have made the discovery more cruel: we held ourselves dignified and dumb; whilst they, poor things, were so much regretting that we could not understand what they said. They finished their visit to us and their remarks, and returned, leaving me to regret my folly upon which I had thoughtlessly entered.

Several weeks were spent in their daily exhibitions in Vauxhall, and, as one can easily imagine, much to the satisfaction of the Indians, and, I believe, much to the amusement of the visitors who came to see them. Within the last week of their exhibition I admitted from charity schools 32,000 children, with their teachers, free of charge; to all of whom I gave instructive lectures on the position of the tribe, their condition, their customs and character: and explained also the modes, which were acted out by 14 living Indians before their eyes; and but one of these schools ever communicated with me after, to thank me for the amusement or instruction; which might not have been a *curious omission*, but I thought it *was*, at the time.

With the amusements at Vauxhall ended my career in London; and contemplating a tour to several of the provincial towns, in company with the Indians, I took my little family to Brighton, and having left them comfortably situated and provided for, I joined the party in Birmingham, where they had arrived and taken lodgings. The idea of moving about pleased the Indians very much, and I found them all in high spirits when I arrived, delighted to have found that the *chickabobboo* was the same there as in London, and was likely to continue much the same in all parts of the kingdom to which they should go. There was an unfortunate offset to this pleasing intelligence, however, which seemed to annoy them very much, and of which they were making bitter complaint. On leaving London for the country, they had spent some days, and exercised all their ingenuity, in endeavouring to clean their beautiful skin dresses, which the soot of London had sadly metamorphosed; and on arriving in Birmingham they had the extreme mortification to anticipate, from appearances, an equal destruction of that soft and white surface which they give to their skin dresses, and which (though it had been entirely lost sight of during the latter part of their stay in London) had, with great pains, been partially restored for a more pleasing appearance in the country.

Though I had several times passed through Birmingham, and on one occasion stopped there a day or two, I entered this time a total stranger, and in rather a strange and amusing manner. On my journey there by the railway, I had fallen in company and conversation with a very amusing man, who told me he was a commercial traveller, and we had had so much amusing chat together, that when we arrived, at a late hour at night, I was quite happy to follow his advice as to the quarters we were to take up in the town, at least for the night. He said it was so late that the hotels would be closed, and that the commercial inn, where he was going, was the only place open, and I should find there everything to make me comfortable, and a very nice sort of people. We took an omnibus for town, and as there was only room for one inside, he got upon the top, and so we went off; and getting, as I supposed, into or near the middle of the town, the bus stopped at a "commercial inn," which was open, and lighted up in front, and a number of passengers getting out, and others down from the top, I was seeing to get my luggage in safe, and the omnibus drove off with my jolly companion still on the top; or this I presumed, as he was not left behind. My only alternative now was, to make the best of it, and be as comfortable as I could; so I got into the "commercial room," and having been told that I should have a bed, I felt quite easy, and told the plump, tidy little landlady, who was waiting upon me herself, that I would have a mug of ale and a biscuit, and then be ready to go to bed. As she turned round to execute my command, she met a party consisting of three young women, and a man leading one of them on his arm, and in his hands carrying three or four carpet-bags and band-boxes, just got down from the same bus, and entering the inn on the same errand that I was on. " Madam," said he, "what have you?"—"Hevery-think, sir, that you can wish." "Well, one thing we must have, that is, two beds."—"They are ready, sir." "Well, ladies," said he, "suppose we take a drop of wet." This agreed to, the "wet" was brought in in a moment, and also my mug of ale.

A very genteel-looking little man whom I had seen in the same carriage with me, and now sitting in the room before me, with his carpet-bag by the side of him, and his umbrella in his hand, addressed me, "Stranger, you'll allow me."—"Certainly, sir." "I think I heard you tell a gentleman in the carriage that you were from New York."—"Yes, I did so." "*I'm* from there. I left there four months ago, and I've gone ahead, or I'll be shot. How long have *you* bin from there, sir?"—"About five years." "Hell! there's been great fixins there in that time; you'd scarcely know New York now; look here, isn't this the darndest strange country you ever saw in your life? rot 'em, I can't get 'em to do anything as I want it done; they are the greatest set of numskulls I ever saw; now see, that little snub of a petticoat that's just gone out there, I suppose she is cock of the walk here too; she's been all civility to you, but I've had a hell of a blow up with her; I was in here not five minutes before you by the watch, and I spoke for a bed and a mug of ale; she brought me the ale, and I told her to bring me a tumbler and a cracker, and she turned upon me in a hell of a flare-up. She said she was very much obliged to me for my himpudence, she didn't allow crackers in her house, and as for 'tumblers,' they were characters she never had anything to do with, thank God; they were a low set of creatures, and they never got any favour about her house. She wanted to know what quarter I came from. I told her I wasn't from *any quarter*, I was from *half*—half the globe, by God, and the better half too—wasn't I right, stranger? She said her house was a hinn, to be sure, but she didn't hentertain blackguards, so there was my hale, and I might drink it hup and be hoff, and be anged, and then she cut her string quicker than lightning; now isn't she a hard un? I don't suppose there is another house open in this darned outlandish place at this time of the night; what the devil shall I do? *you* are fixed snug enough." "Oh, well, never mind," said I, "be quite easy, it is settled in a moment,"—as I rung the bell. The tidy little landlady came in again, and I said, "This gentleman will have a glass if you please, and a biscuit."—"Hif he was a gentleman, Sir," said she, "but I assure you, Sir, is beaviour as'nt been much like it." "Well, well," said I, "never mind it now, you will be good friends after a little better understanding—he comes from a country where a glass is a *tumbler* and a biscuit is a *cracker*: now, if you had known this, there would have been no difficulty between you." "Ho, that I hadmit, but it's very hodd." "Never mind that, you will find him a good fellow, and give him his bed." "Is bed, Sir?—hit's too late; it's been hoccupied hever since you entered the ouse—the only chance his for you and im to turn hin." "Well," said I, "never mind, he and I will manage that; it is after midnight, and I suppose the other houses are all shut?" "I'll hanswer for that: hif you are ready, gentlemen, I'll show you hup." My friend kept by my side, but knowing the gloomy fate that awaited him if he got into the street again, he kept entirely quiet until the little landlady was down stairs. "There," said he, "isn't she a roarer? I could have settled the hash with her myself in a twinkling, if she had only let me have said five words, but her tongue run so slick that I couldn't get the half of a word in edgewise."

My new acquaintance and I talked a little more before we "turned in," but much more after we had got into bed. He could command words and ideas fast enough when he was on his feet; but I found in him something of Jim's peculiarity, that he thought much faster and stronger when on his back; and for half an hour or so I reaped the benefit of the improvement. How long I heard him, and how much he actually said, I never could tell exactly; but what he said before I went to sleep I always distinctly recollected, and a mere sentence or two of it was as follows:—"Well, stranger, here we are: this is droll, ain't it? 'hodd,' as the landlady would call it. I'd a been in the streets to-night as sure as catgut if it hadn't been for you. God knows I am obliged to you. Youv'e got a sort o' way o' gettin' along ur' these ere darned, ignorant, stupid sort o' beings. I can't do it: dod rot 'em! they put me out at every step; they are so eternally ignorant; did you ever see the like? I suppose you are going to stop awhile in Birmingham?" "A few days." "*I* shall be here a week, and be bright and early enough to get into a decenter house than this is, and be glad to join you. I was told in London that the Ioway Indians went on here yesterday. I'm damned anxious to meet them: you've seen them, I suppose?" "Yes, I saw them in London." "Well, *I* did not; I was just too late; but I must go and look 'em up to-morrow: they know me." "Then you have seen them'?" "Oh, dam 'em, yes: I've known 'em for several years: they'll be at home with me at once. I've run buffaloes with White-Cloud, the chief, many and many a time. He and I have camped out more than once. They are a fine set of fellows. I'm going to spend some time with them in Birmingham. I know 'em like a book. Oh yes, they'll know me quick enough. I was all through their country. I went clean up Lake Superior, nearly to Hudson's Bay. I saw all the Chippeways, and the Black-feet, and the Crows, Catlin's old friends. By the way, Catlin, I'm told, is with these Indians, or was, when they were in London—he's all sorts of a man." "Have you seen him?" "Seen him? why, dam it, I raised him, as the saying is: I have known him all my life. I met him a number of times in the Prairie country; he's a roarer." This was about the last that I distinctly recollected before going to sleep; and the next morning my vigilant and wide-awake little bedfellow, being about the room a little before me, where my name was conspicuous on my carpet bag and writing-desk, &c., had from some cause or other thought it would be less trouble and bother to wend his way amongst these "stupid and ignorant beings" alone, than to encounter the Indians and Mr. Catlin, and endeavour to obliterate the hasty professions he had made; and therefore, when I came down and called for breakfast for two, the landlady informed me that my companion had paid his bill and left at an early hour. I was rather sorry for this, for he was quite an amusing little man, and I have never heard of him since.

I found the dumpy little landlady kindly disposed, and she gave me a very good breakfast, amusing me a great deal with anecdotes of the party who called for "a little bit of wet;" she informed me they were a wedding-party, and the man who had the lady on his arm was the bride-groom. While waiting for my breakfast I was much amused with some fun going on in the street before the window. It seems that the house directly opposite had been taken by a couple of tidy-looking young women who were sisters, and that, having established a millinery business on the lower floor, they had several apartments which they were anxious to underlet in order to assist them in paying their heavy rent. Young gentlemen are everywhere in this country considered the most desirable lodgers, as they give less trouble than any others, are less of the time at home, and generally pay best. These young adventurers had been therefore anxious to get such a class of lodgers in their house, and had, the day before, employed a sign-painter to paint a conspicuous board, in bright and glaring letters, which was put up on a post erected in the little garden in front of their house, near the gate. The announcement ran, when the young ladies retired to bed, "*Lodgings for single gentlemen*"—a customary and very innocent way of offering apartments; but owing to the cruelty of some wag during the night it was found in the morning, to the great amusement of the collected crowd, to read, "*Longings for single gentlemen.*" How long this continued to amuse the passers-by, or how it might have affected the future prospects of the poor girls, I cannot of course tell, as I forthwith proceeded to a more pleasant part of the town. Birmingham I found on further acquaintance to be one of the pleasantest towns I visited in the kingdom, and its hotels and streets generally very different from those into which my commercial travelling acquaintance had that night led me.

Mr. Melody had all things prepared for our exhibition when I arrived, having taken the large hall in the Shakspeare Buildings, and also procured rooms for the Indians to sleep in in the same establishment.

The Indians and myself were kindly received in Birmingham, for which, no doubt, they, like myself, will long feel grateful. The work which I had published had been extensively read there, and was an introduction of the most pleasing kind to me, and the novelty and wildness of the manners of the Indians enough to ensure them much attention.

In their exhibition room, which was nightly well attended, we observed many of the Society of Friends, whom we could always easily distinguish by their dress, and also more easily by the kind interest they expressed and exhibited, whenever opportunity occurred, for the welfare of those poor people. The Indians, with their native shrewdness and sagacity, at once discovered from their appearance and manner that they were a different class of people from any they had seen, and were full of inquiries about them. I told them that these were of the same society as their kind friend Dr. Hodgkin, whom they so often saw in London, who is at the head of the *Aborigines Protection Society*, who was the first person in England to invite them to his table, and whom the reader will recollect they called *Ichon-na Wap-pa*(the straight coat); that they were the followers of the great William Penn, whom I believed they had heard something about. They instantly pronounced the name of "Penn, Penn," around the room, convincing me, as nearly every tribe I ever visited in the remotest wildernesses in America had done, that they had heard, and attached the greatest reverence to, the name of Penn.

These inquiries commenced in their private room one evening after the exhibition had closed, and they had had an interview in the exhibition room with several ladies and gentlemen of that society, and had received from them some very valuable presents. They all agreed that there was something in their manners and in their mode of shaking hands with them that was more kind and friendly than anything they had met amongst other people; and this I could see had made a sensible impression upon them.

I took this occasion to give them, in a brief way, an account of the life of the immortal William Penn; of his good faith and kindness in all his transactions with the Indians, and the brotherly love he had for them until his death. I also gave them some general ideas of the Society of Friends in this country, from whom the great William Penn came;—that they were the friends of all the human race; that they never went to war with any people; that they therefore had no enemies; they drink no spirituous liquors; that in America and this country they were unanimously the friends of the Indians; and I was glad to find that in Birmingham we were in the midst of a great many of them, with whom they would no doubt become acquainted. There were here some inquiries about the religion of the Friends, which I told them was the Christian religion, which had been explained to them; that they were all religious and charitable, and, whatever religion the Indians might prefer to follow, these good people would be equally sure to be their friends. They seemed, after this, to feel an evident pleasure whenever they saw parties of Friends entering the room: they at once recognised them whenever they came in, and, on retiring to their own room, counted up the numbers that had appeared, and made their remarks upon them. In one of these conversations I pleased them very much by reading to them a note which I had just received from Mr. Joseph Sturge, with whom I had been acquainted in London, and who was now residing in Birmingham, inviting me to bring the whole party of Indians to his house to breakfast the next morning. I told them that Mr. Sturge was a very distinguished man, and one of the leading men of the Society of Friends. This pleased them all exceedingly, and at the hour appointed this kind gentleman's carriages were at the door to convey the party to his house. Mr. Melody and Jeffrey accompanied us, and there were consequently seventeen guests to be seated at this gentleman's hospitable board, besides a number of his personal friends who were invited to meet the Indians. After receiving all in the most cordial manner, he read a chapter in his Bible, and then we were invited to the table. This interview elicited much interesting conversation, and gained for the Indians and Mr. Melody many warm and useful friends.

Before taking leave, the War-chief arose, and, offering his hand to Mr. Sturge, made the following remarks:—

"My Friend,—The Great Spirit, who does everything that is good, has inclined your heart to be kind to us; and, first of all, we thank Him for it.

"The Chief, White Cloud, who sits by me, directs me to say that we are also thankful to you for this notice you have taken of us, poor and ignorant people, and we shall recollect and not forget it.

"We hope the Great Spirit will be kind to you all. I have no more to say."

The simplicity of this natural appeal to the Great Spirit, and its close (in which they were commended by the poor and unenlightened Indian of the wilderness to the care and kindness of their God), seemed to create surprise in the minds of the audience, and to excite in the Indians' behalf a deep and lively interest.

After the breakfast and conversation were over, the whole party was kindly sent back by the same carriages, and the Indians returned in a state of perfect delight with the treatment they had met with, and the presents they had received.

Poor *Jim* (the student and recorder) was anxious that I should write down the name of *William Penn* in his book, and also that of the gentleman who had just entertained us, that he might be able to repeat them correctly when he got back to the wilderness again, and have something to say about them.

We found on our return that the hour of another engagement was at hand, and carriages were soon prepared to take us to the button-factory of Messrs. Turner and Son, to which we had been kindly invited; and on our arrival we found ourselves most cordially received and entertained. The proprietor led the party through every room in his extensive establishment, and showed them the whole process of striking the buttons and medals from various dies, which pleased them very much, and, after showing and explaining to them all the different processes through which they passed in their manufacture, led them into his ware-room or magazine, where his stock on hand was exhibited, and package after package, and gross upon gross, of the most splendid and costly buttons were taken down, and by his own generous hand presented to them. These were such *brilliant evidences* of kindness, and would be so ornamental to the splendid dresses which they and their wives were to have when they got home, that they looked upon them as more valuable than gold or silver. These were presented to them in the aggregate, and all carried in a heavy parcel by the interpreter; and when they had thanked the gentleman for his munificent liberality and got back to their rooms, a scene of great brilliancy and much interest and amusement was presented for an hour or two, while they had their treasures spread out, covering half of the floor on which they lodged, and making a *per capita* division of them.

In the midst of this exhilarating and dazzling scene, their old friend *Bobasheela* made his appearance, having just arrived from London on his way to Cornwall. He could not, he said, pass within a hundred miles of them without stopping to see them a few days, and smoke a pipe or two with them again. *Bobasheela* was stopped at the door, notwithstanding their love for him; he could not step in without doing sacrilege with his muddy boots to the glittering carpet of buttons which they had formed on the floor, and upon which his eyes were staring, as he thought at the first glance they could have committed no less a trespass than to have plundered a jeweller's shop. A way was soon opened for his feet to pass, and, having taken a hearty shake of the hand with all, he was offered a seat on the floor, and in a few moments found that an equal parcel was accumulating between his knees as in front of each, and that, instead of fourteen, they were now dividing them into fifteen parcels. This he objected to, and with much trouble got them to undo what they had done, and go back to the first regulation of dividing them equally amongst fourteen.

The Shakspeare Buildings afforded the Indians a fine promenade in its large portico overlooking the street, where all Birmingham passed before their eyes, giving them one of the most gratifying privileges they had had, and promising them a rich and boundless means of amusement; but their enjoyment of it was short, for the crowds that assembled in the streets became a hinderance to business, and they were denied the further privilege of their delightful look-out. They were therefore called in, and stayed in, and yet the crowd remained, and could not be dispersed, while their attention seemed fixed upon some object higher up than the portico, which led us at once to surmise its cause, and, searching for the old Doctor, he was not to be found: he was, of course, upon the pinnacle of the house, wrapped in his robe, smiling upon the crowd beneath him, and taking a contemplative gaze over the city and country that lay under his view. I could only get to him by following the intricate mazes through which the old lady (curatress) conducted me, and through which the Doctor said he had required several days of investigation to find his way, and which he had never succeeded in until just at that moment.

Under this rather painful embargo there was no satisfactory way of peeping into the amusements of the streets but by going down the stairs, which Jim and his ever-curious friend the Doctor used daily and almost hourly to do, and, standing in the hall, see all they could that was amusing, until the crowd became such that it was necessary to recall them to their room. On one of these occasions they had espied a miserably poor old woman, with her little child, both in rags, and begging for the means of existence. The pity of the kind old Doctor was touched, and he beckoned her to come to him, and held out some money; but fear was superior to want with her, and she refused to take the prize. The Doctor went for Daniel, who, at his request, prevailed upon the poor woman to come up to their room, by assuring her that they would not hurt her, and would give her much more than white people would. She came up with Daniel, and the Indians, all seated on the floor, lit a pipe as if going into the most profound council; and so they were, for with hearts sympathizing for the misery and poverty of this pitiable-looking object, a white woman and child starving to death amidst the thousands of white people all around her in their fine houses and with all their wealth, they were anxious to talk with her, and find out how it was that she should not be better taken care of. Jeffrey was called to interpret, and Melody, *Bobasheela*, Daniel, and myself, with two or three friends who happened to be with us at the time, were spectators of the scene that ensued. The War-chief told her not to be frightened nor to let her little child be so, for they were her friends; and the Doctor walked up to her, took his hand out from under his robe, put five shillings into hers, and stepped back. The poor woman curtsied several times, and, crossing her hands upon her breast, as she retreated to the wall, thanked "his Honour" for his kindness. "The Lard be with your Honours for your loving kindness, and may the Lard of Haven bless you to al etarnity, for ee niver e thought af sich threatment fram sich fraightful-lukin gantlemin as ee was a thakin you to ba."

The War-chief then said to her, "There, you see, by the money we have been all of us giving out of our purses, that we wish to make you happy with your little child, that you may have something for it to eat; you see now that we don't wish to hurt you, and we shall not; but we want to talk with you a little, and before we talk we always make our presents, if we have anything to give. We are here poor, and a great way from home, where we also have our little children to feed; but the Great Spirit has been kind to us, and we have enough to eat." To this the Indians, who were passing the pipe around, all responded *"How! how! how!"*

The old chief then proceeded to ask the poor woman how she became so poor, and why the white people did not take care of her and her child. She replied that she had been in the workhouse, and her husband was there still; she described also the manner in which she had left it, and how she became a beggar in the streets. She said that when she and her husband were taken into the poorhouse they were not allowed to live together, and that she would rather die than live in that way any longer, or rather beg for something to eat in the streets as she was now doing; and as the cold weather was coming in, she expected her child and herself would be soon starved to death.

The poor Indians, women and all, looked upon this miserable shivering object of pity, in the midst of the wealth and luxuries of civilization, as a mystery they could not expound, and, giving way to impulses that they could feel and appreciate, the women opened their trunks to search for presents for the little child, and by White Cloud's order filled her lap with cold meat and bread sufficient to last them for a day or two. The good old Doctor's politeness and sympathy led him to the bottom of the stairs with her, where he made her understand by signs that every morning, when the sun was up to a place that he pointed to with his hand, if she would come, she would get food enough for herself and her little child as long as they stayed in Birmingham; and he recollected his promise, and made it his especial duty every morning to attend to his pensioners at the hour appointed.[27]

The moral to be drawn from all this was one of curious interest and results in the minds of the Indians, and a long conversation ensued amongst them, in which *Daniel* and their friend *Bobasheela* (who were familiar with the sufferings and modes of treatment of the poor) took part, and which, as Melody and I had withdrawn, afterwards gave us some cause to regret that such a pitiable object of charity had been brought into their presence for the temporary relief they could give her, and which resulted in so glaring an account of the sum total of misery and poverty that was constantly about them, of the extent of which we both began to think it would have been better to have kept them ignorant. Daniel and *Bobasheela* had opened their eyes to the system of poorhouses and other public establishments for the employment and protection of the poor; and until this account, which was already entered in *Jim's* book, had been given them by these two knowing politicians, they had but little idea of this enormous item that was to go into the scales in weighing the blessings of civilization.

Almost daily visits were now being made to their private rooms by parties of ladies and gentlemen of the Society of Friends, with whom they were rapidly advancing into the most interesting acquaintance, and which I observed it was affording Mr. Melody almost unspeakable satisfaction to behold. They were kindly invited to several houses, and treated at their tables with the greatest friendship. Of these, there was one visit that it would be wrong for me to overlook and to neglect to give here the notes that I made of it at the time.

A note was written to me in a bold and legible hand by Miss Catherine Hutton, desiring to know "at what hour it would be suitable for her to come from her house, a few miles out of town, to see the Indians (for whom she had always had a great love), so as not to meet a crowd, for her health was not very good, being in the ninety-first year of her age." This venerable and most excellent lady I held in the highest respect, from a correspondence I had held with her on the subject of the Indians ever since I had been in England, though I never had seen her. Her letters had always teemed with love and kindness for these benighted people, and also with thanks to me for having done so much as I had for their character and history. I therefore deemed it proper to respond to her kindness by proposing to take the whole party to her house and pay her the visit. Her note was answered with that proposition, which gave her great pleasure, and we took a carriage and went to her delightful residence.

We were received with unbounded kindness by this most excellent and remarkable lady, and spent a couple of hours under her hospitable roof with great satisfaction to ourselves, and with much pleasure to her, as her letter to me on the following day fully evinced.[28] After a personal introduction to each one in turn, as she desired, and half an hour's conversation, they were invited into an adjoining room to a breakfast-table loaded with the luxuries she had thought most grateful to their tastes. This finished, another half-hour or more was passed in the most interesting conversation, containing her questions and their answers, and her Christian advice to prepare their minds for the world to which, said she, "we must all go soon, and, for myself, I am just going, and am ready." When we were about to take our leave of her, she called each one up in succession, and, having a quantity of money in silver half-crowns placed on the sofa by her side, she dealt it out to them as they came up, shaking hands at the same time and bidding each one a lasting farewell, embracing each of the women and children in her arms and kissing them as she took leave. This kindness melted their hearts to tears, and brought old *Neu-mon-ya* (the War-chief) up before her at full length, to make the following remarks:—

> "My Friend,—The Great Spirit has opened your heart to feel a friendship for the red people, and we are thankful to Him for it. We have been happy to see your face to-day, and our hearts will never forget your kindness. You have put a great deal of money into our hands, which will help to feed our little children, and the Great Spirit will not forget this when you go before him.

> "My kind Mother,—You are very old. Your life has been good; and the Great Spirit has allowed you to live to see us; and He will soon call you to Him. We live a great way from here, and we shall not look upon your face again in this world; though we all believe that, if we behave well enough, we shall see your face in the world to come."

The chief here stopped, and, shaking her hand again, withdrew. The excellent lady was overwhelmed in tears, and called to her maid, "Betty, bring all the silver that I left in the drawer there; bring the whole of it and divide it among them; my eyes are so weak that I cannot see it—give it to them, dear creatures! May God bless their dear souls!" Such had been the meeting, and such were her parting words as we came away.

The Indians continued to speak in terms of the greatest admiration of this kind old lady, and the certainty that they should never see her face again made them for some days contemplative and sad. They had many civilities extended to them in town, however, which were calculated to dissipate melancholy and contemplation. Their repeated visits to the house and the table of Doctor Percy were exceedingly pleasing to them, where they were amused with experiments in electricity and galvanism, and other chemical results, to them new, and far beyond the reach of their comprehensions.

Their days and nights were now passing away very pleasantly, visited by and visiting so many kind friends, doing all they could to make them happy—giving their nightly amusements at the Shakspearian Rooms, and enjoying the society and western jokes of their old friend *Bobasheela*, and, after their dinners and suppers, their other old friend, *chickabobboo*.

About this time some very kindly-disposed friends proposed that a couple of nights of their exhibitions should be given in the immense room of the Town-hall, and one half of the receipts be presented to the two hospitals, representing that upon such conditions they thought the use of the hall would be granted free of expense, and believing that the results would be beneficial to both parties. Mr. Melody and I at once consented, and, the entertainments on those two nights being for a charitable purpose, the crowds that came in were very great, and the receipts beyond what we expected, the profits being 145*l.* 12*s.*, the half of which, 72*l.* 16*s.*, the Ioways presented to the two hospitals, and on the following day were invited to attend at the Town-hall at eleven o'clock in the morning, to receive an acknowledgment of it from the venerable Presidents of the two institutions, and to hear an address which was prepared to be read and given to them. The Indians met the two kind and excellent gentlemen (both of whom were Friends), and many others, both ladies and gentlemen, of their society; and seeing the results of this meeting likely to be of a very interesting nature, I took pains to make notes of all that was said on the occasion. The venerable Mr. R. T. Cadbury, from the General Hospital, in a very impressive manner, and suited to their understandings, explained to the Indians, through their interpreter, the purpose for which the hospital was built and carried on, after which he read the following resolution, which had been passed at the weekly meeting of the Board of Governors on the preceding day:—

> "Resolved,—That the Chairman be requested to present the thanks of this Board to Mr. Catlin, Mr. Melody, and the Ioway Indians, for the donation of 36*l.* 8*s.*, being a moiety of the net proceeds of two exhibitions made for the benefit of the two hospitals at the Town-hall; and to assure them their generous gift shall be faithfully applied to the relief of the sick and maimed, for whose benefit the said hospital was instituted, and for sixty-five years has been supported by voluntary donations and subscriptions."

After reading this, Mr. Cadbury presented to each of them a copy of the annual report and rules of the institution, and expressed a hope that all of them would reach their distant homes in safety, and that their visit to this country would be beneficial to them.

The chief, *White Cloud*, shook hands with Mr. Cadbury, and replied as follows:—

> "My Friend,—I have very few remarks to make to you. We are all very thankful to you for the speech you have made to us, and for the prayer you have made that we may all reach home safe. Those words pleased all my people here very much, and we thank you for them.
>
> "My Friend,—We have now been some time in England, and, amongst all the words of friendship we have heard, nothing has been more pleasing

to us than the words we have heard from your lips. We have seen some of the greatest men in this country, and none have delighted us so much as you have by the way in which you have spoken; and we believe that the service we have rendered to the hospital will be looked on with mutual satisfaction.

"My Friend,—The Americans have been long trying to civilize us, and we now begin to see the advantages of it, and hope the Government of the United States will do us some good. I hope some of the people of my nation will place their children with white people, that they may see how the white children live.

"My Friend,—I have nothing more to say, but to thank you."

After the speech of White Cloud, Mr. J. Cadbury, at the head of a deputation from the *"Temperance Society"* (to which the Indians had sent also the sum of 36*l.* 8*s.*), presented himself, and read an address from that association, thanking them for the amount received, and advising the Indians to abstain from the use of *"fire-water"* and to practise *charity*, which was one of the greatest of virtues.

Mr. Cadbury then addressed the Indians, in all the fervency and earnestness of prayer, on the all-important subject of temperance. His words and sentences, selected for their simple understandings, were in the simplicity, and consequently the eloquence of nature, and seemed to win their highest admiration and attention. He painted to them in vivid colours the horrors and vice of intemperance, and its consequences; and also the beauty and loveliness of sobriety, and truth, and charity, which he hoped and should pray that they might practise in the wilderness, with constant prayers to the Great Spirit in the heavens, when they returned to their own country.

When this venerable gentleman's remarks were finished, the old Doctor (or Medicine-man) arose from his seat upon the floor, with his pipe in his lips, and, advancing, shook hands with the two Messrs. Cadbury, and, handing his pipe to the chief, spoke as follows:—

"My Friends,—I rise to thank you for the words you have spoken to us: they have been kind, and we are thankful for them.

"My Friends,—When I am at home in the wilderness, as well as when I am amongst you, I always pray to the Great Spirit; and I believe the chiefs and the warriors of my tribe, and even the women also, pray every day to the Great Spirit, and He has therefore been very kind to us.

"My Friends,—We have been this day taken by the hand in friendship, and this gives us great consolation. Your friendly words have opened our ears, and your words of advice will not be forgotten.

"My Friends,—You have advised us to be charitable to the poor, and we have this day handed you 360 dollars to help the poor in your hospitals. We have not time to see those poor people, but we know you will make good use of the money for them; and we shall be happy if, by our coming this way, we shall have made the poor comfortable.

"My Friends,—We Indians are poor, and we cannot do much charity. The Great Spirit has been kind to us though since we came to this country, and we have given altogether more than 200 dollars to the poor people in the streets of London before we came here; and I need not tell you that this is not the first day that we have given to the poor in this city.

"My Friends,—If we were rich, like many white men in this country, the poor people we see around the streets in this cold weather, with their little children barefooted and begging, would soon get enough to eat, and clothes to keep them warm.

"My Friends,—It has made us unhappy to see the poor people begging for something to eat since we came to this country. In our country we are all poor, but the poor all have enough to eat, and clothes to keep them warm. We have seen your poorhouses, and been in them, and we think them very good; but we think there should be more of them, and that the rich men should pay for them.

"My Friends,—We admit that before we left home we all were fond of *'fire-water,'* but in this country we have not drunk it. Your words are good, and we know it is a great sin to drink it. Your words to us on that subject, can do but little good, for we are but a few; but if you can tell them to the white people, who make the *'fire-water,'* and bring it into our country to sell, and can tell them also to the thousands whom we see drunk with it in this country, then we think you may do a great deal of good; and we believe the Great Spirit will reward you for it.

"My Friends,—It makes us unhappy, in a country where there is so much wealth, to see so many poor and hungry, and so many as we see drunk. We know you are good people, and kind to the poor, and we give you our hands at parting; praying that the Great Spirit will assist you in taking care of the poor, and making people sober.

"My Friends,—I have no more to say."

Temperance medals were then given to each of the Indians, and the deputation took leave.

A council was held that evening in the Indians' apartments, and several pipes smoked, during which time the conversation ran upon numerous topics, the first of which was the interesting meeting they had held that day, and on several former occasions, with the Friends, and which good people they were about to leave, and they seemed fearful they should meet none others in their travels. They were passing their comments upon the vast numbers which Daniel and *Bobasheela* had told them there actually were of poor people shut up in the poorhouses, besides those in the streets, and underground in the coal-pits; and concluded that the numerous clergymen they had to preach to them, and to keep them honest and sober, were not too many, but they thought they even ought to have more, and should at least keep all they had at home, instead of sending them to preach to the Indians. *Jim* was busy poring over his note-book, and getting Daniel to put down in round numbers the amount of poor in the poorhouses and in the streets, which they had found in some newspaper. And he was anxious to have down without any mistake the large sum of money they had presented to the hospitals, so that when they got home they could tell of the charity they had done in England; and if ever they got so poor as to have to beg, they would have a good paper to beg with. The sum, in American currency (as they know less of pounds, shillings, and pence), amounted to the respectable one of 370 dollars.

This last night's talk in Birmingham was rather a gloomy one, for it was after leave had been taken of all friends. *Bobasheela* was to start in the morning for Liverpool, and I for London, where I had been summoned to attend as a witness in court, and Mr. Melody and the Indians were to leave for Nottingham and other towns in the north. So at a late hour we parted, and early in the morning set out for our different destinations, bearing with us many warm attachments formed during our short stay in the beautiful town of Birmingham.

For what befel these good fellows in Nottingham and Leeds there will probably be no historian, as I was not with them. I commenced with them in York, where I became again the expounder of their habits and mysteries, and was delighted to meet them on classic ground, where there is so much to engage the attention and admiration of civilized or savage. I had visited York on a former occasion, and had the most ardent wish to be present at this time, and to conduct these rude people into the noble cathedral, and on to its grand tower. I had this pleasure; and in it accomplished one of my favourite designs in accompanying them on their northern tour.

On my return from London I had joined the Indians at Leeds, where they had been exhibiting for some days, and found them just ready to start for York. I was their companion by the railway, therefore, to that ancient and venerable city; and made a note or two on an occurrence of an amusing nature which happened on the way. When we were within a few miles of the town the Indians were suddenly excited and startled by the appearance of a party of fox-hunters, forty or fifty in number, following their pack in full cry, having just crossed the track ahead of the train.

This was a subject entirely new to them and unthought of by the Indians; and, knowing that English soldiers all wore red coats, they were alarmed, their first impression being that we had brought them on to hostile ground, and that this was a "war-party" in pursuit of their enemy. They were relieved and excessively amused when I told them it was merely a fox-hunt, and that the gentlemen they saw riding were mostly noblemen and men of great influence and wealth. They watched them intensely until they were out of sight, and made many amusing remarks about them after we had arrived at York. I told them they rode without guns, and the first one in at the death pulled off the tail of the fox and rode into town with it under his hatband. Their laughter was excessive at the idea of "such gentlemen hunting in open fields, and with a whip instead of a gun; and that great chiefs, as I had pronounced them, should be risking their lives, and the limbs of their fine horses, for a poor fox, the flesh of which, even if it were good to eat, was not wanted by such rich people, who had meat enough at home; and the skin of which could not be worth so much trouble, especially when, as everybody knows, it is good for nothing when the tail is pulled off."

On our arrival in York one of the first and most often repeated questions which they put was, whether there were any of the "good people," as they now called them, the Friends, living there. I told them it was a place where a great many of them lived, and no doubt many would come to see them, which seemed to please and encourage them very much. Mr. Melody having taken rooms for them near to the York Minster, of which they had a partial view from their windows, their impatience became so great that we sallied out the morning after our arrival to pay the first visit to that grand and venerable pile. The reader has doubtless seen or read of this sublime edifice, and I need not attempt to describe it here. Were it in my power to portray the feelings which agitated the breasts of these rude people when they stood before this stupendous fabric of human hands, and as they passed through its aisles, amid its huge columns, and under its grand arches, I should be glad to do it; but those feelings which they enjoyed in the awful silence, were for none but themselves to know. We all followed the guide, who showed and explained to us all that was worth seeing below, and then showed us the way by which we were to reach the summit of the grand or middle tower, where the whole party arrived after a laborious ascent of 273 steps. We had luckily selected a clear day; and the giddy height from which we gazed upon the town under our feet, and the lovely landscape in the distance all around us, afforded to the Indians a view far more wonderful than their eyes had previously beheld. Whilst we were all engaged in looking upon the various scenes that lay like the lines upon a map beneath us, the old Doctor, with his *propensity* which has been spoken of before, had succeeded in getting a little higher than any of the rest of the party, by climbing on to the little house erected over the gangway through which we entered upon the roof; and, upon the pinnacle of this, for a while stood smiling down upon the thousands of people who were gathering in the streets. He was at length, however, seen to assume a more conspicuous attitude by raising his head and his eyes towards the sky, and for some moments he devoutly addressed himself to the Great Spirit, whom the Indians always contemplate as "in the heavens, above the clouds." When he had finished this invocation, he slowly and carefully "descended on to the roof, and as he joined his friends he observed that when he was up there "he was nearer to the Great Spirit than he had ever been before." The War-chief excited much merriment by his sarcastic reply, that "it was a pity he did not stay there, for he would never be so near the Great Spirit again." The Doctor had no way of answering this severe retort, except by a silent smile, as, with his head turned away, he gazed on the beautiful landscape beneath him. When we descended from the tower, the Indians desired to advance again to the centre of this grand edifice, where they stood for a few minutes with their hands covering their mouths, as they gazed upon the huge columns around them and the stupendous arches over their heads, and at last came silently away, and I believe inspired with greater awe and respect for the religion of white men than they had ever felt before.

Our stay of three days in York was too short for the Indians to make many acquaintances; but at their exhibitions they saw many of the Society of Friends, and these, as in other places, came forward to offer them their hands and invite them to their houses.

Amongst the invitations they received was one from the governor of the Castle, who with great kindness conducted us through the various apartments of the prison, explaining the whole of its system and discipline to us. We were shown the various cells for different malefactors, with their inmates in them, which no doubt conveyed to the minds of the Indians new ideas of white men's iniquities, and the justice of civilized laws.

When we were withdrawing we were invited to examine a little museum of weapons which had been used by various convicts to commit the horrid deeds for which they had suffered death or transportation. A small room, surrounded by a wire screen, was devoted to these, and as it was unlocked we were invited in, and found one wall of the room completely covered with these shocking records of crime.

The turnkey to this room stepped in, and in a spirit of the greatest kindness, with a rod in his hand to point with, commenced to explain them, and of course add to their interest, in the following manner:—

> "You see here, gentlemen, the weapons that have been used in the commission of murders by persons who have been tried and hung in this place, or transported for life. That long gun which you see there is the identical gun that Dyon shot his father with. *He was hung.*

"That club and iron coulter you see there, gentlemen, were used by two highwaymen, who killed the gatekeeper, near Sheffield, by knocking out his brains, and afterwards robbed him. *They were both hung.*

"This club and razor here, gentlemen (you see the blood on the razor now), were used by Thompson, who killed his wife. He knocked her down with this club, and cut her throat with this identical razor.

"This leather strap—gentlemen, do you see it? Well, this strap was taken from a calf's neck by Benjamin Holrough, and he hung his father with it. *He was hung here.*

"That hedging-bill, razor, and tongs, gentlemen, were the things used by Healy and Terry, who knocked an old woman down, cut her throat, and buried her. *They were hung in this prison.*

"Now, gentlemen, we come to that hammer and razor you see there. With that same hammer Mary Crowther knocked her husband down, and then with that razor cut his throat. *She was hung.*

"Do you see that club, gentlemen? That is the club with which Turner and Swihill, only nineteen years of age, murdered the bookkeeper near Sheffield. *Both were hung.*

"Do you see this short gun, gentlemen? This is the very gun with which Dobson shot his father. *He was hung.*

"This hat, gentlemen, with a hole in it, was the hat of Johnson, who was murdered near Sheffield. The hole you see is where the blow was struck that killed him."

The Indians, who had looked on these things and listened to these recitals with a curious interest at first, were now becoming a little uneasy, and the old Doctor, who smiled upon several of the first descriptions, now showed symptoms of evident disquiet, retreating behind the party, and towards the door.

"Do you see this knife and bloody cravat, gentlemen? With that same knife John James stuck the bailiff through the cravat, and killed him. *He was executed here.*

"A fire-poker, gentlemen, with which King murdered his wife near Sheffield. *He was hung here.*

"These things, gentlemen—this fork, poker, and bloody shoes—with this poker Hallet knocked his wife down, and stabbed her with the fork; and the shoes have got the blood on them yet. *Hallet was hung.*

"That rope there is the one in which Bardsley was hung, who killed his own father.

"A bloody axe and poker, gentlemen. With that axe and poker an old woman killed a little boy. She then drowned herself. *She was not executed.*

"This shoe-knife, gentlemen, is one that Robert Noll killed his wife with in Sheffield. *He was executed.*

"Another knife, with which Rogers killed a man in Sheffield. He ripped his bowels out with it. *He was hung.*

"A club, and stone, and hat, gentlemen. With this club and stone Blackburn was murdered, and that was his hat: you see how it is all broken and bloody. This was done by four men. *All hung.*

"The hat and hammer here, gentlemen—these belonged to two robbers. One met the other in a wood, and killed him with the hammer. *He was hung.*

"That scythe and pitchfork, you see, gentlemen"——

When our guide had thus far explained, and Jeffrey had translated to the Indians, I observed the old Doctor quite outside of the museum-room, and with his robe wrapped close around him, casting his eyes around in all directions, and evidently in great uneasiness. He called for the party to come out, for, said he, "I do not think this is a good place for us to stay in any longer." We all thought it was as well, for the turnkey had as yet not described one-third of his curiosities; so we thanked him for his kindness, and took leave of him and his interesting museum.

We were then conducted by the governor's request to the apartments of his family, where he and his kind lady and daughters received the Indians and ourselves with much kindness, having his table prepared with refreshments, and, much to the satisfaction of the Indians (after their fatigue of body as well as of mind), with plenty of the *Queen's chickabobboo.*

The sight-seeing of this day and the exhibition at night finished our labours in the interesting town of York, where I have often regretted we did not remain a little longer to avail ourselves of the numerous and kind invitations which were extended to us before we left. After our labours were all done, and the Indians had enjoyed their suppers and their *chickabobboo*, we had a pipe together, and a sort of recapitulation of what we had seen and heard since we arrived. The two most striking subjects of the gossip of this evening were the cathedral and the prison; the one seemed to have filled their minds with astonishment and admiration at the ingenuity and power of civilized man, and the other with surprise and horror at his degradation and wickedness; and evidently with some alarm for the safety of their persons in such a vicinity of vice as they had reason to believe they were in from the evidences they had seen during the day. The poor old Doctor was so anxious for the next morning to dawn, that we might be on our way, that he had become quite nervous and entirely contemplative and unsociable. They had heard such a catalogue of murders and executions explained, though they knew that we had but begun with the list, and saw so many incarcerated in the prison, some awaiting their trial, others who had been convicted and were under sentence of death or transportation, and others again pining in their cells, and weeping for their wives and children (merely because they could not pay the money that they owed), that they became horrified and alarmed; and as it was the first place where they had seen an exhibition of this kind, there was some reason for the poor fellows' opinions that they were in the midst of the wickedest place in the world.

They said that, from the grandeur and great number of their churches, they thought they ought to be one of the most honest and harmless people they had been amongst, but instead of that they were now convinced they must be the very worst, and the quicker Mr. Melody made arrangements to be off the better. The Indians had been objects of great interest, and for the three nights of their amusements their room was well filled and nightly increasing; but all arguments were in vain, and we must needs be on the move. I relieved their minds in a measure relative to the instruments of death they had seen and the executions of which they had heard an account, by informing them of a fact that had not occurred to them—that the number of executions mentioned had been spread over a great number of years, and were for crimes committed amongst some hundreds of thousands of inhabitants, occupying a tract of country a great many miles in every direction from York; and also that the poor men imprisoned for debt were from various parts of the country for a great distance around. This seemed to abate their surprise to a considerable degree; still, the first impression was here made, and made by means of their eyes (which they say they never disbelieve, and I am quite sure they will never get rid of it), that York was the "wicked town," as they continued to call it during the remainder of their European travels. I explained to them that other towns had their jails and their gallows—that in London they daily rode in their buss past prison walls, and where the numbers imprisoned were greater than those in York, in proportion to the greater size of the city.

Their comments were many and curious on the cruelty of imprisoning people for debt, because they could not pay money. "Why not kill them?" they said; "it would be better, because when a man is dead he is no expense to any one, and his wife can get a husband again, and his little children a father to feed and take care of them; when he is in jail they must starve: when he is once in jail he cannot wish his face to be seen again, and they had better kill them all at once." They thought it easier to die than to live in jail, and seemed to be surprised that white men, so many hundreds and thousands, would submit to it, when they had so many means by which they could kill themselves.

They saw convicts in the cells who were to be transported from the country: they inquired the meaning of that, and, when I explained it, they seemed to think that was a good plan, for, said they, "if these people can't get money enough to pay their debts, if they go to another country they need not be ashamed there, and perhaps they will soon make money enough to come back and have their friends take them by the hand again." I told them, however, that they had not understood me exactly—that transportation was only for heinous crimes, and then a man was sent away in irons, and in the country where he went he had to labour several years, or for life, with chains upon him, as a slave. Their ideas were changed at once on this point, and they agreed that it would be better to kill them all at once, or give them weapons and let them do it themselves.

While this conversation was going on, the Recorder Jim found here very interesting statistics for his note-book, and he at once conceived the plan of getting Daniel to find out how many people there were that they had seen in the prison locked up in one town; and then, his ideas expanding, how many (if it could be done at so late an hour) there were in all the prisons in London; and then how many white people in all the kingdom were locked up for crimes, and how many because they couldn't pay money. His friend and teacher, Daniel, whose head had become a tolerable gazetteer and statistical table, told him it would be quite easy to find it all ready printed in books and newspapers, and that he would put it all down in his book in a little time. The inquisitive Jim then inquired if there were any poorhouses in York, as in other towns; to which his friend Daniel replied that there were, and also in nearly every town in the kingdom; upon which Jim started the design of adding to the statistical entries in his book the number of people in poorhouses throughout the kingdom. Daniel agreed to do this for him also, which he could easily copy out of a memorandum-book of his own, and also to give him an estimate of the number of people annually transported from the kingdom for the commission of crimes. This all pleased Jim very much, and was amusement for Daniel; but at the same time I was decidedly regretting with Mr. Melody that his good fellows the Indians, in their visit to York, should have got their eyes open to so much of the dark side of civilization, which it might have been better for them that they never had seen.

Jim's book was now becoming daily a subject of more and more excitement to him, and consequently of jealousy amongst some of the party, and particularly so with the old Doctor; as Jim was getting more rapidly educated than either of the others, and his book so far advanced as to discourage the Doctor from any essay of the kind himself. Jim that night regretted only one thing which he had neglected to do, and which it was now too late to accomplish—that was, to have measured the length of the cathedral and ascertained the number of steps required to walk around it. He had counted the number of steps to the top of the grand tower, and had intended to have measured the cathedral's length. I had procured some very beautiful engravings of it, however, one of which Daniel arranged in his book, and the length of the building and its height we easily found for him in the pocket Guide.

The Doctor, watching with a jealous eye these numerous estimates going into Jim's book, to be referred to (and of course sworn to) when he got home, and probably on various occasions long before, and having learned enough of arithmetic to understand what a wonderful effect a cipher has when placed on the right of a number of figures, he smiled from day to day with a wicked intent on Jim's records, which, if they went back to his tribe in anything like a credible form, would be a direct infringement upon his peculiar department, and materially affect his standing, inasmuch as Jim laid no claims to a knowledge of *medicine*, or to anything more than good eating and drinking, before he left home.

However, the Doctor at this time could only meditate and smile, as his stiff hand required some practice with the pen before he could make those little 0's so as to match with others in the book, which was often left carelessly lying about upon their table. This intent was entirely and originally wicked on the part of the old Doctor, because he had not yet, that any one knew of, made any reference to his measure of the giant woman, since he had carefully rolled up his cord and put it away amongst his other estimates, to be taken home to "astonish the natives" on their return.

CHAPTER XXIII.

Newcastle-on-Tyne—Indians' alarms about jails—Kind visits from Friends—Mrs. A. Richardson—Advice of the Friends—War-Chiefs reply—Liberal presents—Arrive at Sunderland—Kindness of the Friends—All breakfast with Mr. T. Richardson—Indians plant trees in his garden—And the Author also—The Doctor's superstition—Sacrifice—Feast—Illness of the Roman Nose—Indians visit a coalpit—North Shields—A sailors' dinner and a row—Arrive at Edinburgh—A drive—First exhibition there—Visit to Salisbury Crag—To Arthur's Seat—Holyrood House and Castle—The crown of Robert Bruce—The "big gun,"—"Queen Mab"—Curious modes of building—"Flats"—Origin of—Illness of Corsair, the little *pappoose*—The old Doctor speaks—War-chief's speech—A feast of ducks—Indians' remarks upon the government of Scotland—"The swapping of crowns"—The Doctor proposes the crown of Robert Bruce for Prince Albert—Start for Dundee—Indians' liberality—A noble act—Arrival at Dundee—Death of little Corsair—Distress of the Little Wolf and his wife—Curious ceremony—Young men piercing their arms—Indians at Perth—Arrival in Glasgow—Quartered in the Town-hall—The cemetery—The Hunterian Museum—The Doctor's admiration of it—Daily drives—Indians throw money to the poor—Alarm for *Roman Nose*—Two reverend gentlemen talk with the Indians—War-chief's remarks—Greenock—Doctor's regret at leaving.

Newcastle-on-Tyne was the next place where we stopped, and when I arrived there I found Mr. Melody and his friends very comfortably lodged, and all in excellent spirits. The Indians, he told me, had been exceedingly buoyant in spirits from the moment they left York, and the old Doctor sang the whole way, even though he had been defeated in his design of riding outside on the railway train, as he had been in the habit of doing on the omnibus in London. I told them I had remained a little behind them in York to enjoy a few hours more of the society of an excellent and kind lady of the Society of Friends,[29] whom they would recollect to have seen in the exhibition room when they had finished their last night's exhibition, who came forward and shook hands in the most affectionate manner, and left gold in their hands as she bade them good bye, and commended them to the care of the Great Spirit.

I told them that this good lady had only returned from the country on the last evening of their exhibiting in York, and was exceedingly disappointed that she could not have the pleasure of their society at her house. I then sat down and amused them an hour with a beautiful manuscript book, by her own hand, which she had presented to me, containing the portraits of seven Seneca chiefs and braves, who were in England twenty-five years before, and whom she entertained for three weeks in her own house. This interesting work contains also some twenty pages of poetry glowing with piety, and written in a chaste and beautiful style; and an hundred or more pages in prose, giving a full description of the party, their modes, and a history of their success, as they travelled through the kingdom. This was a subject of much pleasure to them, but at the same time increased their regret that they had not seen more of this kind lady before they left the town of York.

Their first inquiries after their arrival in Newcastle were whether they would meet any of the "good people" in that town, and whether that was a place where they had prisons and a gallows like those in London and in York. I answered that they would no doubt find many of the Friends there, for I knew several very kind families who would call upon them, and also that the good lady who gave me the book in York had written letters to several of the Friends in Newcastle to call on them; and that, as to the jails, &c., I believed they were much the same.

In a sort of council which we held there, as we were in the Indian habit of convening one whenever we were leaving an old lodging or taking possession of a new one, it was very gravely and diffidently suggested by the Doctor, as the desire of the whole party, that they presumed *Chippehola*[30] had money enough left in London (in case they should fail in this section of the country to make enough to pay their debts) to keep them clear from being taken up and treated like white men who can't pay what they owe. I approved this judicious suggestion, and assured them they might feel quite easy as long as they were in the kingdom. I told them I was quite sure they had a good and faithful friend in Mr. Melody, and, if anything happened to him, they would be sure to find me ready to take care of them, and that, if we were both to die, they would find all the English people around them their friends. This seemed to satisfy and to cheer them up, and our few days in Newcastle thus commenced very pleasantly. From their first night's exhibition they all returned to their lodgings with peculiar satisfaction that they had observed a greater number of Friends in the crowd than they had seen in any place before, and many of these had remained until everybody else had gone away, to shake hands and converse with them. They found roast beef and beef-steaks and *chickabobboo* also, the same as in other places, and altogether there was enough around them here to produce cheerful faces.

I need not describe again to the reader the nature and excitement of the dances, &c., in their exhibitions, which were nightly repeated here as they had been in London; but incidents and results growing out of these amusements were now becoming exceedingly interesting, and as will be found in the sequel of much importance, I trust, to those poor people and their descendants. Very many of the Society of Friends were nightly attending their exhibitions, not so much for the purpose of witnessing or encouraging their war-dances and customs, as for an opportunity of forming an acquaintance with them, with a view to render them in some way an essential good. With this object a letter was addressed to me by Mrs. Anna Richardson (with whom I had formerly corresponded on the subject of the Indians), proposing that a number of the Friends should be allowed to hold a conversation with them in their apartments, on some morning, for the purpose of learning the true state of their minds relative to the subjects of religion and education, and to propose some efforts that might result to their advantage, and that of their nation. Mr. Melody and myself embraced this kind proposal at once, and the Indians all seemed delighted with it when it was made known to them. The morning was appointed, and this kind and truly charitable lady came with fifteen or twenty of her friends, and the Indians listened with patience and apparent pleasure to the Christian advice that was given them by several, and cheerfully answered to the interrogatories which were put to them.

The immediate appeal and thanks to the "Great Spirit, who had sent these kind people to them," by the War-chief in his reply, seemed to impress upon the minds of all present the conviction of a high and noble sentiment of religion in the breasts of these people, which required but the light of the Christian revelation. His replies as to the benefits of education were much as he had made them on several occasions before, that, "as for themselves, they were too far advanced in life to think of being benefited by it, but that their children might learn to read and write, and that they should be glad to have them taught to do so." Here seemed to dawn a gleam of hope, which that pious lady, in her conversation and subsequent correspondence with me, often alluded to, as the most favourable omen for the desire which the Friends had of rendering them some lasting benefit. Mr. Melody on this occasion produced a little book printed in the Ioway language, in the missionary school already in existence in the tribe, and also letters which he had just received from the Rev. Mr. Irvin, then conducting the school, giving an encouraging account of it, and hoping that the Indians and himself might return safe, and with means to assist in the noble enterprise. This information was gratifying in the extreme, and all seemed to think that there was a chance of enlightening these benighted people. The heart of this Christian woman reached to the American wilderness in a letter that she directed to this reverend gentleman, believing that there, where were the wives and children of the chiefs and warriors who were travelling, was the place for the efforts of the Society of Friends to be beneficially applied; and thus, I believe, formed the chain from which I feel confident the most fortunate results will flow.[31]

Several subsequent interviews were held with the Indians by these kind people, who took them to their houses and schools, and bestowed upon them many tangible proofs of their attachment to them, and anxiety for their welfare. The Indians left Newcastle and these suddenly made friends with great reluctance, and we paid a visit of a couple of days to Sunderland. Here they found also many of the "good people" attending their exhibitions, and received several warm and friendly invitations to their houses. Amongst these kind attentions there was one which they never will forget: they were invited to breakfast at the table of Mr. T. Richardson, in his lovely mansion, with his kind family and some friends, and after the breakfast was over all were invited into his beautiful garden, where a spade was ready, and a small tree prepared for each one to plant and attach his name to. This ceremony amused them very much, and, when they had all done, there was one left for *Chippehola*, who took the spade and completed the interesting ceremony. This had been kindly designed for their amusement, and for the pleasing recollections of his family, by this good man; and with all it went off cheerfully, except with the Doctor, who refused for some time, but was at length induced to take the spade and plant his tree. I observed from the moment that he had done it that he was contemplative, and evidently apprehensive that some bad luck was to come from it—that there was *medicine* in it, and he was alarmed. He was silent during the rest of the interview, and after they had returned to their rooms he still remained so for some time, when he explained to me that "he feared some one would be sick—some one of those trees would die, and he would much rather they had not been planted." He said "it would be necessary to make a great feast the next day," which I told him would be difficult, as we were to leave at an early hour. This puzzled him very much, as it was so late that, "if they were to try to give it that night, there would not be time for the ducks to be well cooked." They all laughed at him for his superstition, and he got the charm off as well as he could by throwing some tobacco, as a sacrifice, into the fire.

We travelled the next day to North Shields, and the gloom that was still evidently hanging over the old man's brow was darkened by the increased illness of the *Roman Nose*, who had been for some weeks slightly ailing, but on that day was attacked for the first time with some fever. The Doctor's alarm was such that he stayed constantly by him, and did not accompany his friend Jim and one or two others with Daniel to the coalpit. This, from the repeated representations of Daniel and their old friend *Bobasheela*, was one of the greatest curiosities in the kingdom, and they were not disappointed in it. In this enterprise I did not accompany them, but from their representations ascertained that they descended more than two thousand feet and then travelled half a mile or so under the sea—that there were fifty horses and mules at that depth under the ground, that never will come up, drawing cars loaded with coal on railways, and six or seven hundred men, women, and children, as black as negroes, and many of these who seldom come up, but sleep there at nights. This scene shocked them even more than the sights they had seen in York, for they seemed to think that the debtors' cells in a prison would be far preferable to the slavery they there saw, of "hundreds of women and children drawing out, as they said, from some narrow places where the horses could not go, little carriages loaded with coal; where the women had to go on their hands and knees through the mud and water, and almost entirely naked, drawing their loads by a strap that was buckled around their waists; their knees and their legs and their feet, which were all naked, were bleeding with cuts from the stones, and their hands also; they drew these loads in the dark, and they had only a little candle to see the way." This surprising scene, which took them hours to describe to their companions, became more surprising when Daniel told them of "the vast number of such mines in various parts of the kingdom, and of the fact that many people in some parts have been born in those mines, and gone to school in them, and spent their lives, without ever knowing how the daylight looked."

Daniel reminded them of the hundreds of mines he had pointed out to them while travelling by the railroads, and that they were all under ground, like what they had seen. Here was rich subject for Jim, for another entry in his book, of the statistics of England; and Daniel, always ready, turned to the page in his own note-book, and soon got for Jim's memorandum the sum total of coalpits and mines in the kingdom, and the hundreds of thousands of human *civilized* beings who were imprisoned in them.

It happened, on the second day that we were stopping in North Shields, much to the amusement of the Indians, that there was a sailors' dinner prepared for an hundred or more in the large hall of the hotel where we were lodging; and, from the rooms which the Indians occupied, there was an opportunity of looking through a small window down into their hall, and upon the merry and noisy group around the table. This was a rich treat for the Indians; and, commencing in an amusing and funny manner, it became every moment more and more so, and, finally (when they began to dance and sing and smash the glasses, and at length the tables, and from that to "set-to's," "fisticuffs," and "knockdowns," by the dozens, and, at last, to a general *mêlée*, a row, and a fight in the street) one of the most decidedly exciting and spirited scenes they had witnessed in the country.

It afforded them amusement also for a long time after the day on which it took place, when they spoke of it as the "great fighting feast."

Two days completed our visit to North Shields, and on the next we were in comfortable quarters in Edinburgh. The Indians were greatly delighted with the appearance of the city as they entered it, and more so daily, as they took their omnibus drives around and through the different parts of it.

The Doctor, however, who was tending on his patient, *Roman Nose*, seemed sad, and looked as if he had forebodings still of some sad results to flow from planting the trees; but he took his seat upon the bus, with his old joking friend Jim, by the side of the driver, smiling occasionally on whatever he saw amusing, as he was passing through the streets. Their novel appearance created a great excitement in Edinburgh; and our announcements filled our hall with the most respectable and fashionable people.

Their dances called forth great applause; and, in the midst of it, the War-chief, so delighted with the beauty of the city, and now by seeing so numerous and fashionable an audience before him, and all applauding, arose to make a speech. As he straightened up, and, wrapping his buffalo robe around him, extended his long right arm, the audience gave him a round of applause, occasioned entirely by the dignified and manly appearance he made when he took the attitude of the orator, and he commenced:—

> "My friends, I understand by the great noise you have made with your hands and feet, that something pleases you, and this pleases us, as we are strangers amongst you, and with red skins. (Applause.)

> "My friends, we have but just arrived in your beautiful city, and we see that you are a different people from the English in London, where we have been. In going into a strange place, amongst strange people, we always feel some fear that our dances and our noise may not please—we are showing you how we dance in our own country, and we believe that is what you wish to see. (Applause and 'How, how, how!')

> "My friends, we are delighted with your city, what we have seen of it—we have seen nothing so handsome before—we will try to please you with some more of our dances, and then we will be happy to shake hands with you. ('How, how, how!')

> "This is all I have to say now." (Great applause.)

We were now in the most beautiful city in the kingdom, if not one of the most beautiful in the world; and the Indians, as well as ourselves, observed the difference in the manners and appearance of the people. The Indians had been pleased with their reception in the evening, and, in their drive during the day, had been excited by the inviting scenery overtowering the city,—the castle, with its "big gun," gaping over the town—the *Salisbury Crag*, and *Arthur's Seat*—all of which places they were to visit on that day; and, having swallowed their breakfasts and taken their seats in their carriage, seemed to have entered upon a new world of amusement. Their views from, and runs over, these towering peaks afforded them great amusement; and the castle, with its crown of Robert Bruce, and other insignia of royalty—its mammouth gun, and the little room in which King James I. of England was born; and in Holyrood House,—the blood of Rizzio upon the floor, and the bed in which

Queen Mary had slept—were all subjects of new and fresh excitement to them.

Nor was their amusement less whilst they were riding through the streets, at the constant variety and sudden contrasts—from the low and poverty-stricken rabble of High-street and its vicinity, to the modern and splendid sections of the city—of crossing high bridges over gardens, instead of rivers; of houses built upon the sides of the hills and on rocks; and many other amusing things that they talked about when they got back.

To Mr. Melody and Jeffrey also, and to Daniel, all these scenes were new; and the Indians, therefore, had companions and guides enough, and enough, also, to explain to them the meaning of all they saw.

I had been in Edinburgh on a former occasion, and was now engaged in looking up and conversing with old friends, whose former kindness now claimed my first attention; and in hunting for one of them, I found his office had been removed to another part of the city; and, making my way towards it as well as I could, I was amused at the instructions given to me when I inquired of a man whom I met in the street, and who, it happened, was acquainted with my friend and his location, and who relieved me instantly from further embarrassment by the following most lucid and simple direction, as he pointed down the street:—"You have only to take the first turning to the right, Sir, and it is the top flat at the bottom." This seemed queer and amusing to me, though not in the least embarrassing, for I had been long enough in Edinburgh before to learn that a "flat" was a "story" or floor; and long enough in London to know that one *end* of a street is the "top" and the other the "bottom."

To a stranger, however, such an answer as the one I received might have been exceedingly bewildering, and increased his difficulties rather than diminished them.

The old law maxim of "*Cujus est solum, ejus est usque ad cœlum,*" would scarcely apply to real estate in the city of Edinburgh; for houses are not only *rented* by floors or *flats*, but titles, in fee simple and by deed, are given for floor above floor, oftentimes in the same house; a custom that is difficult to account for, unless from the curious fact that so many of the houses in Edinburgh are built so high, by the sides of hills and precipitous ledges, that an adjoining tenant may oftentimes step from the surface of his cultivated fields into the tenth or twelfth story of his neighbour's back windows, and, by this singular mode of conveyance, able to walk into a comfortable dwelling without the expense of building, and without curtailing the area of his arable ground. By thus getting, for a trifle, the fee simple for the upper story, and of course the privilege of building as many stories on the top of it as he should require, when he could afford the means to do it, his neighbour below was called a "flat." The law, which is generally cruel to most flats, relinquished one of its oldest and most sacred maxims, to support the numerous claims of this kind which the side-hills and ledges in the building-grounds of the city had produced; and so numerous were the *flats*, and so frequent the instances of this new sort of tenure, that the term "flat" has become carelessly and erroneously applied to all the floors or stories of buildings in Edinburgh that are to be let or sold separately from the rest of the house.

It was arranged that our stay in Edinburgh was to be but for a few days; and, with this view, we had begun to see its sights pretty rapidly during the two first since our arrival. Many fashionable parties were calling on the Indians in their apartments, and leaving them presents; and at their second night's exhibition the room was crowded to great excess with the fashion and nobility of the city. The Indians discovered at once that they never before were in the midst of audiences so intellectual and genteel. There was nothing of low and vulgar appearance in any part of the room; but all had the stamp of refinement and gentility, which stimulated their pride, and they did their utmost.

In the midst of their amusements on that evening there was a general call upon me from the ladies, to explain why the little "pappoose in its cradle" was not shown, as announced in the bills; to which I was sorry to reply that it was so ill that it could not be seen. This having been interpreted to the Indians by Jeffrey, and also heard by the Little Wolf's wife, the mother of the child, and then nursing it in the room behind their platform, she suddenly arranged it, sick as it was, in its beautifully ornamented little cradle, and, having slung it upon her back, and thrown her pictured robe around her, walked into the room, to the surprise of the Indians, and to the great satisfaction of the gentlemen as well as the ladies of the whole house. Her appearance was such, when she walked across the platform, that it called forth applause from every quarter. Many were the ladies who advanced from their seats to the platform, to examine so interesting a subject more closely; and many presents were bestowed upon the mother, who was obliged to retire again with it, from the feeble state it was then in. This fine little child, of ten or twelve months old, and the manner in which it was carried in its Indian cradle upon its mother's back, had formed one of the most interesting parts of the exhibition the whole time that the Indians were in London, and since they had left. Its illness now becoming somewhat alarming, with the increasing illness also of the *Roman Nose*, was adding to the old Doctor's alarms, growing out of the *planting of the little trees*, which he had insisted was ominous of something that would happen, but what, he did not attempt to predict.

He was daily prescribing and attending his patients, but, being without the roots which he uses in his own country, he was evidently much at a loss; and the ablest advice was procured for both of the patients while in that city.

The Doctor, on this occasion, (though somewhat depressed in spirits, owing to his superstitious forebodings about the sick, seeing such a vast concourse of ladies present, and all encouraging him with their applause as he made his boasts in the eagle dance,) made an effort for a *sensation*, as he did on his first night in London. When the dance was done, he advanced to the edge of the platform, and, with his usual quizzical look and smile from under his headdress of buffalo horns and eagle quills, addressed the audience. His speech was translated by Jeffrey, and, though it was highly applauded, fell much short of the effect amongst the ladies which he had produced on former occasions. He sat down somewhat in a disappointed mood, when his cruel companion, Jim, told him that his attempt "was an entire failure, and that he would never take with the ladies in Edinburgh." The old man replied to him that he had better try himself, and, if he would lie flat on his back and make a speech, perhaps *he* might please the ladies of Edinburgh. After another dance, and amidst the roar of applause, old *Neu-mon-ya* (the War-chief) arose, and, in the best of his humour, said,—

> "My friends, I thank the Great Spirit who conducted us safe across the Great Salt Lake that His eye is still upon us, and that He has led us to your city. No city that we have seen is so beautiful as yours; and we have seen a great deal of it as we have been riding in our carriage to-day. ('*How, how, how!*')

> "My friends, the Great Spirit has made us with red skins, and, as all our modes of life are different from yours, our dances are quite different, and we are glad that they do not give any offence when we dance them. Our dresses, which are made of skins, are not so fine and beautiful as yours, but they keep us warm, and that we think is the great thing. ('*How, how, how!*' Applause and 'Hear, hear.')

> "My friends, we have been to-day to see your great fort. We were much pleased with it, and the 'big gun;' we think it a great pity it is broken. We saw the room where the king of England was born, and we feel proud that we have been in it. ('*How, how, how!*' Much laughter.)

> "My friends, we saw there the crowns of your kings and queens as we were told. This we don't think we quite understand yet, but we think *Chippehola* will tell us all that,—it may be all right. (Laughter and 'Hear.')

> "My friends, we went to another great house where we saw many things that pleased us—we saw the bed in which your Queen slept: this was very

pleasing to us all; it was much nearer than we got to the Queen of England. (Great laughter.)

"My friends, this is all I have to say." ('Bravo!')

After this night's exhibition, and the sights of the day which had pleased them so much, there was subject enough for a number of pipes of conversation; and to join them in this Mr. Melody and I had repaired to their room, where we found them in the midst of a grand feast of ducks, which they said it was always necessary to give when they entered a new country, and which in this case they had expended some of their own money in buying. Daniel and Jeffrey were seated with them, and we were obliged to sit down upon the floor, and take each a duck's leg at least, and a glass of the *Queen's chickabobboo* (champagne), which had been added at the expense of Daniel and Jeffrey, as the ordinary *chickabobboo* did not answer the object of a feast of that description. After the feast was over, and the War-chief had returned thanks to the Great Spirit, according to their invariable custom, the pipe was lit, and then the gossip for the evening commenced. They had already learned from Daniel that there were jails and poorhouses here as in other places, and were now remarking that they had not yet seen any of the "good people" here, and began to fear they had lost all chance of meeting any of them again. They seemed to be much at a loss to know how it was that here were the crowns and swords of kings and queens, and the houses they had lived in, and the beds they had slept on, and that there are none of them left. They believed, though they were not yet quite certain of it, that this country must have been conquered by England. These inquiries were all answered as nearly as I could explain them; and the result was, that "it was a great pity, in their estimations, that so fine a country and people should not continue to have a king of their own to put on the crown again, instead of leaving it in the castle to be shut up in a dark room." They seemed to think it "very curious that the Scotch people should like to keep the crown for people to look at, when they could not keep the king to wear it;" and they thought "it would be far better to take out the beautiful red and green stones and make watch-seals of them, and melt the gold into sovereigns, so that some of it might get into poor people's pockets, than to keep it where it is, just to be looked at and to be talked of."

They thought "the crown was much more beautiful than the one they saw in London belonging to the Queen, and which was kept in the great prison where they saw so many guns, spears, &c."[32] The joker, Jim, thought that "if he were the Queen he should propose to *swap*, for he thought this decidedly the handsomest crown." The old Doctor said, that "if he were the Queen of England he should be very well suited to wear the one they had seen in London, and he would send and get this one very quickly, and also the beautiful sword they saw, for Prince Albert to wear." In this happy and conjectural mood we left them, receiving from Daniel further accounts of the events and history of the country which they had seen so many evidences of during their visits in the early part of the day.

Our stay in this beautiful city was but four days, contemplating another visit to it in a short time; and at the close of that time the party took a steamer for Dundee, with a view to make a visit of a few days to that town, and afterwards spend a day or two in Perth. I took the land route to Dundee, and, arriving there before the party, had announced their arrival and exhibition to take place on the same evening. An accident however that happened on the steamer compelled it to put back to Edinburgh, and their arrival was delayed for a couple of days.

During this voyage there was an occurrence on board of the steamer, which was related to me by Mr. Melody and Daniel, which deserves mention in this place. It seems that on board of the steamer, as a passenger, was a little girl of twelve years of age and a stranger to all on board. When, on their way, the captain was collecting his passage-money on deck, he came to the little girl for her fare, who told him she had no money, but that she expected to meet her father in Dundee, whom she was going to see, and that he would certainly pay her fare if she could find him. The captain was in a great rage, and abused the child for coming on without the money to pay her fare, and said that he should not let her go ashore, but should hold her a prisoner on board, and take her back to Edinburgh with him. The poor little girl was frightened, and cried herself almost into fits. The passengers, of whom there were a great many, all seemed affected by her situation, and began to raise the money amongst them to pay her passage, giving a penny or two apiece, which, when done, amounted to about a quarter of the sum required. The poor little girl's grief and fear still continued, and the old Doctor, standing on deck, wrapped in his robe, and watching all these results, too much touched with pity for her situation, went down in the fore-cabin where the rest of the party were, and, relating the circumstances, soon raised eight shillings, one shilling of which, the Little Wolf, after giving a shilling himself, put into the hand of his little infant, then supposed to be dying, that its dying hand might do one act of charity, and caused it to drop it into the Doctor's hand with the rest. With the money the Doctor came on deck, and, advancing, offered it to the little girl, who was frightened and ran away. Daniel went to the girl and called her up to the Doctor, assuring her there was no need of alarm, when the old Doctor put the money into her hand, and said to her, through the interpreter, and in presence of all the passengers, who were gathering around, "Now go to the cruel captain and pay him the money, and never again be afraid of a man because his skin is red; but be always sure that the heart of a red man is as good and as kind as that of a white man. And when you are in Dundee, where we are all going, if you do not find your father as you wish, and are amongst strangers, come to us, wherever we shall be, and you shall not suffer; you shall have enough to eat, and, if money is necessary, you shall have more."

Such acts of kindness as this, and others that have and will be named, that I was a witness to while those people were under my charge, require no further comment than to be made known: they carry their own proof with them that the Doctor was right in saying that "the hearts of red men are as good as those of the whites."

As I was in anxious expectation of their arrival, I met the party with carriages when they landed, and I was pained to learn that the babe of the Little Wolf, which he had wrapped and embraced in his arms, was dying, and it breathed its last at the moment they entered the apartments that were prepared for them. My heart was broken to see the agony that this noble fellow was in, embracing his little boy, and laying him down in the last gasp of death, in a foreign land, and amongst strangers. We all wept for the heartbroken parents, and also for the dear little "Corsair," as he was called (from the name of the steamer on which he was born, on the Ohio river in the United States). We had all become attached to the little fellow, and his death caused a gloom amongst the whole party. The old Doctor looked more sad than ever, and evidently beheld the symptoms of *Roman Nose* as more alarming than they had been.

A council was called, as the first step after their arrival, and a pipe was passed around in solemn silence; after which it was asked by the War-chief if I knew of any of the "good people" in that town; to which I answered that "I was a stranger there, and did not know of any one." It seemed it was an occasion on which they felt that it would be an unusual pleasure to meet some of them, as the Little Wolf and his wife had expressed a wish to find some. It occurred then to Mr. Melody that he had a letter to a lady in that town, and, on delivering it, found she was one of that society, and, with another kind friend, she called and administered comfort to these wretched parents in the midst of their distress. They brought the necessary clothes for the child's remains, and, when we had the coffin prepared, laid it out with the kindest hands, and prepared it for the grave; and their other continued and kind offices tended to soothe the anguished breasts of the parents while we remained there.

It is a subject of regret to me that I have lost the names of those two excellent ladies, to whom my public acknowledgments are so justly due. After they had laid the remains of the child in the coffin, each of the young men of the party ran a knife through the fleshy part of their left arms, and, drawing a white feather through the wounds, deposited the feathers with the blood on them in the coffin with the body. This done, the father and mother brought all they possessed, excepting the clothes which they had on, and presented to them, according to the custom of their country, and also all the fine presents they had received, their money, trinkets, weapons, &c. This is one of the curious modes of that tribe, and is considered necessary to be conformed to in all cases where a child dies. The parents are bound to give away all they possess in the world. I believe, however, that it is understood that, after a certain time, these goods are returned, and oftentimes with increased treasures attending them.

There now came another pang for the heart of this noble fellow, the Little Wolf, and one which seemed to shake his manly frame more than that he had already felt. His child he could not take with him, and the thought of leaving it in a strange burying-ground, and "to be dug up," as he said he knew it would be, seemed to make his misery and that of his wife complete. However, in the midst of his griefs, he suggested that, if it were possible to have it conveyed to their kind friends in Newcastle-on-Tyne, he was sure those "good people," who treated them so kindly, would be glad to bury it in their beautiful burying-ground which he had seen, where it would be at home, and he and his wife should then feel happy. Mr. Melody at once proposed to take it there himself, and attend to its burial, which pleased the parents very much, and he started the next day with it. He was received with the greatest kindness by Mrs. A. Richardson and their other kind friends, who attended to its burial in the society's beautiful cemetery.[33]

Our visit to the delightful little town of Perth was made, where we remained, and the Indians astonished and pleased with their wild and unheard-of modes, for two days. We then were within fifteen miles of Merthyl Castle, the seat of Sir William Drummond Stewart, the well-known and bold traveller of the prairies and Rocky Mountains of America, whose friendly invitation we received to visit his noble mansion, but which I shall long regret came so late that other engagements we had entered into in Edinburgh and Glasgow prevented us from complying with it.

Our way was now back, and, having repeated their exhibitions a few nights longer in Edinburgh, and, as before, to crowded and fashionable houses, we commenced upon our visit to the noble city of Glasgow. On our arrival, the party were taken in an omnibus from the station to the town-hall, in which it was arranged their exhibitions were to be given, and in a private room of which the Indians were to lodge.

They were pleased with the part of the city they saw as they entered it, and were in good spirits and cheer, and prepared for the few days they were to stop there. The same arrangement was at once made by Mr. Melody, as in other places, to give them their daily ride in an omnibus for their health, and for the purpose of giving them a view of everything to be seen about the town. In their drives about the city of Glasgow there was not so much of the picturesque and change to amuse them as they saw in Edinburgh, yet everything was new and pleasing.

The beautiful cemetery attracted their highest admiration of anything they saw, with all the party but the Doctor, whose whole and undivided admiration was withheld from everything else to be centred in the noble Hunterian Museum: the vapour-baths, conservatories, &c., which had before arrested his attention, were all sunk and lost sight of in this. After each and every of his visits to it he returned dejected and cast down with the conviction of his own ignorance and white man's superior skill. He wished very much to see the great man who made all those wonderful preparations of diseases, and the astonishing models in wax, as he would be so proud to offer him his hand; but, being informed that he had been dead for many years, he seemed sad that there was no way of paying him the tribute of his praise.

Their exhibitions, which were given nightly, as they had been given in the Egyptian Hall, were nightly explained by me in the same way, and fully and fashionably attended. The same kind of excitement was repeated—speeches were made, and rounds of applause—young ladies falling in love—Indians' talks at night, and their suppers of beef-steaks and *chickabobboo*.

Another present of Bibles, equal in number to the number of Indians, was handed on to the platform from an unknown hand, and each one had the Indian name of its owner handsomely written in its front.

Scarcely a day or an evening passed but they received more or less Bibles from the hands of the kind and Christian people who were witnessing their amusements or inviting them to their houses; and from the continued access to their stock during their whole career, together with toys, with cloths and knives, and other presents, their baggage was becoming actually of a troublesome size.

In taking their daily drives about town they had several times passed through some of the most populous and at the same time impoverished parts of the city; and the great numbers of poor and squalid-looking and barefooted creatures they saw walking in the snow had excited their deepest pity, and they had got in the daily habit of throwing pennies to them as they passed along. The numbers of the ragged poor that they saw there they represented as surpassing all they had seen in their whole travels. They inquired whether there were any poor-houses there, and, being informed that there were a number, and all full, they seemed to be yet even more surprised. They were in the habit daily, until Mr. Melody and myself decided it was best to check it, of each getting some shillings changed into pennies before they started on their ride, to scatter among the poor that they passed. Their generosity became a subject so well known in a few days, that their carriage was followed to their door, where gangs of beggars were stationed great part of the day to get their pennies "when the savages went out." Some pounds of their money they thus threw out into the streets of this great and splendid city, in spite of all we could do to prevent them.

Our apprehensions were now becoming very great, and of course very painful, for the fate of the poor *Roman Nose*: he seemed daily to be losing flesh and strength, and one of the most distinguished physicians, who was attending on him, pronounced his disease to be pulmonary consumption. This was the first decided alarm we had about him, and still it was difficult to believe that so fine and healthy a looking man as he appeared but a few months before should be thus rapidly sinking down with such a disease. He was able to be walking and riding about, but was weak, and took no part in the exhibitions.

About this time, as I was entering the Indians' room one morning, I met two gentlemen coming down the stairs, who recognised me, and said they had proposed to the interpreter and the Indians to have had a little time with them to talk upon the subjects of religion and education, and to know whether missionaries could not be sent into their country to teach and christianise them; and they were afraid they might not have been understood, for they were answered that the Indians did not wish to see them. At that moment Jeffrey was coming up the stairs, and, as it could not have been him whom they saw, I presumed it might have been Daniel who refused them admittance, as he might have been unable to understand the Indians. Jeffrey told them that they had got almost tired of talking with so many in London, but still they could go up, and the Indians, he thought, would be glad to see them. Mr. Melody happened at the moment to be passing also, and he invited them up. They were introduced to the Indians and their object explained by Jeffrey. The War-chief then said to them, as he was sitting on the floor in a corner of the room, that he didn't see any necessity of their talking at all, for all they would have to say they had heard from much more intelligent-looking men than they were, in London, and in other places, and they had given their answers at full length, which *Chippehola* had written all down.

"Now, my friends," said he, "I will tell you that when we first came over to this country we thought that where you had so many preachers, so many to read and explain the good book, we should find the white people all good and sober people; but as we travel about we find this was all a mistake. When we first came over we thought that white man's religion would make all people good, and we then would have been glad to talk with you, but now we cannot say that we like to do it any more." ('*How, how, how!*' responded all, as Jim, who was then lying on a large table, and resting on one elbow, was gradually turning over on to his back, and drawing up his knees in the attitude of speaking.)

The War-chief continued:—

"My friends—I am willing to talk with you if it can do any good to the hundreds and thousands of poor and hungry people that we see in your streets every day when we ride out. We see hundreds of little children with their naked feet in the snow, and we pity them, for we know they are hungry, and we give them money every time we pass by them. In four days we have given twenty dollars to hungry children—we give our money only to children. We are told that the fathers of these children are in the houses where they sell fire-water, and are drunk, and in their words they every moment abuse and insult the Great Spirit. You talk about sending *black-coats* among the Indians: now we have no such poor children among us; we have no such drunkards, or people who abuse the Great Spirit. Indians dare not do so. They pray to the Great Spirit, and he is kind to them. Now we think it would be better for your teachers all to stay at home, and go to work right here in your own streets, where all your good work is wanted. This is my advice. I would rather not say any more." (To this all responded '*How, how, how!*')

Jim had evidently got ready to speak, and showed signs of beginning; but White-cloud spoke to him, and wished him not to say anything. It was decided by these gentlemen at once to be best not to urge the conversation with them; and Mr. Melody explained to them the number of times they had heard and said all that could be said on the subject while in London, and that they were out of patience, and of course a little out of the humour for it. These gentlemen, however, took great interest in them, and handed to each of the chiefs a handsome Bible, impressing upon them the importance of the words of the Great Spirit, which were certainly all contained in them, and which they hoped the Indians might have translated to them. And as I was descending the stairs with them, one of them said to me that he never in his life heard truer remarks, or a lesson that more distinctly and forcibly pointed out the primary duties of his profession.

A few days more, the incidents of which I need not name, finished our visit to the city of Glasgow; and an hour or more by the railway, along the banks of the beautiful Clyde, and passing Dumbarton Castle, landed us in the snug little town of Greenock, from which we were to take steamer to Dublin.

The Indians gave their dances and other amusements there for three or four evenings before we took leave. They were looked upon there as great curiosities, but scarcely formed any acquaintances or attachments, except in one branch of our concern. All were anxious to leave and be on the way to Dublin, except the Doctor, who thought it was bad policy to leave so quick; and though he got on to the steamer with all the rest, he did it very reluctantly, without assigning any reason for it until we were on the voyage, when he acknowledged to Daniel that the reason why he disliked to leave so soon was, that "one of the little maids in the hotel where they lodged used to come in every night, after all were asleep, and lie by the side of him on his buffalo robe." For this simple acknowledgment all seemed rather to sympathise with the polite old gentleman; but it was now too late for a remedy, for we were near to the desired city of Dublin.

CHAPTER XXIV.

Arrival in Dublin—Decline of the *Roman Nose*—Exhibition in the Rotunda—Feast of ducks—First drive—Phœnix Park—Stags—Indians' ideas of game-laws and taxes—Annual expenses of British government—National debt—Daniel enters these in Jim's book—Indians called "Irishmen"—Author's reply—Speech of the War-chief—Jim's rapid civilization—New estimates for his book—Daniel reads of "Murders, &c.," in Times newspaper—Jim subscribes for the Times—Petition of 100,000 women—Society of Friends meet the Indians in the Rotunda—Their advice, and present to the chiefs 40*l.*—Indians invited to Zoological Gardens—Presented with 36*l.*—Indians invited to Trinity College—Conversation with the Rev. Master on religion—Liberal presents—They visit the Archbishop of Dublin—Presents—All breakfast with Mr. Joseph Bewly, a Friend—Kind treatment—Christian advice—Sickness of *Roman Nose*—Various entertainments by the Friends—A curious beggar—Indians' liberality to the poor—Arrival at Liverpool—Rejoicing and feast—Council—*Roman Nose* placed in an hospital—Arrival in Manchester—Exhibition in Free Trade Hall—Immense platform—Three wigwams—Archery—Ball-play, &c.—Great crowds—*Bobasheela* arrives—Death of the *Roman Nose*—Forms of burial, &c.

In Dublin, where we arrived on the 4th of March, after an easy voyage, comfortable quarters were in readiness for the party, and their breakfast soon upon the table. The Indians, having heard that there were many of "the good people" (the Friends) in Dublin, and having brought letters of introduction to some of them, had been impatient to reach that city; and their wish being successfully and easily accomplished, they now felt quite elated and happy, with apparently but one thing to depress their spirits, which was the continued and increasing illness of the *Roman Nose*. He was gradually losing flesh and strength, and getting now a continual fever, which showed the imminent danger of his condition. He had the ablest medical advice that the city could afford, and we still had some hopes of his recovery. Rooms had been prepared for the exhibitions of the Indians in the Rotunda, and, on the second night after their arrival, they commenced with a respectable audience, and all seemed delighted and surprised with their picturesque effect.

There was much applause from the audience, but no speeches from the Indians, owing to their fatigue, or to the fact that they had not yet rode about the city to see anything to speak about. They returned from their exhibition to their apartments, and after their supper they were happy to find that their beef-steaks were good, and that they had found again the *London chickabobboo*.

A very amusing scene occurred during the exhibition, which had greatly excited the Indians, though they had but partially understood it, and now called upon me to explain it to them. While speaking of the modes of life of the Ioway Indians, and describing their way of catching the wild horses on the prairies, a dry and quizzical-looking sort of man rose, and, apparently half drunk, excited the hisses of the audience whilst he was holding on to the end of a seat to steady him. It was difficult to get him down, and I desired the audience to listen to what he had to say. "Ee—you'l escuse me, sir, to e—yax e—yif you are ye man woo was lecturing e—year some time see—ynce, e—on ther Yindians and the—r wild e—yorses? —e—(hic)—e—and the—r breathin, he—(hic)—e—in thee—ir noses?" The excessive singularity of this fellow set the whole house in a roar of laughter, and all felt disposed to hear him go on. "Yes," I replied, "I am the same man." "Ee—e—r wal, sir, e—yerts all—(hic), e—yits all gammon, sir, e—yer, y—ers, (hic) yers tried it on two fillies, sir, e—yand—(hic) yand it didn't se—seed, sir." The poor fellow, observing the great amusement of the ladies as he looked around the room was at once disposed to be a little witty, and proceeded—"Ee—(hic)—ye—yer tried it e—yon se—rl *young ladies*, e—yand (hic) se—seded yerry well!" The poor fellow seemed contented with his wit thus far rather than try to proceed further; and he sat down amidst the greatest possible amusement of the audience, many of whom, notwithstanding, did not seem to understand his meaning, when I deemed it necessary to explain that he referred to my account of Indians breaking wild horses by breathing in their noses, which it would seem he had tried in vain, but by experimenting on young ladies he had met with great success.[34]

The Indians had become very much attached to Daniel, who had been so long a companion and fellow-traveller with them, and felt pleasure with him that he was again upon his native soil. He had described to them that they were now in a different country again, and they resolved to have their necessary feast of ducks the next morning for breakfast, so as not to interfere with their drive, in which they were to open their eyes to the beauties of Dublin, when Daniel was to accompany them, and explain all that they saw. They invited him to the feast, and thought it as well to call upon him now as at a future time for the bottle or two of the *Queen's chickabobboo* (champagne) which he had agreed to produce when he got on to his native shore again.

Nothing more of course could be seen until their feast was over, and they were all in their buss as usual, with four horses, which was ready and started off with them at ten o'clock the next morning. The Doctor, in his familiar way, was alongside of the driver, with his buffalo horns and eagle crest, and his shining lance, with his faithful companion Jim by his side, and they caused a prodigious sensation as they were whirled along through the principal streets of Dublin. One may think at first glance that he can appreciate all the excitement and pleasure which the Doctor took in those drives, taking his first survey of the shops and all the curious places he was peeping into as he rode along; but on a little deliberation they will easily see that his enjoyment might have been much greater than the world supposed who were gazing at him, without thinking how much there was under his eye that was novel and exciting to a savage from the wilderness.

After passing through several of the principal streets they were driven to the Phœnix Park, where they left their carriage, and, taking a run for a mile or two, felt much relieved and delighted with the exercise. The noble stags that started up and were bounding away before them excited them very much, and they were wishing for their weapons which they had left behind. However, they had very deliberately and innocently agreed to take a regular hunt there in a few days, and have a saddle or two of venison, but wiser Daniel reminding them of the *game-laws* of this country, of which they had before heard no account, knocked all their sporting plans on the head.

Nothing perhaps astonished them since they came into the country more than the idea that a man is liable to severe punishment by the laws, for shooting a deer, a rabbit, or a partridge, or for catching a fish out of a lake or a river, without a licence, for which he must pay a tax to the government, and that then they can only shoot upon certain grounds. The poor fellows at first treated the thing as ridiculous and fabulous; but on being assured that such was the fact, they were overwhelmed with astonishment. "What!" asked one of them, "if a poor man is hungry and sees a fine fish in the water, is he not allowed to spear it out and eat it?" "No," said Daniel, "if he does, he must go to jail, and pay a heavy fine besides. A man is not allowed to keep a gun in his house without paying a tax to the government for it, and if he carries a weapon in his pocket he is liable to a fine." "Why is that?" "Because they are afraid he will kill somebody with it." "What do you call a tax?" said Jim. "Let that alone," said Daniel, "until we get home, and then I will tell you all about it." Here was a new field opening to their simple minds for contemplation upon the beautiful mysteries and glories of civilization, in which a few hours of Daniel's lectures would be sure to enlighten them. They dropped the subject here however, and took their carriage again for the city and their lodgings, laughing excessively as they were returning, and long after they got back, at cabs they were constantly passing, which they insisted on it had got turned around, and were going sideways.[35] When they had returned and finished their first remarks about the curious things they had seen, Daniel began to give them some first ideas about taxes and fines which they had inquired about, and which they did not as yet know the meaning of. He explained also the game-laws, and showed them that in such a country as England, if the government did not protect the game and the fish in such a manner, there would soon be none left, and, as it was preserved in such a way, the government made those who wished to hunt or to fish, pay a sum of money to help meet the expenses of the government, and he explained the many ways in which people pay taxes. "All of this," said he, "goes to pay the expenses of the government, and to support the Queen and royal family." He read to them from a newspaper that the actual cost of supporting the royal family and attendants was 891,000*l.* sterling (4,455,000 dollars) per annum; that the Queen's pin-money (privy purse) is 60,000*l.* (300,000 dollars); the Queen's coachmen, postilions, and footmen 12,550*l.* (62,750 dollars).

He read from the same paper also that the expenses of the navy were 5,854,851*l.* (being about 29,274,255 dollars) per annum, and that the expenses of the army were still much greater, and that these all together form but a part of the enormous expenses of the government, which must all be raised by taxes in different ways, and that the people must pay all these expenses at last, in paying for what they eat and drink and wear, so much more than the articles are worth, that a little from all may go to the government to pay the government's debts. He also stated that, notwithstanding so much went to the government, the nation was in debt at this time to the amount of 764,000,000*l.* (3,820,000,000 dollars). This was beyond all their ideas of computation, and, as it could not be possibly appreciated by them, Daniel and they had to drop it, as most people do (and as the *country* probably *will* before it is paid), as a mystery too large for just comprehension.

Jim wanted these estimates down in his book however, thinking perhaps that he might some time be wise enough to comprehend them or find some one that could do it. And when Daniel had put them down, he also made another memorandum underneath them to this effect, and which astonished the Indians very much—"The plate that ornamented the sideboard at the banquet at the Queen's nuptials was estimated at 500,000*l.* (2,500,000 dollars)."

By the time their statistics had progressed thus far their dinner was ready, which was a thing much more simple to comprehend, and consequently more pleasing to them; so their note-book was shut, and taxes and game-laws and national debt gave way to roast-beef and *chickabobboo*.

Their drive through the city had tended to increase the curiosity to see them, and their exhibition-room on the second night was crowded to excess. This was sure to put the Indians into the best of humour; and seeing in different parts of the room quite a number of Friends, gave them additional satisfaction.

In a new country again, and before so full and fashionable an audience, I took unusual pains to explain the objects for which these people had come to this country, their personal appearance, and the modes they were to illustrate. When I had got through, and the Indians were sitting on the platform and smoking their pipe, a man rose in the crowd and said, "That's all gammon, sir!—these people are not Indians. I have seen many Indians, sir, and you can't hoax me!" Here the audience hissed, and raised the cry of "Put him out!—shame!" &c. I stepped forward, and with some difficulty got them silent, and begged they would let the gentleman finish his remarks, because, if they were fairly heard and understood, they might probably add much to the amusements of the evening. So he proceeded: "I know this to be a very great imposition, and I think it is a pity if it is allowed to go on. I have seen too many Indians to be deceived about them. I was at Bombay six years, and after that at Calcutta long enough to know what an Indian is. I know that their hair is always long and black, and not red: I know that these men are *Irishmen*, and painted up in this manner to gull the public. There's one of those fellows I know very well—I have seen him these three years at work in M'Gill's carpenter's shop, and saw him there but a few days ago; so I pronounce them but a raw set, as well as impostors!"

When he sat down I prevented the audience from making any further noise than merely laughing, which was excessive all over the room. I said that "to contradict this gentleman would only be to repeat what I had said, and I hoped at least he would remain in the room a few minutes until they would execute one of their dances, that he might give his opinion as to my skill in teaching 'raw recruits' as he called them." The Indians, who had been smoking their pipes all this time without knowing what the delay had been about, now sprang upon their feet and commenced the war-dance; all further thoughts of "imposition" and "raw recruits" were lost sight of here and for the rest of the evening. When their dance was done they received a tremendous roar of applause, and after resting a few minutes the Doctor was on his feet, and evidently trying very hard in a speech to make a sensation (as he had made on the first night in London) among the ladies. Jeffrey interpreted his speech; and although it made much amusement, and was applauded, still it fell very far short of what his eloquence and his quizzical smiles and wit had done on the former occasion. Being apprehensive also of Jim's cruel sarcasms when he should stop, and apparently in hopes, too, of still saying something more witty, he, unfortunately for its whole effect, continued to speak a little too long after he had said his best things; so he sat down (though in applause) rather dissatisfied with himself, and seemed for some time in a sort of study, as if he was trying to recollect what he had said, a *peculiarity possibly* belonging to Indian orators.

When the Doctor had finished, all arose at the sound of the war-whoop given by the War-chief, and they gave with unusual spirit the discovery dance, and after that their favourite, the eagle dance. The finish of this exciting dance brought rounds of deafening applause and "bravo!" in the midst of which the War-chief arose, and, throwing his buffalo robe around him, said,—

"My friends—We see that we are in a new city, a strange place to us, but that we are not amongst enemies, and this gives us great pleasure. (*'How, how, how!'* and 'Hear, hear.')

"My friends—It gives me pleasure to see so many smiling faces about us, for we know that when you smile you are not angry; we think you are amused with our dancing. It is the custom in our country always to thank the Great Spirit first. He has been kind to us, and our hearts are thankful that he has allowed us to reach your beautiful city, and to be with you tonight. (*'How, how, how!'*)

"My friends—Our modes of dancing are different from yours, and you see we don't come to teach you to dance, but merely to show you how the poor Indians dance. We are told that you have your dancing-masters; but the Great Spirit taught us, and we think we should not change our mode. (*'How, how, how!'*)

"My friends—The interpreter has told us that some one in the room has said we were not Indians—that we were *Irishmen*! Now we are not in any way angry with this man; if we *were* Irishmen, we might be perhaps. ('Hear, hear.' 'Bravo!')

"My friends—We are rather sorry for the man than angry; it is his ignorance, and that is perhaps because he is too far off: let him come nearer to us and examine our skins, our ears, and our noses, full of holes and trinkets—Irishmen don't bore their noses. (Great laughter, and 'Bravo!')

"My friends—Tell that man we will be glad to see him and shake hands with him, and he will then be our friend at once." ("Bravo!" and cries of "Go, go!" from every part of the room: "You *must* go!")

The gentleman left his seat upon this in a very embarrassed condition, and, advancing to the platform, shook the War-chief and each one of the party by the hand, and took a seat near to them for the rest of the evening, evidently well pleased with their performances, and well convinced that they were not Irishmen.

After this the Indians proceeded by giving several other dances, songs, &c.; and when it was announced that their amusements for the evening were finished, they seated themselves on the edge of the platform to meet those who desired to give them their hands. Half an hour or so was spent in this ceremony, during which time they received many presents, and, what to them was more gratifying, they felt the affectionate hands of a number of the "good people" they were so anxious to meet, and who they saw were taking a deep interest in their behalf already. They returned to their apartments unusually delighted with their reception, and, after their supper and *chickabobboo*, Jim had some dry jokes for the Doctor about his speech; assuring him that he never would "go down" with the Irish ladies—that his speech had been a decided failure—and that he had better hereafter keep his mouth entirely shut. They had much merriment also about the "mistake the poor man had made in calling them Irishmen," and all applauded the War-chief for the manner in which he had answered him in his speech.

The Indians in their drive during the morning had observed an unusual number of soldiers in various parts of the city, and, on inquiring of Daniel why there were so many when there was no war and no danger, they learned to their great surprise that this country, like the one they had just left, had been subjugated by England, and that a large military force was necessary to be kept in all the towns to keep the people quiet, and to compel them to pay their taxes to the government. They thought the police were more frequent here also than they had seen them in London, and laughed very much at their carrying clubs to knock men down with. They began to think that the Irish must be very bad people to want so many to watch them with guns and clubs, and laughed at Daniel about the wickedness of his countrymen. He endeavoured to explain to them, however, that, if they had to work as hard as the Irishmen did, and then had their hard earnings mostly all taken away from them, they would require as strong a military force to take care of them as the Irish did. His argument completely brought them over, and they professed perfectly to understand the case; and all said they could see why so many soldiers were necessary. The police, he said, were kept in all the towns, night and day, to prevent people from stealing, from breaking into each other's houses, from fighting, and from knocking each other down and taking away their property. The insatiate Jim then conceived the idea of getting into his book the whole number of soldiers that were required in England, Scotland, and Ireland to keep the people at work in the factories, and to make them pay their taxes; and also the number of police that were necessary in the different cities and towns to keep people all peaceable, and quiet, and honest. Daniel had read to them only a day or two before an article in the 'Times' newspaper, setting forth all these estimates, and, being just the thing he wanted, copied them into his book.

The reader sees by this time that, although Jim's looks were against him, as an orator or lecturer, when he should get back to his own country—and also that though his imagination could not take its wings until he was flat upon his back—still that he was, by dint of industry and constant effort, preparing himself with a magazine of facts which were calculated to impress upon the simple minds of the people in his country the strongest proofs of the virtue and superior blessings of civilization.

These people had discernment enough to see that such an enormous amount of soldiers and police as their list presented them would not be kept in pay if they were not necessary. And they naturally put the question at once—"What state would the country be in if the military and police were all taken away?" They had been brought to the zenith of civilization that they might see and admire it in its best form; but the world who read will see with me that they were close critics, and *agree* with me, I think, that it is almost a pity they should be the teachers of such statistics as they are to teach to thousands yet to be taught in the wilderness. As I have shown in a former part of this work, I have long since been opposed to parties of Indians being brought to this country, believing that civilization should be a gradual thing, rather than open the eyes of these ignorant people to all its mysteries at a glance, when the mass of its poverty and vices alarms them, and its luxuries and virtues are at a discouraging distance—beyond the reach of their attainment.

Daniel was at this time cutting a slip from the 'Times,' which he read to Jim; and it was decided at once to be an admissible and highly interesting entry to make, and to go by the side of his former estimates of the manufacture and consumption of *chickabobboo*. The article ran thus:—"The consumption of ardent spirits in Great Britain and Ireland in the last year was 29,200,000 gallons, and the Poor Law Commissioners estimate the money annually spent in ardent spirits at 24,000,000*l.* (120,000,000 dollars); and it is calculated that 50,000 drunkards die yearly in England and Ireland, and that one-half of the insanity, two-thirds of the pauperism, and three-fourths of the crimes of the land are the consequences of drunkenness."

This, Jim said, was one of the best things he had got down in his book, because he said that the *black-coats* were always talking so much about the Indians getting drunk, that it would be a good thing for him to have to show; and he said he thought he should be able, when they were about to go home, to get *Chippehola*[36] to write by the side of it that fourteen Ioways were one year in England and never drank any of this *fire-water*, and were never drunk in that time.

Daniel and Jeffrey continued to read (or rather Daniel to read, and Jeffrey to interpret) the news and events in the 'Times,' to which the Indians were all listening with attention. He read several amusing things, and then of a *"Horrid murder!" a man had murdered his wife and two little children.* He read the account; and next—*"Brutal Assault on a Female!"*—*"A Father killed by his own Son!"*—*"Murder of an Infant and Suicide of the Mother!"*—*"Death from Starvation!"*—*"Execution of Sarah Loundes for poisoning her Husband!"*—*"Robbery of 150l. Bank of England Notes!"* &c. &c.

They had read so many exciting things in one paper, and were but half through the list, when Jim, who had rolled over on his back and drawn up his knees, as if he was going to say something, asked how much was the price of that newspaper; to which Daniel replied that there was one printed each day like that, and the price fivepence each. "Well," said Jim, "I believe everything is in that paper, and I will give you the money to get it for me every day. Go to the man and tell him I want one of every kind he has: I will take them all home with me, and I will some time learn to read them all."

A clever idea entered (or originated in) the heavy brain of Jim at this moment. He went to a box in the corner of the room, from which he took out, and arranged on the floor, about twenty handsomely-bound Bibles, when he made this memorable and commercial-like vociferation, in tolerably plain English: "I guess em swap!" He had been much amused with several numbers of 'Punch,' which he had long pored over and packed away for amusement on the prairies; and believing that his plan for "swapping" would enable him to venture boldly, he authorized Daniel to subscribe for Punch also, provided Punch would take Bibles for pay. Daniel assured him that that would be "no go," as he thought Punch would not care about Bibles; but told him that he would at all events have the 'Times' for him every morning, as he wished, and was now going to read to them a very curious thing that he had got his thumb upon, and commenced to read:—

"Lord R. Grosvenor and Mr. Spooner attended yesterday at the Home-office with Sir George Grey to present a memorial to the Queen from the women of England, signed by 100,000, praying that the bill for preventing trading in seduction may pass into a law. The following is a copy of the petition:—

"'TO THE QUEEN.

"'We, the undersigned women of Great Britain and Ireland, placed by Divine Providence under the sway of the British Sceptre, which God has committed to your Majesty's hands, most humbly beg leave to make known to our beloved Sovereign the heavy and cruel grievance that oppresses a large portion of the female population of the realm. A system exists, by which not only are undue facilities and temptations held out to the immoral, the giddy, and the poor, to enter upon a life of infamy, degradation, and ruin, but unwary young females and mere children are frequently entrapped, and sold into the hands of profligate libertines. Agents are sent into the towns and villages of the United Kingdom, whose ostensible object is to engage young girls for domestic service, or other female employments, but whose real design is to degrade and ruin them. Female agents are also employed in London and many of our large towns to watch the public conveyances, and decoy the simple and inexperienced into houses of moral pollution and crime, by offers of advice or temporary protection. By such and other means the entrapping of innocent young women is reduced to a regular trade, the existence of which is, in the highest degree, discreditable to the nation. Despite the efforts of right-minded men and of benevolent institutions to suppress, by means of the existing laws, this vile trade in female innocence, thousands of the most helpless of your Majesty's subjects are annually destroyed, both in body and soul. We therefore appeal to your Majesty, beseeching you to extend your Royal protection around the daughters of the poor, by promoting such vigorous laws as the wisdom of your Majesty's counsellors may see good to devise, and thereby deliver your Majesty's fair realm from a system of profligacy so offensive to Almighty God, and so fatal to the personal, social, temporal, and spiritual well-being of the women of England.'"

"Fish! fish!" exclaimed Jim, as Daniel finished reading. Some laughed excessively, and the poor Indian women groaned; but Jim, lying still on his back, and of course his ideas circulating freely, roared out again "*Fish! fish! chickabobboo! money! money!*—put that all in my book." Daniel said, "There is no need of that, for it is in your paper, which is all the same, and I will mark a black line around it." "Then be careful not to lose the paper," said Jim, "for I like that very much: I'll show that to the *black-coats* when I get home."

Thus the talk of that night had run to a late hour, and I took leave.

The next morning I received two invitations for the Indians, both of which were calculated to give them great pleasure: the one was an invitation to visit the Zoological Gardens, then in their infant but very flourishing state, when the directors very kindly proposed to admit the public by shilling tickets, and to give the receipts to the Indians. This, therefore, was very exciting to their ambition; and the other invitation was equally or more so, as it was from several gentlemen of the Society of Friends, who proposed that, as there were a great many of that society in Dublin, and who all felt a deep interest in the welfare of the Indians, but who had, many of them, a decided objection to attend their war-dances, &c., they should feel glad to meet them at some hour that might be appointed, in their exhibition room, for the purpose of forming an acquaintance with them, and of having some conversation with them on the subject of education, agriculture, &c., with a view to ascertain in what way they could best render them some essential service. This invitation was embraced by the Indians with great pleasure, and at the time appointed they met about one hundred ladies and gentlemen, all of that society, to whom I introduced them by briefly explaining their objects in visiting this country, their modes of life, their costumes, &c. After that, several ladies, as well as gentlemen, asked them questions relative to their religious belief and modes of worship; to all of which the War-chief answered in the most cheerful manner; and, as he constantly replied with appeals to the Great Spirit, who, he said, directed all their hearts, they all saw in him a feeling of reverence for the Great Spirit, which satisfied all that they were endowed with high sentiments of religion and devotion.

Mr. Melody here stated that he had just received very interesting and satisfactory letters from the reverend gentlemen conducting a missionary school, which was prospering, in their tribe, parts of which letters he read, and also presented a small book already printed in the Ioway language by a printing-press belonging to the Missionary Society, and now at work at their mission. This gave great satisfaction to the visitors, who saw that these people had friends at home who were doing what they could to enlighten their minds.

The friendly feelings of all present were then conveyed to them by several who addressed them in turn, expressing their deep anxiety for their worldly welfare and their spiritual good, and in the kindest and most impressive language exhorted them to temperance, to a knowledge of our Saviour, and to the blessings of education, which lead to it. They impressed upon their minds also the benefits that would flow from the abandonment of their hunters' life and warfare, and the adoption of agricultural pursuits. It was then stated that it was the object of the meeting to make them a present of something more than mere professions of friendship, and desired of me to ascertain what would be most useful and acceptable to them. The question being put to them, the White Cloud replied that "anything they felt disposed to give they would accept with thankfulness, but, as the question had been asked, he should say that *money* would be preferable to anything else, for it was more easily carried, and when in America, and near their own country, they could buy with it what their wives and little children should most need." It was then proposed that a hat should be passed around, for the purpose, by which the sum of 40*l.* was received, and handed to the chief, to divide between them. Besides this very liberal donation, a number of beautifully-bound Bibles were presented to them, and several very kind and lovely ladies went to the shops, and returned with beautiful shawls and other useful presents for the women and children; and one benevolent gentleman, who had been of the meeting, and whose name I regret that I have forgotten, brought in with his own hands, a large trunk filled with pretty and useful things, which he took pleasure in dividing amongst them, and in presenting the trunk to the wife of the chief.

Thus ended this very kind and interesting meeting, which the Indians will never forget, and which went far to strengthen their former belief that the "good people," as they called them, would be everywhere found to be their genuine friends.

Their invitation to the Zoological Gardens was for the day following, and they were there highly entertained by the young men who were the founders of that institution. They met in those peculiarly beautiful grounds a great number of the fashionable ladies and gentlemen of Dublin; and, after an hour or two delightfully spent amongst them, received from the treasurer of the institution the sum of 36*l.* that had been taken at the entrance. Nothing could have been more gratefully received than were these two kind presents; nor could anything have afforded them more convincing proofs of the hospitality and kindness of the people they were amongst.

The exhibitions at the Rotunda were continued on every evening, and the Indians took their daily ride at ten o'clock in the morning, seeing all that was to be seen in the streets and the suburbs of Dublin, and after their suppers and their *chickabobboo* enjoyed their jokes and their pipe, whilst they were making their remarks upon the occurrences of the day, and listening to Daniel's readings of the 'Times' newspaper, to which the *Chemokemon*[37] (as they now called him), Jim, had become a subscriber. This boundless source of information and amusement, just now opened to their minds, was engrossing much of their time; and Daniel and Jeffrey were called upon regularly every night, after their suppers, to tell them all that was new and curious in the paper of the day; and Jim desired a daily entry in his book of the number of *murders* and *robberies* that appeared in it. All this Daniel, in his kindness, did for him, after reading the description of them; and in this way the ingenious Jim considered he had all things now in good train to enable him to enlighten the Indian races when he should get back to the prairies of his own country.

Poor Jim, whose avarice began to dawn with his first steps towards civilization, and who, having his wife with him to add her share of presents to his, and was now getting such an accumulation of Bibles that they were becoming a serious item of luggage, related here a curious anecdote that occurred while he was in the Zoological Gardens:— The Bibles they had received, and were daily receiving, as "the most valuable presents that could be made them," he had supposed must of course have some considerable intrinsic value; and he felt disposed, as he was now increasing his expenses, by taking the 'Times' newspaper and in other ways, to try the experiment of occasionally selling one of his bibles to increase his funds, and, on starting to go to the gardens, had put one in his pouch to offer to people he should meet in the crowd; and it seems he offered it in many cases, but nobody would buy, but one had been *given* to him by a lady; so he came home with one more than he took; and he said to us, "I guess em no good—I no sell em, but I get em a heap."

A very friendly invitation was received about this time from the President of Trinity College for the party to visit that noble institution, and Mr. Melody and myself took great pleasure in accompanying them there. They were treated there with the greatest possible kindness; and, after being shown through all its parts—its library, museum, &c.—a liberal collection was made for them amongst the reverend gentlemen and their families, and presented to them a few days afterwards.

I took the War-chief and several of the party to visit the Archbishop of Dublin and his family, who treated them with much kindness, and presented to each a sovereign, as an evidence of the attachment they felt for them. This unexpected kindness called upon them for some expression of thanks in return; and the War-chief, after offering his hand to the Archbishop, said to him:—

> "My friend, as the Great Spirit has moved your heart to be kind to us, I rise up to thank Him first, and then to tell you how thankful we feel to you for what your hand has given us. We are poor, and do not deserve this; but we will keep it, and it will buy food and clothing for our little children.
>
> "My friend, we are soon going from here, and we live a great way. We shall never see your face again in this world, but we shall hope that the Great Spirit will allow us to meet in the world that is before us, and where you and I must soon go."

The Archbishop seemed much struck with his remarks; and, taking him again by the hand, said to him that he believed they would meet again in the world to come, and, commending them to the care of the Great Spirit, bade them an affectionate farewell.

An invitation was awaiting them at this time, also, to breakfast the next morning with Mr. Joseph Bewley, a Friend, and who lived a few miles out of the city. His carriages arrived for them at the hour, and the whole party visited him and his kind family and took their breakfast with them. After the breakfast was over, the chief thanked this kind gentleman for his hospitality and the presents very liberally bestowed; and the party all listened with great attention to the Christian advice which he gave them, recommending to them also to lay down all their weapons of war, and to study the arts of peace. These remarks seemed to have made a deep impression on their minds, for they were daily talking of this kind man and the advice and information he gave them.

Having finished our exhibitions by advertisement, but being detained a few days longer in Dublin than we expected by the illness of the *Roman Nose*, an opportunity was afforded the Indians to attend a number of evening parties, to which they were invited by families of the Society of Friends, and treated with the greatest kindness and attention.

The Indians had thus formed their notions of the beautiful city of Dublin by riding through it repeatedly in all its parts—by viewing, outside and in, its churches, its colleges, its gardens, and other places of amusement; and of its inhabitants, by meeting them in the exhibition rooms, and in their own houses, at their hospitable boards. They decided that Edinburgh was rather the most beautiful city; that in Glasgow they saw the most ragged and poor; and that in Dublin they met the warmest-hearted and most kind people of any they had seen in the kingdom. In Dublin, as in Glasgow, they had been in the habit of throwing handfuls of pence to the poor; and at length had got them baited, so that gangs of hungry, ragged creatures were daily following their carriage home to their door, and there waiting under their windows for the pence that were often showered down upon their heads.

Out of the thousands of beggars that *I* met while there (and many of whom extracted money from my pocket by their wit or drollery when I was not disposed to give it), there was but one of whom I shall make mention in this place. In my daily walk from my hotel to the Rotunda, there was an old, hardy-looking veteran, who used often to meet me and solicit with great importunity, as I had encouraged him by giving to him once or twice when I first met him. I was walking on that pavement one day with an American friend whom I had met, and, observing this old man coming at some distance ahead of us on the same pavement, I said to my friend, "Now watch the motions of that old fellow as he comes up to beg—look at the expression of his face." When we had got within a few rods of him the old man threw his stomach in, and one knee in an instant seemed out of joint, and his face! oh, most pitiable to look upon. We approached him arm-in-arm, and while coming towards him I put my hand in my pocket as if I was getting out some money, which brought this extraordinary expression from him: "My kind sir, may the gates of Heaven open to receive you!"—(by this time we had got by him, and, seeing that my hand remained stationary in my pocket, as he had turned round and was scowling daggers at me)—"and may you be kicked out the moment you get there!"

There is an inveteracy in the Irish begging and wit that shows it to be native and not borrowed; it is therefore more irresistible and more successful than in any other country perhaps in the world. I speak this, however, merely as an opinion of my own, formed on the many instances where the very reasons I assigned for not giving were so ingeniously and suddenly turned into irresistible arguments for giving, that my hand was in my pocket before I was aware of it.

The Indians however gave from other motives; not able to appreciate their wit, they had discernment enough to see the wretchedness that existed among the poor people in the lanes and outskirts of the city, and too much pity in their hearts not to try with their money to relieve them; and in that way I fully believe that they gave a very considerable proportion of the money they had received since they entered the city.

The symptoms of the poor *Roman Nose*, whose case was now decided to be almost hopeless, were a little more favourable, and it was agreed, with his united wish, that we should start for Liverpool by steamer; and on the morning when we went on board, the Indians were more strongly than ever confirmed in their belief that the Friends were the people who had taken the deepest interest in their welfare, by meeting nearly all they had seen in their numerous visits, down at the wharf, to shake hands with them, and wish them an everlasting farewell! Such proof as this, which brought even tears in their eyes, will be the last to be forgotten by them or by me, and should be the last to be overlooked in the public acknowledgment I am now making.

Our voyage across the Channel was easy and pleasant; and amongst the numerous and fashionable people on board, poor Jim had the mortification of trying to test the intrinsic value of his numerous stock of Bibles by occasionally offering one that he carried in his pouch. "I no sell 'em—they no like 'em," was his reply again; and he began to doubt the value of them, which he was greatly disappointed to find they had fixed much above their market-price.

On landing at the wharf in Liverpool the Indians recognised the spot where they first set their feet upon English soil, and they raised the yell (not unlike the war-whoop) which is given by war-parties when, returning from battle, they are able to see their own village. This gathered a great crowd in a few moments, that was exceedingly difficult to disperse, and it instilled new ambition and strength into the poor *Roman Nose*, who thought in his weakness that they were near home; but he rallied only to look out and realize that he was too far from his home ever to see it again.

Lodgings had been prepared for them, to which they immediately repaired; and, as their sinking companion was so rapidly declining, they were all in sadness, though they tried, poor fellows, to be gay and cheerful. Their exhibitions had been advertised to commence, and they proceeded with them. Before they commenced, however, a feast was made to thank the Great Spirit for having conducted them quite around England to the place from whence they started, and also for the benefit of the health of their fellow-warrior, the *Roman Nose*.

A council was also held, when Mr. Melody and I were called in, and by some it was proposed to start for home, and by others to go to Paris and see a King, as they had tried, but in vain, to see the Queen of England. A visit to Paris had been a favourite theme with them for some months past, and all at length joined in the wish to see the King and Queen of France.

The most skilful physicians were called to attend the poor *Roman Nose*, and they advised us to place him in an hospital. He was consulted, and, wishing to go, was removed there, where the interpreter, Jeffrey, stayed, and every attention was paid him. A few nights of exhibitions in Liverpool finished our stay in that town, and brought us to an engagement we had made, for four nights, in the Free Trade Hall in Manchester.

The Indians saw that their fellow-warrior was to sink to the grave in a few days, and yet, like philosophers, they said it was the will of the Great Spirit, and they must not complain. They said they would give their exhibitions for the four nights, as they were promised to the public, and then stop until their companion was dead and buried; our exhibitions were consequently made to immense crowds on those evenings, and to the same people who had seen the Ojibbeways with such a relish when they first arrived. The different appearance of this tribe, and difference in their modes, made them subjects of new and fresh interest, and no doubt that their exhibitions, if they had been continued, would have been nightly filled for a length of time. They here gave their exhibitions the additional interest of erecting three wigwams into a sort of Indian village on the immense platform, and stationed their targets at the two ends, giving a fair illustration of their skill in archery, as they shot for prizes across the breadth of the immense hall.

Their exhibitions gained them much applause here, as in other places, with which they were well pleased, and they had many invitations from kind families in town, but which they declined, as they said they were sad, as one of their number was dying. Thus their amusements in Manchester, and for the kingdom, were finished, and they retired to their private apartments, awaiting the end of the poor *Roman Nose*, which was now daily expected. Mr. Melody and Jeffrey stayed by him, and I went to see him, and so did several of the Indians, on each day until his death.

While the Indians were thus resting in their quarters, they were surprised and cheered by the sudden arrival of their old friend, *Bobasheela*, who had just come from Cornwall to see them again before their departure for America, as he supposed, from seeing by the papers that they had arrived in Liverpool.

They thus amused themselves from day to day, lying still, not wishing to ride about, or to admit company, or to attend to the invitations from various quarters given to them. Their time was now chiefly taken up in repairing their dresses, &c., in anticipation of going before the King of France, and listening to the amusing and shocking things which Daniel was daily reading in Jim's newspaper, and minuting down in his note-book, as he required. He wished Daniel and his friend *Bobasheela* to find in his paper, if they could, how many churches there were in England, and how many *black-coats* (as he called them) there were who were constantly reading the good book and preaching to them. This they could not do at the moment, but *Bobasheela* told him he could get it all out of a book that had lately been published, and would give it to him the next day. This was done according to promise, and by Daniel recorded in his book.

Bobasheela's anxieties were now turned towards the poor suffering *Roman Nose*, and he went to Liverpool to see him, and arrived with some of the Indians just in time to see him breathe his last. Alas! poor, fine fellow! he went down gradually and regularly to the grave; and though amongst strangers and far away from all of the graves of his relatives, he died like a philosopher, and (though not a Christian) not *unlike* a Christian. He said repeatedly to Jeffrey that he should live but so many days, and afterwards so many hours, and seemed to be perfectly resigned to the change that was to take place. He said that his time had come; he was going to the beautiful hunting-grounds, where he would soon see his friends who had gone before him: he said that when he shut his eyes he could plainly see them, and he felt sure it was only to change the society of his friends here for that of his dear parents and other friends, and he was now anxious to be with them. He said the road might be long, but it did not matter where he started from; the Great Spirit had promised him strength to reach it. He told his friend *Bobasheela* that in his pouch he would find some money, with which he wished him to buy some of the best vermilion, and, if possible, some green paint, such as *Chippehola* used to get for him in London, and have them put in his pouch with his flint and steel, and to be sure to be placed in his grave, that he might be able to make his face look well among his friends where he was going. He wished him, and Daniel also, to have his arrows examined in his quiver, and repaired with new and sharp blades, as he recollected that, before he was sick, many of them were injured by shooting at the target, and during his illness others might have been destroyed. He had requested his silver medal, which was given to him by the American government for saving the lives of ten of his defenceless enemies, to be suspended by a blue ribbon over his head while he was sick, that he might see it until he died, and in that position it hung when I was last with him—his eyes were upon it, and his smile, until he drew his last breath. After his death his friend *Bobasheela*, and Jeffrey and the Doctor, laid him in his coffin, and, placing in it, according to the Indian mode, his faithful bow and quiver of arrows, his pipe and tobacco to last him through the "journey he was to perform," having dressed him in all his finest clothes, and painted his face, and placed his bow and quiver and his pouch by his side, and his medal on his breast, the coffin was closed, and his remains were buried, attended by his faithful friends around him, by the officers of the institution, and many citizens, who sympathized in his unlucky fate.

Thus ended the career of *No-ho-mun-ya* (or the Roman Nose), one of the most peaceable and well-disposed and finest men of the party, or of the tribe from which he came.

The reader will now contemplate the Indians and their friend *Bobasheela* again in their private rooms in Manchester, spending a week or so together, smoking their pipes, with their faces painted black, recounting the deeds of the vanished warrior, and recapitulating the events of their tour through England, Scotland, and Ireland, and trying to cheer the view that was ahead of them by drinking *chickabobboo*. These few days passed heavily by, and they soon became anxious to throw off the gloom that was cast over them, by seeing something new, and by resuming the exercise and excitements of the dance. Their thoughts were now on Paris, and I was there making arrangements for their reception. The reader will therefore, with my help, *imagine* himself across the Channel (and probably for the first time in his life without being sea-sick), and ready to commence, with the Indians and me, amidst new scenes and new scenery, the following chapter.

CHAPTER XXV.

The Author arrives in Paris—Victoria Hotel—Mr. Melody and his Indians arrive—Doctor missing, and found on the top of the hotel—Alarm of servants—First drive in Paris—Visit to Mr. King, the American ambassador—French *chickabobboo*—M. Vattemare—Indians visit the Hôtel de Ville—Préfet de police—Magnificent salons—The "big looking-glasses"—The Préfet's lady—Refreshments and *chickabobboo*—Speech of the War-chief—Reply of the Préfet—Salle Valentino taken for the exhibition—Daniel arrives with the Collection from London—Indians visit the King in the palace of the Tuileries—Royal personages—Conversation—War-chief presents the calumet—His speech to the King—Eagle-dance—War-dance—Little Wolf presents his tomahawk and whip to the King—His speech—Refreshments and "Queen's *chickabobboo*"—Drinking the King's and Queen's health, and health of the Count de Paris—"Vive le Roi"—Jim's opinion of the King—An Indian's idea of descents—Presents in money from the King—Mode of dividing it—A drive—Ladies leading dogs with strings—The number counted in one drive—The Indians' surprise—An entry for Jim's book—Jim laments the loss of the Times newspaper and *Punch*—He takes Galignani's Messenger—Indians dine at W. Costar's—The Doctor's compliment to a lady's fine voice—Indians visit the Royal Academy of Sciences—Curious reception—M. Arago—Indians' suspicions and alarms—Jim's remarkable speech—Opening of the exhibition in Salle Valentino—Great excitement—Speech of the War-chief—Shaking hands—Public opinion of the Author's Collection.

Having long before resolved to take my collection to Paris before returning it to my own country, and the Indians being ambitious to see the King of the French, it was mutually agreed that my whole collection should be opened in Paris, and that their dances and other amusements should for a short time be given in it, as they had been given in London.

Under this arrangement, with my wife and my four dear little children, I repaired to Paris as soon as possible, leaving Daniel to ship over and accompany my collection, whilst Mr. Melody conducted his party of Indians.

In crossing the Channel, and receding from its shores, as I was seated on the deck of a steamer, I looked back, and, having for the first time nothing else to do, and a little time to reflect upon England, and what I had seen of it in five years, I took out of my pocket my little note-book, where I had entered, not what England is, and what she does (and which all the world knows), but the points in which her modes are different from those in my own country. I would have a few leisure hours to run over these curious entries, and time to reflect upon them, as we sailed along, and I began to read thus:—

"London, 1844. The essential Differences between England and the United States.

"The United States much the largest; but England is a great deal older.

"New-Yorkers cross the streets diagonally; the Londoners cross them at right angles.

"In England the odd pennies are wrapped in a paper, and handed back with 'I thank you, Sir.'

"Streets in London have tops and bottoms; in America they have upper and lower ends.

"In England a man's wife is 'very bad;' in America, 'very ill;' and in France, 'bien malade.'

"Americans 'turn to the *right* as the law directs;' the English turn to the *left*.

"English mutton and babies are much the fattest.

"Gooseberries in England much the largest, but not so sweet.

"Pigs in the American cities are seen promenading in the streets; in London, only seen hanging by their hind legs.

"In England men are 'knocked up;' in America they are 'knocked down.'

"'*Top-coats*' are very frequent in England, in America nothing is known higher than an '*over-coat.*'

"In the United States a man is 'smart;' in England he is 'clever.'

"English ladies are more luscious, but not quite so——"

Just when I had read thus far, the steward tapped me on the shoulder and told me that "I was wanted below immediately, for my lady was very ill." I closed my book and ran below, where I found my poor wife and little family all dreadfully sick. I waited on them a while and got sea-sick myself. My musings on England and America were thus broken off; and from the time that we launched forth amidst the clatter upon a French wharf, I had as much as I could do to keep my little children and my luggage together, and all recollections of England and my native country vanished in the confusion and din that was around me in the new world we were entering upon. Custom-houses and railways and diligences have been a thousand times described, and I need say nothing of them, except that we got through them all, and into the *Victoria Hotel*, in Paris, where we found rest, fine beds, kind attentions, and enough to eat.

A few days after my arrival in Paris, Mr. Melody made his appearance with his party of Ioways, for whom apartments were prepared in the same hotel, and after much fatigue and vexation the immense hall in Rue St. Honoré (Salle Valentino) was engaged as the place for their future operations. Daniel in the mean time was moving up with the Indian collection of eight tons weight, and in a few days all parties were on the ground, though there was to be some delay in arranging the numerous collection, and in getting the Indians introduced to the King, which was the first object. They had entered the city at a late hour at night, and for several days it had been impossible to attend to the necessary arrangements for driving them about; and they became excessively impatient to be on wheels again, to get a glimpse of the strange and beautiful things which they knew were about them. In the mean time they were taking all the amusement to themselves that they could get, by looking out of the windows; and their red and crested heads in Paris soon drew a crowd together in the streets, and thousands of heads protruding from the windows and house-tops. The Doctor soon found his way to the roof, and from that regaled his eyes, at an early hour, with a bird's-eye view of the boundless mystery and confusion of chimneys and house-tops and domes and spires that were around him.

The servants in the house were at first alarmed, and the good landlady smiled at their unexpected appearance; and she roared with laughter when she was informed that the beds were all to be removed from their rooms, that they spread their own robes, and, in preference, slept upon the floor. All in the house, however, got attached to them in a few days, and all went pleasantly on.

The first airing they took in Paris was in an omnibus with four, as they had been driven in London; but, to the old Doctor's exceeding chagrin, there was no seat for him to take outside by the side of the driver. He was easily reconciled however to his seat with the rest, and they thus soon had a glance at a number of the principal streets of the city, and were landed at the American Embassy, to pay their first respects to Mr. King, at that time the minister to France. They were received by Mr. King and his niece with great kindness; and after a little conversation, through the interpreter, Mr. King invited them to the table, loaded with cakes and fruit, and offered them a glass of wine, proposing their health, and at the same time telling them that, though he was opposed to encouraging Indians to drink, yet he was quite sure that a glass or two of the *vin rouge* of the French would not hurt them. The colour of it seemed to cause them to hesitate a moment, while they were casting their eyes around upon me. They understood the nod of my head, and, hearing me pronounce it *chickabobboo*, took the hint and drank it off with great pleasure. Mr. Melody here assured Mr. King of the temperate habits of these people; and I explained to the party the origin and meaning of *chickabobboo*, which pleased them all very much. They partook of a second glass, and also of the cakes and fruit, and took leave, the War-chief having thanked Mr. King and his niece for their kindness, and having expressed his great pleasure at meeting so kind an American gentleman so far from home.

The Indians were now in their omnibus again, and Mr. Melody and myself in our carriage, with a kind friend, Mons. A. Vattemare, who had obtained for the Indians an invitation to visit the *Hotel de Ville*, where we were now to drive. In this drive from St. Germain we recrossed the Seine by Pont Neuf, and had a fine view of all the bridges, and the palace of the Tuileries, and the Louvre. The omnibus stopped a moment on the middle of the bridge, and they were much excited by the view. A few minutes more brought us in front of the *Hotel de Ville*, where several thousands of people were assembled; it having been heard in the streets, in all probability, from the servants or police, that a party of savages were to be there at that hour.

There was a great outcry when they landed and entered the hall, and the crowd was sure not to diminish whilst they were within.

We were all presented to His Excellency the *Préfet de Police* by my friend Mons. Vattemare, and received with great kindness, and conducted through all the principal apartments of that noble edifice, which are finished and furnished in the most sumptuous style, and in richness of effect surpassing even the most splendid halls of the palaces of the Tuileries or St. Cloud. The gorgeousness of the carpets on which they stood, and the tapestry that was around them, and the incredible size of the mirrors that were reflecting them in a hundred directions, were subjects till then entirely new to them; and they seemed completely amazed at the splendour with which they were surrounded. From these splendid salons we were conducted into the *salle à manger*, and opportunely where the table was spread and the plates laid for a grand banquet. This was a lucky occurrence, affording us, as well as the Indians, an opportunity of seeing the richness of the plate upon which those elegant affairs are served up, and which but a choice few can ever behold.

Retiring from and through this suite of splendid salons, we entered an antechamber, where we were presented to the elegant lady of the *Préfet* and several of their friends, who brought us to a table loaded with fruit and cakes and other refreshments, and wine of several sorts and the best in quality. The corks of several bottles of champagne were drawn, and, as the sparkling wine was running, each one smiled as he whispered the word *chickabobboo*. The *Préfet* drank their health in a glass of the "*Queen's chickabobboo*" as they called it, and then, with his own hand, presented each a handsome silver medal, and also one to Mr. Melody and myself.

The War-chief by this time felt called upon for some acknowledgment on their part for this kind treatment, and, advancing to the *Préfet*, shook hands with him, and addressed him thus:—

"My friend and father, your kindness to us this day makes our hearts glad, and we thank you for it. We are strangers here, and poor ignorant children from the wilderness. We came here with heavy hearts, having just buried one of our warriors, and your kindness has driven away our sorrow. ('*How, how, how!*')

"My father, the splendour of the rooms, and other things you have just shown us, blind our eyes with their brightness, and we now see that white men can do anything.

"My father, we were astonished at what we saw in London, where we have been, but we think your village is much the most beautiful. We thank the Great Spirit, who has opened your great house to us to-day, and also your lady, who has been kind to us.

"My father, I have done."

At the close of his speech the *Préfet* assured him of his kindly feelings towards them, and his anxiety for their welfare; and after a general shake of hands we took leave, and descended to the street, and, passing through a dense crowd, took our carriages and drove back to our hotel. Thus ended their first day's drive and visits in Paris, furnishing them with a rich fund for a talk after their dinner and *chickabobboo*, which was to be *vin rouge* in Paris, instead of ale, which they had been in the habit of drinking in England.

Nothing could exceed the exhilarated flow of spirits in which they returned, and the admiration they were expressing of the beauty of the city, and the splendour of the rooms they had been in. They were decided that they should be pleased with Paris; and as Palaces, Kings, and Queens were yet before them, they seemed to be perfectly happy. During their curious remarks on what they had seen, they already were saying that they had seen many thousands of people, and were glad that they saw nobody in rags or begging. They thought the French people all had enough to eat, and *that*, they said, was a great pleasure to them; for it made their hearts sore, when riding out, if they saw poor people, who had nothing to eat, as they had seen in some places.

The Indians decided that the houses of Paris were much more beautiful than they had seen in any place; and they thought, from their cheerful looks, that either the people had their debts more paid up than the English people, or else that they had not so much money as to distress their looks for fear of losing it. We were all pleased with the appearance of Paris, and compelled to feel cheerful from the buoyant feelings that were displayed all around us. Like the Indians, I was pleased with the neat and cleanly appearance of the poorest in the streets, and surprised at the beauty and elegance of their houses, which want, in my estimation, but one more embellishment, which it would be quite easy to give, to render the effect of their streets more beautiful than words can describe. That would be, to paint their window-blinds green, which, by contrast, would make the walls appear more white and clean, and break with pleasing variety the white monotony that now prevails throughout.

This first day's drive about the city had created a prodigious excitement and curiosity where they had gone, and given to the Indians just peep enough, amidst the beauties of Paris, to create a restlessness on both sides for a more familiar acquaintance, and which it had been thought most prudent to defer until they had made their visit to the Palace, for which their application had been made to the King by the American minister, and to which we were daily expecting a reply. In the mean time, Mr. Melody, and Jeffrey, and the Indians kept quiet, entertaining an occasional party of some American friends, or distinguished, personages, who were sending in their cards, and seeking interviews with them. During all this delay they had enough to amuse them, by talking of what they had already seen, and what they expected they were going to see, and cleaning and preparing their dresses for the great occasion. I, in the mean time, with my man Daniel, and others, was arranging my collection on the walls of the *Salle Valentino*; and, by the kind and friendly aid of Mons. Vattemare, obtaining my licence from the authorities, and also conforming to the other numerous and vexatious forms and ceremonies to be gone through before the opening of my exhibition to public view.

The Minister of the Interior had kindly granted an order for the admission of my whole collection into the kingdom, by my paying merely a nominal duty, but there were still forms and delays to submit to in the customs, which were tedious and vexatious, but by the aid of my above-mentioned good friend, they had all been overcome; and my collection was now nearly ready for the public examination, when I received a letter from the American minister, informing me, that "on a certain day, and at a certain hour, His Majesty would see Mr. Catlin and Mr. Melody, with the Ioway Indians, in the Palace of the Tuileries." There was great rejoicing amongst the good fellows when they heard this welcome letter read, and several of them embraced me in their arms, as if I had been the sole cause of it. Their doubts were now at an end: it was certain that they should see the King of France, which, they said, "would be far more satisfactory, and a greater honour, than to have seen the Queen of England." Whatever the poor fellows thought, such was their mode of exultation. "The Ojibbeways," they said, "were subjects of the Queen, but we will be subjects of Louis Philippe."

They had yet a few days to prepare, and even without their drives or company they were contented, as the time passed away, and they were preparing for the interview. On the morning of the day for their reception, the long stem of a beautiful pipe had been painted a bright blue, and ornamented with blue ribbons, emblematical of peace, to be presented by the chief to the King. Every article of dress and ornament had been put in readiness; and, as the hour approached, each one came out from his toilet, in a full blaze of colour of various tints, all with their wampum and medals on, with their necklaces of grizly bears' claws, their shields, and bows, and quivers, their lances, and war clubs, and tomahawks, and scalping knives. In this way, in full dress, with their painted buffalo robes wrapped around them, they stepped into the several carriages prepared for them, and all were wheeled into the *Place Carousel*, and put down at the entrance to the Palace. We were met on the steps by half a dozen huge and splendid looking porters, in flaming scarlet livery and powdered wigs, who conducted us in, and being met by one of the King's *aides-de-camp*, we were conducted by him into His Majesty's presence, in the reception hall of the *Tuileries*.

The royal party were advancing towards us in the hall, and as we met them, Mr. Melody and myself were presented; and I then introduced the party, each one in person, according to his rank or standing, as the King desired. A sort of *conversazione* took place there, which lasted for half an hour or more, in which I was called upon to explain their weapons, costumes, &c., and which seemed to afford great amusement to the royal personages assembled around and amongst us, who were—their Majesties the *King* and the *Queen*, the *Duchess of Orleans* and *Count de Paris*, the *Princess Adelaide*, the *Prince* and *Princess de Joinville*, the *Duke* and *Duchess d'Aumale*, and his *Royal Highness* the *Duke de Brabant*.

His Majesty in the most free and familiar manner (which showed that he had been accustomed to the modes and feelings of Indians) conversed with the chiefs, and said to Jeffrey, "Tell these good fellows that I am glad to see them; that I have been in many of the wigwams of the Indians in America when I was a young man, and they treated me every where kindly, and I love them for it.—Tell them I was amongst the Senecas near Buffalo, and the Oneidas—that I slept in the wigwams of the chiefs—that I was amongst the Shawnees and Delawares on the Ohio; and also amongst the Cherokees and Creeks in Georgia and Tennessee, and saw many other tribes as I descended the Ohio river the whole length, and also the Mississippi to New Orleans, in a small boat, more than fifty years ago." This made the Indians stare, and the women, by a custom of their country, placed their hands over their mouths, as they issued groans of surprise.

"Tell them also, Jeffrey, that I am pleased to see their wives and little children they have with them here, and glad also to show them my family, who are now nearly all around me. Tell them, Jeffrey, that *this* is the Queen; *this lady* is my sister; *these* are two of my sons, with their wives; and *these little lads* [the

Count de Paris and the *Duc de Brabant*] are my grandsons; *this one*, if he lives, will be King of the Belgians, and *that one* King of the French."

N°. 15.

The King then took from his pocket two large gold medals with his own portrait in relief on one side of them, and told me he wished to present them to the two chiefs with his own hand, and wished Jeffrey to explain to them, that after presenting them in that way, he wished them to hand them back to him that he might have a proper inscription engraved on them, when he would return them, and silver medals of equal size to each of the others, with their names engraved upon them. After the medals were thus presented and returned, the War-chief took out from under his robe the beautiful pipe which he had prepared, and advancing towards the King, and holding it with both hands, bent forward and laid it down at his Majesty's feet as a present. Having done so he reached down, and taking it up, placed it in his Majesty's hand (Plate No. 15), and then, assuming his proud attitude of the orator, addressed their Majesties in these words:—

> "Great Father and Great Mother,—the Great Spirit, to whom we have a long time prayed for an interview with you, kindly listens to our words to-day and hears what we say. Great Father, you have made to us to-day rich presents, and I rise to return thanks to you for the chief and his warriors and braves who are present; but, before all, it is necessary that we should thank the Great Spirit who has inspired your heart and your hand thus to honour us this day.

"Great Father, we shall bear these presents to our country and instruct our children to pronounce the name of him who gave them.

"Great Father, when the Indians have anything to say to a great chief, they are in the habit of making some present before they begin. My chief has ordered me to place in your hands this pipe and these strings of wampum as a testimony of the pleasure we have felt in being admitted this day into the presence of your Majesty.

"My Great Father and my Great Mother, you see us this day as we are seen in our country with our red skins and our coarse clothes. This day for *you* is like all other days; for *us* it is a great day—so great a day that our eyes are blinded with the lustre of it.

"Great Father, the chief, myself, and our warriors have for a long time had the desire to come and see the French people, and our Great Father the President of the United States has given us permission to cross the Great Lake. We desired to see the Great Chief of this country, and we now thank the Great Spirit for having allowed us to shake the hand of the Great Chief in his own wigwam.

"Great Father, we are happy to tell you that when we arrived in England, we had much joy in meeting our old friend Mr. Catlin, who has lived amongst us and whom we are happy to have here, as he can tell you who we are.

"Great Father and Great Mother, we will pray to the Great Spirit to preserve your precious lives; we will pray also that we may return safe to our own village, that we may tell to our children and to our young men what we have seen this day.

"My Parents, I have no more to say."

When the War-chief had finished his speech, the King told Jeffrey to say that he felt very great pleasure in having seen them, and he hoped that the Great Spirit would guide them safe home to their country, to their wives and little children.

The King and Royal Family then took leave; and as they were departing, some one of them being attracted to the Indian drum which Jeffrey had brought in his hand, and had left upon the floor in another part of the room, and inquiring what it was, was told that it was their *drum* which they had brought with them, supposing it possible they might be called upon to give a dance. This information overtook the King, and he said, "By all means; call the Queen:" and in a few moments the august assembly were all back to witness the dance, for which purpose all parties moved to the *Salle du Bal*. Their Majesties and the ladies were seated, and the Indians all seating themselves in the middle of the floor, commenced moderately singing and beating the drum, preparatory to the Eagle Dance, in which they were in a few moments engaged.

During this novel and exciting scene, her Majesty desired me to stand by the side of her to explain the meaning of all its features, which seemed to astonish and amuse her very much.

The Doctor led off first in the character (as he called it) of a soaring eagle, sounding his eagle whistle, which he carried in his left hand, with his fan of the eagle's tail, while he was brandishing his lance in the other.

At the first pause he instantly stopped, and, in the attitude of an orator, made his boast of an instance where he killed an enemy in single combat, and took his scalp. The Little Wolf, and *Wash-ka-mon-ya*, and others, then sprang upon their feet, and sounding their chattering whistles,[38] and brandishing their polished weapons, gave an indescribable wildness and spirit to the scene. When the dance was finished, the Indians had the pleasure of receiving their Majesties' applause, by the violent clapping of their hands, and afterwards by expressions of their pleasure and admiration, conveyed to them through the interpreter.

This was exceedingly gratifying to the poor fellows, who were now seated upon the floor to rest a moment previous to commencing with the war-dance, for which they were preparing their weapons, and in which the Little Wolf was to take the lead. For this, as the drum beat, he threw aside his buffalo robe and sprang upon the floor, brandishing his tomahawk and shield, and sounding the frightful war-whoop, which called his warriors up around him. Nothing could have been more thrilling or picturesque than the scene at that moment presented of this huge and terrible-looking warrior, frowning death and destruction on his brow, as he brandished the very weapons he had used in deadly combat, and, in his jumps and sudden starts, seemed threatening with instant use again! The floors and ceilings of the Palace shook with the weight of their steps, and its long halls echoed and vibrated the shrill-sounding notes of the war-whoop. (Plate No. 16.)

In the midst of this dance, the Little Wolf suddenly brandished his tomahawk over the heads of his comrades, and, ordering them to stop, advanced towards the King, and boasting in the most violent exclamations of the manner in which he had killed and scalped a Pawnee warrior, placed in his Majesty's hands his *tomahawk* and the *whip* which was attached to his wrist, and then said,—

"My Great Father, you have heard me say that with that *tomahawk* I have killed a Pawnee warrior, one of the enemies of my tribe; the blade of that tomahawk is still covered with his blood, which you will see. That whip is the same with which I whipped my horse on that occasion.

"My Father, since I have come into this country I have learned that peace is better than war, and I *'bury the tomahawk'* in your hands—I fight no more."

His Majesty deigned graciously to accept the arms thus presented, after having cordially shaken the hand of the Ioway brave.

Their Majesties and attendants then withdrew, taking leave of the Indians in the most gracious and condescending manner, expressing their thanks for the amusement they had afforded them, and their anxiety for their welfare, directing them to be shown into the various apartments of the palace, and then to be conducted to a table of wine and other refreshments prepared for them.

We were now in charge of an officer of the household, who politely led us through the various magnificent halls of the Palace, explaining every thing as we passed, and at length introduced us into a room with a long table spread and groaning under its load of the luxuries of the season, and its abundance of the "*Queen's chickabobboo.*" These were subjects that required no explanations; and all being seated, each one evinced his familiarity with them by the readiness with which he went to work. The healths of the King and the Queen were drank, and also of the Count de Paris, and the rest of the Royal family. The *chickabobboo* they pronounced "first-rate;" and another bottle being poured it was drank off, and we took our carriages, and, after a drive of an hour or so about the city, were landed again in our comparatively humble, but very comfortable, apartments.

The party returning from the Tuileries found their dinner coming up, and little was said until it was over, and they had drank their *chickabobboo*, and seated themselves upon their buffalo robes, which were spread upon the floor, and lighted the pipe. I have before said that the pipe is almost indispensable with Indians, where there is to be any exertion of the mind in private conversation or public speaking, and that generally but one pipe is used, even in a numerous company, each one drawing a few whiffs through it, and passing it on into the hands of his next neighbour.

In this manner they were now seated, and passing the pipe around as I came in, and took a seat with them. They were all quite merry at the moment by trying to sound the "*Vive le Roi!*" which I had taught them at the King's table when they were drinking his Majesty's health. It puzzled them very much, but the adept Jim took it directly, and as the rest found he had got it they seemed quite satisfied, thinking most probably that they could learn it at their pleasure.

Nº. 16.

"Well, Jim," said I, "what do you think of the King, Louis Philippe?" He reached for the pipe, and taking a puff or two handed it to the Doctor, and rolling over on to his back, and drawing up his knees, said, "I think he is a great man and a very good man. I believe he is a much greater chief than the Queen of England, and that he governs his people much better, because we don't see so many poor people in the streets—we think that his people all have enough to eat. His wigwam is very grand and very bright, and his *chickabobboo* the best that we have had. We did not see the King with his fine dress on, but as his servants all around him were beautifully dressed, like gentlemen, we know that the King and Queen must look very elegant when they are in full dress. We saw the King's two sons, and he told us that his grandson was to be the King when he dies—now we don't understand this!" It seemed that his teacher, Daniel, had overlooked the *doctrine of descents* during their close investigations of the statistics and politics of England, and the poor fellow was yet quite in the dark to know "how a grandson (a mere child) would be taken in case of the King's death, instead of one of his sons, either of whom he said he thought would make a very good king if he would take a trip for a year or two, as his father did, on the Mississippi and Missouri, amongst the different tribes of Indians." This was considered a pretty clever thing for Jim to say, and it raised a laugh amongst the Indians; he was encouraged to go on, and turned his conversation upon the gold and silver medals, with which he was very much pleased. They were delighted with the idea that the King's portrait was on one side, and that he was to have their names engraved on the other; and they were not less delighted when I told them that the gentleman who had come in with me and was now sitting by my side, had come from the King to bear them some other token of his Majesty's attachment to them. The object of his visit being thus made known to them, he turned out into the lap of the chief 500 francs to be divided according to their custom. This of course put a stop to conversations about descents and Palaces, &c., for the time, and all went to counting until it was divided into thirteen parcels, one of which for the interpreter. Jeffrey, however, very kindly surrendered his share, and insisted that they should divide it all amongst themselves. It was accordingly made into twelve parcels, each one, old and young, taking an equal share, according to the Indian mode of dividing in all the tribes I have visited.

The War-chief rose and addressed the young man who was commissioned to bear the present to them:—

> "My Friend, we have seen your King (our Great Father) this day, and our hearts were made glad that we were allowed to see his face. We now receive the token of his friendship which he has sent through your hands, and our hearts are again glad. (*'How, how, how!'*)
>
> "My Friend, we wish you to say to the King, our Great Father, that we are thankful for his kindness, and that we shall pray that the Great Spirit may be kind to him and his children.
>
> "My Friend, we are all much obliged to you, and we shall be glad to offer you the pipe with us. (*'How, how, how!'*)"

The pipe was passed a few times around, with some further anecdotes of their visit to the palace, when the messenger arose and took leave of them. In counting the money, Jim had lost his attitude, so there was little more of the sentimental from him, as the conversation was running upon the King's bounty, rather than his greatness, or the splendour of things they had seen during the day. From the liberal additions to their private purse while in Dublin, and by what they were now receiving, they were beginning to feel a little purse proud. Jim was talking of having a *brick house* to live in when he got home, and the Doctor of heading a war party to go against the *Ojibbeways*. The War-chief told him he had better pay his debts first, and that he had slain enough in his own tribe, without going amongst his enemies for the purpose. The *Little Wolf* was going to get money enough to buy thirty horses, and lead a war party against his old enemies, the *Pawnees*; but Mr. Melody reminded him that he was to go to war no more, as he had "buried the tomahawk in his Majesty's hands."

Thus musing and moralizing on the events of the day, I left them to their conversation and their pipe, to attend, myself, where my presence was necessary, in arranging my collection, and preparing my rooms for their exhibitions. In this I had a real task—a scene of vexation and delay that I should wish never to go through again, and of which a brief account may be of service to any one of my countrymen who may be going to Paris to open a public exhibition; at least, my hints will enable him, if he pays attention to them, to begin at the right time, and at the right end of what he has got to do, and to do it to the best advantage.

His first step is, for any exhibition whatever, to make his application to the Prefect of Police for his licence, which is in all cases doubtful, and in all cases also is sure to require two or three weeks for his petition to pass the slow routine of the various offices and hands which it must go through. If it be for any exhibition that can be construed into an interference with the twenty or thirty theatre licences, it may as well not be applied for or thought of, for they will shut it up if opened.

It is also necessary to arrange in time with the overseer of the poor, whether he is to take one-eighth or one-fifth of the receipts for the hospitals—for the *hospice*, as he is termed, is placed at the door of all exhibitions in Paris, who carries off one-eighth or one-fifth of the daily receipts every night. It is necessary also, if catalogues are to be sold in the rooms, to lodge one of them at least two weeks before the exhibition is to open in the hands of the Commissaire de Police, that it may pass through the office of the Prefect, and twenty other officers' hands, to be read, and duly decided that there is nothing revolutionary in it; and then to sell them, or to give them away (all the same), it is necessary for the person who is to sell, and who alone *can* sell them, to apply personally to the Commissaire de Police, and make oath that he was born in France, to give his age and address, &c., &c., before he can take the part that is assigned him. It is then necessary, when the exhibition is announced, to wait until seven or eight guards and police, with muskets and bayonets fixed, enter and unbar the doors, and open them for the public's admission. It is necessary to submit to their friendly care during every day of the exhibition, and to pay each one his wages at night, when they lock up the rooms and put out the lights. In all this, however, though expensive, there is one redeeming feature. These numbers of armed police, at their posts, in front of the door, and in the passage, as well as in the exhibition rooms, give respectability to its appearance, and preserve the strictest order and quiet amongst the company, and keep a constant and vigilant eye to the protection of property. During the time I was engaged in settling these tedious preliminaries, and getting my rooms prepared for their exhibition, the Indians were taking their daily rides, and getting a passing glimpse of most of the out-door scenes of Paris. They were admitting parties of distinguished visitors, who were calling upon them, and occasionally leaving them liberal presents, and passing their evenings upon their buffalo skins, handing around the never-tiring pipe, and talking about the King, and their medals, and curious things they had seen as they had been riding through the streets. The thing which as yet amused the Doctor the most was the great number of women they saw in the streets leading dogs with ribbons and strings. He said he thought they liked their dogs better than they did their little children. In London, he said he had seen some little dogs leading their masters, who were blind, and in Paris they began to think the first day they rode out that one half of the Paris women were blind, but that they had a great laugh when they found that their eyes were wide open, and that instead of their dogs leading them, they were leading their dogs. The Doctor seemed puzzled about the custom of the women leading so many dogs, and although he did not in any direct way censure them for doing it, it seemed to perplex him, and he would sit and smile and talk about it for hours together. He and Jim had, at first, supposed, after they found that the ladies were not blind, that they cooked and ate them, but they were soon corrected in this notion, and always after remained at a loss to know what they could do with them.

On one of their drives, the Doctor and Jim, supplied with a pencil and a piece of paper, had amused themselves by counting, from both sides of the omnibus, the number of women they passed, leading dogs in the street, and thus made some amusement with their list when they got home. They had been absent near an hour, and driving through many of the principal streets of the city, and their list stood thus:—

Women leading one little dog

Women leading two little dogs

Women leading three little dogs

Women with big dogs following (no string)

Women carrying little dogs

Women with little dogs in carriages

The poor fellows insisted on it that the above was a correct account, and Jim, in his droll way (but I have no doubt quite honestly), said that "It was not a very good day either."

I was almost disposed to question the correctness of their estimate, until I took it into my head to make a similar one, in a walk I was one day taking, from the Place Madeleine, through a part of the Boulevard, Rue St. Honoré, and Rue Rivoli, and a turn in the garden of the Tuileries. I saw so many that I lost my reckoning, when I was actually not a vast way from the list they gave me as above, and quite able to believe that their record was near to the truth. While the amusement was going on about the ladies and the little dogs, Daniel, who had already seen many more of the sights of Paris than I had, told the Indians that there was a *Dog Hospital* and a *Dog Market* in Paris, both of them curious places, and well worth their seeing. This amused the Doctor and Jim very much. The Doctor did not care for the *Dog Market*, but the *Hospital* he *must* see. He thought the hospital must be a very necessary thing, as there were such vast numbers; and he thought it would be a good thing to have an hospital for their mistresses also. Jim thought more of the market, and must see it in a day or two, for it was about the time that they should give a feast of thanksgiving, and "a *Dog Feast* was always the most acceptable to the Great Spirit." It was thus agreed all around, that they should make a visit in a few days to the Dog Market and the Dog Hospital.

Jim got Daniel to enter the above list in his book as a very interesting record, and ordered him to leave a blank space underneath it, in order to record any thing else they might learn about dogs while in Paris.

Poor Jim! he was at this time deeply lamenting the loss of the pleasure he had just commenced to draw from the 'Times' newspaper, for which he had become a subscriber, and his old and amusing friend 'Punch,' which Daniel had been in the habit of entertaining them with, and which he had been obliged to relinquish on leaving England. His friend Daniel, however, who was sure always to be by him, particularly at a late hour in the evenings, relieved him from his trouble by telling him that there was an English paper printed in Paris every day, 'Galignani's Messenger,' which republished nearly all the murders, and rapes, and robberies, &c. from the 'Times;' and also, which would make it doubly interesting, those which were daily occurring in Paris. Jim was now built up again, and as he could already read a few words was the envied of all the party. He was learning with Daniel and Jeffrey a few words in French also, to which the others had not aspired; he, could say quite distinctly "*vive le roi*;" he knew that "*bon jour*" was "good morning," or "how do do?" that "*bon*" was "good," that "*mauvais*" was "bad," and that "very sick" was "*bien malade*." He requested Daniel to get Galignani's paper daily for him, for which he and the Doctor had agreed to pay equal shares. He seemed now quite happy in the opinion that his prospects for civilization were again upon a proper footing, and the old Doctor, who profited equally by all of Daniel's readings, was delighted to lend his purse to share in the expense. Daniel at this moment pulled the last number of Galignani out of his pocket, the first sight of which pleased them very much, and after reading several extracts of *horrid murders, highway robberies,* &c., from the 'Times,' he came across a little thing that amused them,—the great number and length of the names of the little Prince of Wales, which he read over thus:— (The author regrets very much that he took no memorandum of this, but refers the reader to the London papers for it.)

There was a hearty laugh by the whole troop when Daniel got through, but when Mr. Melody repeated the name of a poor fellow who used to dress deer skins for a living in the vicinity of *St. Louis*, they all laughed still more heartily, and *Chippehola* set in and laughed also. He had forgotten a part of this poor fellow's name, but as far as he recollected of his sign board, it ran thus:— "*Haunus, hubbard, lubbard, lamberd, lunk, vandunk, Peter, Jacobus, Lockamore, Lavendolph*, dresses deer skins of all animals, and in all ways, alum dressed."

Such was a part of the gossip of an evening, while my days were occupied in preparing my rooms for the admission of the public. During this delay, one of the gentlemen who visited the Indians most frequently, as his native countrymen, was Mr. W. Costar, formerly of New York, but now living in Paris, and whose kind lady invited the whole party to dine at her house.

The Indians had expressed the greatest pleasure at meeting this American gentleman in Paris, as if they claimed a sort of kindred to him, and met the invitation as one of great kindness, and the interview as one in which they were to feel much pleasure. They were particularly careful in dressing and preparing for it, and when ready, and the time had arrived, Mr. Melody and I accompanied them to this gentleman's house, where a most sumptuous dinner was served, and besides his accomplished lady and lovely daughters, there were several ladies of distinction and of title, seated, to complete the honours that were to be paid to the Indians.

It was a matter of great surprise to all the fashionable guests who were present, that those rude people from the wilderness, used to take their meals from the ground, were so perfectly composed and so much at ease at the table, and managed so well with the knife and fork, and even so gracefully smiled over their glasses of wine when a lady or a gentleman proposed the health of any one. Just before we had finished our dessert, a number of fashionable ladies, the Countess of L———, the Baron and Baroness de G———, and several others who had begun to assemble for the evening soirée, arrived, and were ushered into the dining room, where they had the curiosity of seeing the Indians as they were seated in all their trinkets and ranged around the table; and from the lips of all escaped the instant exclamations of, "Bless me! what a fine and noble-looking set of men they are! How much at ease they seem! Why, those are polished gentlemen," &c. &c.

From the dinner table they were invited to the salon, where a large party had gathered, who were delighted with the wild and picturesque appearance of the "Peaux Rouges."

The Indians saw some fine dancing and waltzing, and heard some splendid playing on the piano, and singing.

The Doctor's complete fascination by the playing and singing of a beautiful young lady was so conspicuous as to become the principal event of the evening, and after he had stood and smiled upon her in profound admiration during her fourth or fifth song, he *amused* many of the party, and *shocked* others, by the extraordinary and unexpected, though perfectly just remark, that "her voice was as soft and sweet as that of a wolf!"

This startling compliment I must leave for the estimates of the world, mentioning only the two facts, that the Doctor's *totem* (or *arms*) is the wolf; and that in my travels in the prairies of America I have often thought that the soft, and plaintive, and silvery tones of the howling prairie wolf oftentimes surpassed in sweetness the powers of the human voice.

M. Vattemare, in his kind endeavours to promote the interest of the Indians, and that of myself, had obtained an invitation from the Members of the Royal Academy of Sciences for the Indians to visit them at one of their sittings, which was a great honour; but the poor Indians left Paris without ever having been able to learn how or in what way that honour arrived. Messrs. Melody and Vattemare and myself accompanied the whole party to their rooms, and, being ushered and squeezed and pushed into a dense crowd of gentlemen, all standing, and where the Indians were not even offered a seat, they were gazed and scowled at, their heads and arms felt, their looks and capacities criticised like those of wild beasts, without being asked a question, or thanked for the kindness of coming, and where they were offered not even a glass of cold water. The Indians and ourselves were thus eyed and elbowed about in this crowd for half an hour, from which we were all glad to escape, deciding that it was entirely too scientific for us, and a style of politeness that we were not perhaps sufficiently acquainted with duly to appreciate.

The various conjectures about the objects of this visit were raised after we got home, and they were as curious as they were numerous. The Indians had reflected upon it with evident surprise, and repeatedly inquired of M. Vattemare and myself for what purpose we had taken them there. M. Vattemare told them that these were the greatest scientific men of the kingdom. This they did not understand, and he then, to explain, said they were the great *medicine men*, the learned doctors, &c. They then took the hint a little better, and decided alarm with it, for they said they recollected to have seen in some of their faces, while examining their heads and arms, decided expressions of anxiety to dissect their limbs and bones, which they now felt quite sure would be the case if any of them should die while in Paris. The War-chief, who seldom had much to say while speaking of the events of the day, very gravely observed on this occasion, that "he had been decidedly displeased, and the chief also, but it would be best to say no more about it, though if any of the party got sick, to take great care what physicians were called to visit them."

M. Vattemare, in his kind interest for all parties, here exerted his influence to a little further degree, and persuaded the Indians to believe that those distinguished men, the great philosopher M. Arago and others, who were present, would be their warmest friends, but that with these transcendently great and wise men, their minds and all their time were so engrossed with their profound studies, that they had no time or desire to practise politeness; that they were the eyes which the public used, to look deep into and through all things strange or new that came to Paris; and that the public were after that, polite and civil, in proportion as those learned men should decide that they ought or ought not to be.

Jim here took a whiff or two on his pipe, and, turning over on his back and drawing up his knees and clasping his hands across his stomach (Plate No. 17), said—

"We know very well that the King and the Queen and all the royal family are pleased with us, and are our friends, and if that is not enough to make us respected we had better go home. We believe that the King is a much greater man, and a much *better* man, than any of those we saw there, and better than the whole of them put together. We know that there are many kind people in this great city who will be glad to shake our hands in friendship, and there are others who would like to get our skins, and we think that we saw some such there to-day. We met some kind people yesterday, where we went to dine—we love those people and do not fear them. If we should get sick they would be kind to us, and we think much more of that kind lady and gentleman than we do of all the great doctors we have seen this day—we hope not to see them any more. This is the wish of the chiefs, and of our wives and little children, who are all alarmed about them."

This finished the conversation for the present about the learned society, though the impression was one of a most unfavourable kind on their minds, and was a long time in wearing away.

Nº 17.

The time had at length arrived for the opening of my collection and the commencement of the illustrations of the Indians. It had been for some days announced, and the hour had approached. The visitors were admitted into the rooms where my numerous collection of 600 paintings and some thousands of articles of Indian manufactures were subjects of new and curious interest to examine until the audience were mostly assembled, when, at a signal, the Indians all entered the room from an adjoining apartment, advancing to and mounting the platform, in Indian file, in full dress and paint, and armed and equipped as if for a battle-field. They sounded the war-whoop as they came in, and nothing could exceed the thrill of excitement that ran through the crowd in every part of the Hall. There was a rush to see who should get nearest to the platform, and be enabled most closely to scan "*les Sauvages horribles,*" "*les Peaux Rouges,*" *ou* "*les nouvelles Diables à Paris.*"

The chief led the party as they entered the room, and, having ascended the platform, erected the flag of his tribe in the centre, and in a moment the party were all seated around it, and lighting their pipe to take a smoke, whilst I was introducing them and their wives to the audience. This having been done in as brief a time as possible, they finished their pipe and commenced their amusements in Paris by giving the *discovery-dance*. This curious mode forms a part and the commencement of the war-dance, and is generally led off by one of the War-chiefs, who dances forward alone, pretending to be skulking and hunting for the track of his enemy, and when he discovers it he beckons on his warriors, who steal into the dance behind him, and follow him up as he advances, and pretends at length to discover the enemy in the distance, ordering all to be ready for the attack.

The Doctor was the one who opened the *bal* on this occasion, and it was a proud and important moment for him: not that the fate of nations unborn, or the success of their enterprise, depended upon the event, but what to him was perhaps as high an incentive—that his standing with the ladies of Paris would probably be regulated for the whole time they should be there by the sensation he should make at the first dash. He therefore put on his most confident smile as he went into the dance: as he tilted about and pointed out the track where his enemy had gone, he made signs that the enemy had passed by, and then, beckoning up his warriors, pointed him out amongst a group of beautiful ladies who had taken an elevated and conspicuous position in front. He sounded the war-whoop, and all echoed it as he pointed towards the ladies, who screamed, and leapt from their seats, as the Indians' weapons were drawn! Here was an excitement begun, and the old Doctor smiled as he turned his head and his weapons in other directions, and proceeded with the dance. At the end of its first part their feet all came to a simultaneous stop, when the Doctor advanced to the front of the platform, and, brandishing his spear over the heads of the audience, made the most tremendous boast of the manner in which he took a prisoner in a battle with the Pawnees, and drove him home before his horse rather than take his life: he then plunged into the most agitated dance alone, and acting out the whole features of his battle in time to the song and beating of the drum; and at the close, rounds of applause awaited him in every part of the crowd. These the Doctor received with so complaisant a smile of satisfaction, as he bowed his head gracefully inclined on one side, that another and another burst of applause, and another bow and smile, followed; satisfying him that the path was cleared before him. He then shook his rattle of deer's hoofs, and, summoning his warriors, they all united in finishing with full and wild effect this spirited dance. Though in the midst of a dancing country, their mode of dancing was quite new, and was evidently calculated to amuse, from the immense applause that was given them at the end of their first effort.

The dancers had now all taken their seats, except the Doctor, who was lingering on his feet, and had passed his spear into his left hand, evidently preparing to push his advantage a little further with the ladies, by making a speech, as soon as silence should be sufficiently restored to enable him to be heard. This little delay might or might not have been a fortunate occurrence for the Doctor, for it afforded Jim an opportunity to remind him how much he had lost by his last two or three speeches, which so completely put him out, that he sat down, apparently well pleased and satisfied with what he had already accomplished.

My kind friend M. Vattemare, who had now become a great favourite of the Indians, went forward, and offered them his hand to encourage them, assuring them of the great pleasure the audience were taking, and encouraging them to go on with all the spirit they could, as there were some of the most distinguished people of Paris present—the Minister of the Interior and his lady, the Prêfet de Police, several foreign ambassadors, and a number of the editors of the leading journals, who were taking notes, and would speak about them in the papers the next morning.

The *eagle-dance* was now announced to the audience as the next amusement; and after a brief description of it, the *Little Wolf* sprang upon his feet, and sounding his eagle whistle, and shaking the eagle's tail in his left hand, while he brandished his tomahawk in his right, he commenced. His fellow-warriors were soon engaged with him, and all excited to the determination to make "a hit." As after the first, they were complimented by rounds of applause, and sat down to their pipe with peculiar satisfaction. The War-chief took the first few whiffs upon it, and, rising, advanced to the front of the platform, and in the most dignified and graceful attitude that the orator could assume, extended his right hand over the heads of the audience, and said—

"My Friends,—It gives us great pleasure to see so many pleasant faces before us to-night, and to learn from your applause that you are amused with our dances. We are but children; we live in the woods, and are ignorant, and you see us here as the Great Spirit made us; and our dances are not like the dances of the French people, whom we have been told dance the best of any people in the world. (*'How, how, how!'* and immense applause.)

"My Friends,—We come here not to teach you to dance—(a roar of applause and laughter)—we come here not to teach you anything, for you are a great deal wiser than we, but to show you how we red people look and act in the wilderness, and we shall be glad some nights to go and see how the French people dance. (Great applause and *'How, how, how!'*)

"My Friends,—We are happy that the Great Spirit has kept us alive and well, and that we have been allowed to see the face of our Great Father your King. We saw him and your good Queen, and the little boy who will be king, and they all treated us with kind hearts, and we feel thankful for it. (*'How, how, how!'*)

"My Friends,—We have crossed two oceans to come here, and we have seen no village so beautiful as Paris. London, where the *Saganoshes* live, is a large village, but their wigwams are not so beautiful as those in Paris, and in their streets there are too many people who seem to be very poor and hungry. (*'How, how, how!'*)

"My Friends,—I have no more to say at present, only, that, when my young men have finished their dances, we shall be glad to shake hands with you all, if you desire it." (*"How, how, how!"*)

The old man resumed his seat and his pipe amidst a din of applause; and at this moment several trinkets and pieces of money were tossed upon the platform from various parts of the room.

After the eagle-dance they strung their bows, and, slinging their quivers upon their backs, commenced shooting at the target for prizes. The hall in which their dances were given was so immensely large that they had a range of 150 feet to throw their arrows at their targets, which formed by no means the least amusing and exciting part of their exhibitions. Their ball-sticks were also taken in hand, and the ball, and their mode of catching and throwing it, beautifully illustrated. After this, and another dance, a general shake of the hands took place, and a promenade of the Indians through the vast space occupied by my collection. They retired from the rooms and the crowd in fine glee, having made their *début* in Paris, about which they had had great anxiety, somebody having told them that the French people would not be pleased with their dancing, as they danced so well themselves.

The Indians being gone, *I* became the lion, and was asked for in every part of the rooms. The visitors were now examining my numerous works, and all wanted to see me. My friend M. Vattemare was by my side, and kindly presented me to many gentlemen of the press, and others of his acquaintance, in the rooms. There were so many who said they were waiting "for the honour," &c., that I was kept until a very late hour before I could leave the room.

There were a number of fellow-artists present, who took pleasure in complimenting me for the manner in which my paintings were executed; and many others for my perseverance and philanthropy in having laboured thus to preserve the memorials of these dying people. I was complimented on all sides, and bowed, and was bowed to, and invited by cards and addresses left for me. So *I* went home, as well as the Indians, elated with the pleasing conviction that *mine* was a "hit," as well as *theirs*.

The leading journals of the next day were liberal in their comments upon the Indians and my collection, pronouncing my labours of great interest and value, and the exhibition altogether one of the most extraordinary interest ever opened in Paris, and advising all the world to see it.[39] Thus were we started in the way of business after the first night's exhibition, and that after remaining there just one month before we could meet and pass all the necessary forms and get quite ready.

CHAPTER XXVI.

Indians at Madame Greene's party—Their ideas of waltzing—The Doctor's admiration of the young ladies—The King's fête, first of May—Indians in the Palace—Royal Family in the balcony—Grand and sublime scene on the river—Indians in a crowd of nobility in the Duc d'Aumale's apartments—Messenger to Indians' apartments with gold and silver medals—Medals to the women and children—Consequent difficulties—Visit to the Hospital of Invalids—Place Concorde—Column of Luxor—The fountains—Visit to the Triumphal Arch—Jim's description of an ugly woman—Victor Hugo—Madame Georges Sands—Indians visit the Louvre—M. de Cailleux—Baron de Humboldt—Illness of the wife of Little Wolf—A phrenologist visits the Indians—The phrenologist's head examined—Two Catholic priests visit the Indians—Indians visit the Garden of Plants—Alarm of the birds and animals—The "poor prisoner buffalo"—Visit to the *Salle aux Vins*—Astonishment of the Indians—The war-whoop—*Chickabobboo*—Cafés explained—Indians visit *Père la Chaise*—A great funeral—A speech over the grave—Hired mourners—Visit the *School of Medicine*—and *"Dupuytren's Room"*—Excitement of the Doctor—Visit to the *Foundling Hospital*—Astonishment and pity of the Indians—Entries in Jim's note-book, and Doctor's remarks—Visit the *Guillotine*—Indians' ideas of *hanging* in England, and *beheading* in France—Curious debate—Visit to the *Dog Market*—Jim's purchase and difficulty—The *Dog Hospital*—Alarm of the "petites malades"—Retreat—*Bobasheela* arrives from London—Great rejoicing—Jim's comments on the Frenchwomen—The *little foundlings* and the *little dogs*.

Having thus commenced upon our operations in the Salle Valentino, it was thought best to change the lodgings of the Indians to some point more near to the place of their exhibitions, and rooms were at length procured for them in the same building with their hall, and communicating with it. To these apartments they were removed, and arrangements were made for two open carriages to drive them an hour each day for their recreation and amusement. By this arrangement we had the sights of Paris before us, and easily within our reach, to be visited at our leisure. Our exhibitions were given each night from eight to ten, and each afternoon from one to three o'clock; so that they had the mornings for sight-seeing, and their evenings, from ten to twelve, to visit the theatres or parties, whenever they were invited and felt disposed to attend.

The first evening-party they were invited to attend in Paris was that of the lady of *Mr. Greene*, the American banker. They were there ushered into a brilliant blaze of lamps, of beauty, and fashion, composed chiefly of Americans, to whom they felt the peculiar attachment of countrymen, though of a different complexion, and anywhere else than across the Atlantic would have been strangers to.

They were received with great kindness by this polite and excellent lady and her daughters, and made many pleasing acquaintances in her house. The old Doctor had luckily dressed out his head with his red crest, and left at home his huge head-dress of horns and eagles' quills, which would have been exceedingly unhandy in a *squeeze*, and subjected him to curious remarks amongst the ladies. He had loaded on all his wampum and other ornaments, and smiled away the hours in perfect happiness, as he was fanning himself with the tail of a war-eagle, and bowing his head to the young and beautiful ladies who were helping him to lemonade and *blanc-mange*, and to the young men who were inviting him to the table to take an occasional glass of the "*Queen's chickabobboo.*" Their heavy buffalo robes were distressing to them (said the Doctor) in the great heat of the rooms, "but then, as the ladies were afraid of getting paint on their dresses, they did not squeeze so hard against us as they did against the other people in the room, so we did not get so hot as we might have been."

It amused the Doctor and Jim very much to see the gentlemen take the ladies by the waist when they were dancing with them, probably never having seen waltzing before. They were pleased also, as the Doctor said, with "the manner in which the ladies showed their beautiful white necks and arms, but they saw several that they thought had better been covered." "The many nice and sweet and frothy little things that the ladies gave them in tea-saucers to eat, with little spoons, were too sweet, and they did not like them much; and in coming away they were sorry they could not find the good lady to thank her, the crowd was so great; but the *chickabobboo* (champagne), which was very good, was close to the door, and a young man with yellow hair and moustaches kept pouring it out until they were afraid, if they drank any more, some of the poor fellows who were dancing so hard would get none."

The scene they witnessed that night was truly very brilliant, and afforded them theme for a number of pipes of gossip after they got home.

It has been said, and very correctly, that there is no end to the amusements of Paris, and to the Indians, to whose sight every thing was new and curious, the term, no doubt, more aptly applied than to the rest of the world. Of those never-ending sights there was one now at hand which was promising them and "all the world" a fund of amusement, and the poor fellows were impatient for its arrival. This splendid and all-exciting affair was the King's fête on the 1st of May, his birthday as some style it, though it is not exactly such, it is the day fixed upon as the annual celebration of his birth. This was, of course, a holiday to the Indians, as well as for everybody else, and I resolved to spend the greater part of it with them.

Through the aid of some friends I had procured an order to admit the party of Indians into the apartments of the Duke d'Aumale in the Tuileries, to witness the grand concert in front of the Palace, and to see the magnificent fireworks and illumination on the Seine at night. We had the best possible position assigned us in the wing of the Palace, overlooking the river in both directions, up and down, bringing all the bridges of the Seine, the Deputies, and Invalides, and other public buildings, which were illuminated, directly under our eyes. During the day, Mr. Melody, and Jeffrey, and Daniel had taken, as they called it, "a grand drive," to inspect the various places of amusement, and the immense concourse of people assembled in them. Of these, the Barrières, the Champs Elysées, &c., they were obliged to take but a passing glance, for to have undertaken to stop and to mix with the dense crowds assembled in them would have been dangerous, even to their lives, from the masses of people who would have crowded upon them. The Indians themselves were very sagacious on this point, and always judiciously kept at a reasonable distance on such occasions. It was amusement enough for them during the day to ride rapidly about and through the streets, anticipating the pleasure they were to have in the evening, and taking a distant view from their carriages, of the exciting emulation of the *May-pole*, and a glance at the tops of the thousand booths, and "flying ships," and "merry-go-rounds" of the Champs Elysées.

At six o'clock we took our carriages and drove to the Tuileries, and, being conducted to the splendid apartments of the Duke d'Aumale, who was then absent from Paris, we had there, from the windows looking down upon the Seine and over the Quartier St. Germain, and the windows in front, looking over the garden of the Tuileries and Place Concorde, the most general and comprehensive view that was to be had from any point that could have been selected. Under our eyes in front, the immense area of the garden of the Tuileries was packed with human beings, forming but one black and dotted mass of some hundreds of thousands who were gathered to listen to the magnificent orchestra of music, and to see and salute with "Vive le Roi!" "Vive la Reine!" and "Vive le Comte de Paris!" the Royal Family as they appeared in the balcony. Though it appeared as if every part of the gardens was filled, there was still a black and moving mass pouring through Rue Rivoli, Rue Castiglione, Rue Royale, and Place Concorde, all concentrating in the garden of the Tuileries. This countless mass of human beings continued to gather until the hour when their Majesties entered the balcony, and then, all hats off, there was a shout as vast and incomputable as the mass itself of "Vive le Roi!—Vive le Roi!—Vive la Reine!—Vive le Comte de Paris!" The King then, with his chapeau in his hand, bowed to the audience in various directions; so did her Majesty the Queen and the little Comte de Paris. The band then struck up the national air, and played several pieces, while the Royal Family were seated in the balcony, and the last golden rays of the sun, that was going behind the Arc de Triomphe, was shining in their faces. Their Majesties then retired as the twilight was commencing, and the vast crowd began to move in the direction of the Seine, the Terrace, and Place Concorde, to witness the grand scene of illumination and "feu d'artifice" that was preparing on the river.

As the daylight disappeared, the artificial light commenced to display its various characters, and the Indians began to wonder. This scene was to be entirely new to them, and the reader can imagine better than I can explain what was their astonishment when the King's signal rocket was fired from the Tuileries, and in the next moment the whole river, as it were, in a blaze of liquid fire, and the heavens burst asunder with all their luminaries falling in a chaos of flames and sparkling fire to the earth! The incessant roar and flash of cannons lining the shore of the river, and the explosion of rockets in the air, with the dense columns of white, and yellow, and blue, and blood-red smoke, that were rising from the bed of the river, and all reflected upon the surface of the water, heightened the grandeur of its effect, and helped to make it unlike anything on earth, save what we might imagine to transpire in and over the deep and yawning crater of a huge volcano in the midst of its midnight eruption.

This wonderful scene lasted for half an hour, and when the last flash died away, all eyes like our own seemed to turn away from the smoking desolation that seemed to be left below, and the dense mass was dividing and pouring off in streams through the various streets and avenues, some seeking their homes with their little children, and hundreds of thousands of others, to revel away the night amidst the brilliant illuminations and innocent amusements of the Champs Elysées.

We turned our eyes at that moment from the scene, and, in turning around, found ourselves blockaded by a phalanx of officers in gold lace and cocked hats, and ladies, attachés of the royal household, Deputies, Peers of France, and other distinguished guests of the Royal Family, who had been viewing the scene from other windows of the Palace, and had now gathered in our rooms to look at "*les Peaux Rouges.*" My good friend M. Vattemare was present on this occasion, and of great service to us all, as there were in this crowd the incumbents of several high offices under the Crown, and others of distinction with whom he was acquainted, and to whom he introduced us all, converting the rooms and the crowd in a little time into a splendid soirée, where conversation and refreshments soon made all easy and quite happy.

The servants of the Duke's household conducted us into the several apartments, explaining the paintings and other works of art, and also took us into the Duke's bedchamber, where were the portraits of himself and the Duchess, and others of the Royal Family. There was, we learned, in another part of the Palace, a grand *bal* on that evening, and that accounted for the constant crowds of fashionable ladies and gentlemen who were pouring into our apartments, and who would have continued to do so in all probability for the greater part of the night had we not taken up the line of march, endeavouring to make our way to our carriages on our way home. This was for some time exceedingly difficult, as we had a succession of rooms and halls to pass through before we reached the top of the staircase, all of which were filled with a dense mass of ladies and gentlemen, who had got information that the Ioway Indians were in the Duke's apartments, and were then making their way there to get a peep at them. We crowded and squeezed through this mass as well as we could, and were all laughing at Jim's remarks as we passed along. He thought the people had all left the King and Queen to see the Indians. "Come see Ingins" (said he in English) "at Salle Valentino—see em dance—better go back, see King, see Queen—Ingins no good." Mr. Melody gave the poor fellow the first idea that his words were thrown away, as these people were all French, and did not understand English; so Jim said, "I spose em no buy Bible then?" and began to whistle. We soon descended the grand escalier, and, taking our carriages, were in a few minutes entering the Indians' apartments in Salle Valentino.

Jim got home a little provoked, as the Doctor was showing a very handsome eyeglass which had been presented to him: two or three of the women had also received presents in money and trinkets, but Jim's wife, as well as himself, was amongst the neglected or overlooked. He then took out of his pouch and throwing it down upon the table one of his beautiful gilt bound little Bibles, and said, "Me no sell em." "Did you try, Jim?" "Yes, me try em, but me no sell em—folks call em *Onglaise*. Onglaise no good, I guess, I no sell em." Poor Jim! he looked quite chapfallen at the moment, and much more so when Daniel afterwards told him that he ought to have had an auction or other sale of his Bibles before he left England, for the French didn't care much about Bibles, and if they did they wouldn't buy his, for they were in the English language, which they could not read. Jim's regrets were now very great, to think they had so little oversight as to come away without thinking to make some conversion of them into ready cash. Daniel told him, however, that he thought there would be nothing lost on them, as they would sell better in America than they would have sold in England, and he had better pack them away until they went home.

The conversation running upon Bibles, Jim was asked, as there was some sympathy expressed for him, how many he and his wife had, to which he replied, "I no know—I guess a heap." It was in a few moments ascertained more correctly from his wife, who had the immediate charge of them, that they had twenty-eight, and the account soon returned from the whole party, that in all they had received about 120 since they arrived in England.

They took their suppers, which were ready when they got back, and their *chickabobboo* (vin rouge) with their pipe, and engaged M. Vattemare for some time to explain the meaning of the many beautiful decorations they had seen worn on the breasts and shoulders of the officers they had met in the palace. The explanations of these things pleased them very much: as to the fireworks, they said that was such great *medicine* to them, that they did not care about talking on the subject until they had taken more time to think.

Just as M. Vattemare and I were about to leave the room, I found Jim and the Doctor interrogating Daniel about the "big guns that spoke so loud: they thought they must have very large mouths to speak so strong," and were anxious to see them. Daniel told them that those which made the loudest noise were at the Hospital of the Invalides, and it was then agreed that they should go there the next day to see them.

Jim said they had all been delighted at what Daniel read in his paper about their going before the King and Queen, and that he must be sure to bring the paper at an early hour the next morning, to let them hear what was said about the Indians being in the palace the second time, and in the rooms of the Duke, to see the fireworks.

The rest of their evening was taken up in "thinking" on what they had seen, and the next morning, as he had promised, Daniel came in with the paper and read a long account of the amusements of the day and evening, and also of the hundreds of thousands in the crowd who moved along in front of the Duke d'Aumale's apartments to look at the Indians, in preference to look at the King and the Queen. It was decided (as he read) that the crowd was much more dense and remained at a much later hour in front of that wing of the palace than in front of the balcony, where the Royal Family and the orchestra of music were. This pleased them all very much; and after their breakfasts, while they were yet in this cheerful train of feelings, the young man who had brought them the money from the King made his appearance, and I was instantly sent for. On arriving I was informed by him that he had come from his Majesty with the gold and silver medals, to be presented in his Majesty's name to each one individually. This announced, the Indians of course put all other occupations aside, and, being all seated on the floor, at the request of the chief, the medals were called out by the inscriptions on them and presented accordingly. The first presented was a gold medal to White Cloud, the chief: the inscription on the back of it read thus:—

"Donné à *Mu-hu-she-kaw*, par le Roi: 1845."

The next presented was to the War-chief—a gold medal of equal size, and inscription in the same form. Silver medals, of equal size with inscriptions, were then presented to all the warriors and women and children. This last part of the list, women and children, seemed to startle them a little. The idea of women and children receiving medals was entirely new to them, and put them quite at a stand. There was no alternative but to take them, and be thankful for them; but it seemed curious enough to them—a subject not to be named, however, until the messenger had departed with their thanks to his Majesty for his kindness. This was done by the War-chief, and the gentleman departed.

The old Doctor and *Wa-ton-ye*, the two unmarried men of the party, were the only ones who seemed to show anything like decided dissatisfaction in their faces, though Jim and Little Wolf were fumbling theirs over in their fingers, evidently in a struggle of feeling whether to be dissatisfied or not. The Little Wolf was a warrior of decided note, who had taken several scalps, and his wife had never taken one, and yet her medal was equal to his own; however, by the operation he had got two medals instead of one. Jim felt a little touched, and, though never having done much more in war than his squaw had, was preparing to make a great harangue on the occasion, and even rolled over on his back, and drew up his knees, for the purpose, but, taking the shining metal from his wife's hands, and placing it by the side of his own, he thought they would form a beautiful ornament, both hanging together, symbolic of an affectionate husband and wife, and he was silent. The poor old Doctor, though, who had taken *one prisoner* certain, and *possibly* some scalps, and (as the old War-chief had one day told him) undoubtedly "many lives," who could only dangle one medal (having no wife), and that one no better than those given to the women and children, lost all traces of the complaisant smiles that had shone on his face a little time before, and, rising suddenly up, and wrapping his robe around him, he found his way to the house-top, where he stood in silent gaze upon the chimneys and tiles, more suited to the meditations that were running through his troubled mind. *Wa-ton-ye*, in the mean time, with smothered feelings that no one ever heard vent given to, hung his with its tri-coloured ribbon upon a nail in the wall just over his head, and, drawing his buffalo robe quite over him, hid his face, and went to sleep.

White Cloud and the War-chief sat during the while, with their families hanging about their shoulders and knees, well pleased, and smiling upon the brightness of his Majesty's familiar features in shining gold, as they turned their medals around in various lights. Theirs were of a more precious metal, and each, from the number of his family with him, became the owner of *three*, instead of *one*, over which the poor Doctor was yet pondering on the house-top, as he stood looking off towards the mountains and prairies.

When their carriages were at the door, to make their visit to the *Hôpital des Invalides*, as promised the night before, the Doctor was unwilling to break the charm of his contemplations, and *Wa-ton-ye* could not be waked, and the rest drove off in good cheer and delight. They hung their medals on their necks, suspended by their tri-coloured ribbons, the meaning of which having been explained to them, and they were soon at the mouths of the huge cannon, whose "big mouths" had "spoken so loudly" the night before.

After taking a good look at them, and getting something of their curious history, they entered that wonderful and most noble institution, an honour to the name of its founder and to the country that loves and upholds it, the *Hospital* of *Invalids*. Nothing on earth could have struck these people as more curious and interesting (a race of warriors themselves) than this institution, with its 3800 venerable inmates, the living victims of battles, wounded, crippled, fed, and clothed, and made happy, the living evidences of the human slaughter that must have taken place in the scenes they had been through. If this scene convinced them of the destructiveness of civilized modes of warfare, it taught them an useful lesson of civilized sympathy for those who are the unfortunate victims of war and carnage.

The moral that was drawn from this day's visit was an important one to them, and I took the opportunity, and many others afterwards, to impress it upon their minds. It pleased them to hear that these old veterans, with one leg and one arm, were the very men who were chosen to come to the big guns, and fire them off, on the day of the King's fete—the same guns that they fought around, and over, when they were taking them from the enemies.

Returning from the "*Invalides*," our carriages were stopped in Place Concorde for a view of the beautiful fountains playing, which pleased and astonished them, as they do all foreigners who pass. The Egyptian obelisk column of Luxor, of seventy-two feet, in one solid piece of granite, and brought from Egypt to Paris, was shown and explained to them, and our carriage driven to the ground where the *guillotine* had stood on which the blood of Kings and Queens had been shed, and where the father of Louis Philippe was beheaded. These extraordinary and almost incredible facts of history, and that so recent, filled their minds with amazement, and almost with incredulity. Our drive that day was continued through the broad avenue of the Champs Elysées to the *triumphal arch* at the Barrière d'Etoile, and our view from the top of it was one of the finest they thought in the world. We were not quite as high as when we were on the tower of the York cathedral, but the scene around us was far more picturesque and enchanting.

When we returned we found the old Doctor and *Wa-ton-ye* seated upon their buffalo robes, and playing at cards, quite in good humour, and their medals put away, as if nothing had happened to put them out. They were much amused at the descriptions of what the others had seen, and particularly so at Jim's description of an ugly woman he saw on top of the Arc de Triomphe, and who followed him around, he said, and looked him in the face until he was frightened. Here the Doctor, who had been out of humour, and was disposed to be a little severe on Jim, replied that "it was laughable for such an ill-looking, big-mouthed fellow as him to be talking about any one's ill looks, and to be alarmed at any one's ugliness, looking out over such a set of features as he had on the lower part of his face." Jim, however, having two medals, took but little notice of the Doctor's severity, but proceeded to tell about the ugly woman he saw. He said, "her eyes had all the time two white rings clear around them, and the end of her nose turning up, as if she had always smelled something bad, had pulled her upper-lip up so high that she could not shut her mouth or cover her teeth. She had two great rows of teeth, and there was black all between them, as if a charge of gunpowder had gone off in her mouth, and her skin was as white as snow, excepting on her cheeks, and there it was quite red, like a rose."

"Stop, stop, Jim," said I, "let me write that down before you go any further."

But this was all. He said he could not bear to look at her, and therefore he did not examine her any further. He also made some fun about two English ladies, who were up there when they were on the Arc de Triomphe. He said, "he had sat down by the side of the railing with his wife, where these ladies came to them. One of them asked if they could speak English, to which he made no reply, but shook his head. He said they had a great many things to say about him, and one of them wanted to feel his face (his chin, he supposed), to see if he had any beard; and when she did not find any, she said something which he did not understand, but he said it tickled them very much, and then he said she put her hand on his shoulder, which was naked, and took hold of his arm, and said several things, about which they had a great deal of laugh, which he understood, and which he would not like to mention, for his wife did not understand them, and he did not wish her to know what they were laughing about."

The hour having approached for their afternoon's exhibition, the conversation was here broken off. I was, however, obliged to delay a few minutes for some account they wished me to give them of the guillotine, which I had spoken of while in the Place Concorde. I briefly described it to them, and they all expressed a wish to go some day and see it, and I promised to take them.

The exhibition in the afternoon was attended by many more fashionable ladies and gentlemen than that of the evening; and so many carriages driving up to the door, in a pleasant day, was always sure to put the Doctor into the best of humour, and generally, when he was in such a mood, there would be wit and drollery enough in him, and his good friend Jim, to influence the whole group. They were usually in good spirits, and, when so, were sure to please; and thus were they on that, the first of their morning's entertainments; and it happened luckily, for we had in the rooms some of the most fashionable and literary personages of Paris—amongst these, the famous writers, *Victor Hugo, Madame Georges Sands*, and several others, to whom the Indians and myself were personally introduced.

The old Doctor was told by M. Vattemare, who was again there, to do his best, and all did their parts admirably well, and much to the astonishment of the ladies, several of which old dames I found had really supposed, until now, that the *"sauvages"* were little more than wild beasts. After the Indians had finished their amusements and retired from the rooms, *I* was left *lion* again and "lord of all the visitors were now surveying." Then it was that *my* embarrassment came, losing in a great measure the pleasure that I could have drawn from the society of such persons who came to praise, by not speaking the French language.

However, I had generally the benefit of my friend M. Vattemare or others around me ready to help me through the difficulty. It gave me daily pleasure to find that my works were highly applauded by the press, as well as by personal expressions in the room, and in all the grades of society to which I was then being invited.

Our second evening soon approached, and we found the hall fashionably filled again, and of course the Indians, though in a strange country, in good spirits and gratified, as their very appearance while entering the room got them rounds of applause. After their exhibition was over in the usual way I got *my* applause, and so our mutual efforts were daily and nightly made to instruct and amuse the Parisians, which I shall always flatter myself we did to a considerable extent.

While our exhibitions were now in such a train, we were studying how to make the most valuable use of our extra time, by seeing the sights of Paris and its environs.

The *Louvre* was one of the first objects of our attention; and having procured an order from the Director to visit it on a private day, we took an early hour and made our entry into it. We were received by the Director with kindness, and he conducted the party the whole way through the different galleries, pointing out and explaining to them and to us the leading and most interesting things in it.

The Director, M. de Cailleux, had invited several of his distinguished friends to meet him on the occasion, and it was to them, as well as to us, interesting to see the Indians under such circumstances, where there was so much to attract their attention and calculated to surprise them. M. Vattemare was with us on this occasion, and of very great service in his introductions and interpretations for us. Amongst the distinguished persons who were present, and to whom I was introduced on the occasion, was the Baron de Humboldt.

He accompanied us quite through the rooms of the Louvre, and took a great deal of interest in the Indians, having seen and dealt with so many in the course of his travels. I had much conversation with him, and in a few days after was honoured by him with a private visit to my rooms, when I took great pleasure in explaining the extent and objects of my collection.

The view of the Louvre was a great treat to the Indians, who had had but little opportunity before of seeing works of art. In London we thought we had showed them all the sights, but had entirely forgotten the exhibitions of paintings; and I believe the poor fellows had been led to think, before they saw the Louvre, that mine was the greatest collection of paintings in the world. They had a great deal of talk about it when they got home and had lit their pipe. The one great objection they raised to it was, that "it was too long—there were too many things to be seen; so many that they said they had forgotten all the first before they got through, and they couldn't think of them again." There was one impression they got while there, however—that no length of room or number of pictures would easily eradicate from their memories, the immense number of marks of bullets on the columns of the portico, and even inside of the building, shot through the windows in the time of the Revolution of July. This appalling scene was described to them on the spot by M. Vattemare, which opened their eyes to an historical fact quite new to them, and of which they soon taxed him and me for some further account.

The poor fellows at this time were beginning to sympathize with the noble fellow the Little Wolf, whose wife had been for some weeks growing ill, and was now evidently declining with symptoms of quick consumption. The buoyant spirits of the good and gallant fellow seemed to be giving way to apprehensions; and although he joined in the amusements, he seemed at times dejected and unhappy. There were days when her symptoms seemed alarming, and then she would rally and be in the room again in all the finery of her dress and trinkets, but was evidently gradually losing strength and flesh, and decided by her physician to be in a rapid decline. She was about this time advised to keep to her chamber and away from the excitement of the exhibition and sight-seeing, in which the rest of the party were daily engaged.

By this time the Ioways had made so much noise in Paris that they were engaging the attention of the scientific, the religious, and the ethnologic, as well as the mere curious part of the world, and daily and almost hourly applications were being made to Mr. Melody and myself for private interviews with them for the above purposes. We were disposed to afford every facility in our power in such cases, but in all instances left the Indians to decide who they would and who they would not see.

Amongst those applicants there was a phrenologist, who had been thrusting himself into their acquaintance as much as possible in their exhibition rooms, and repeatedly soliciting permission to go to their private rooms to make some scientific examinations and estimates of their heads, to which the Indians had objected, not understanding the meaning or object of his designs. He had become very importunate however, and, having brought them a number of presents at different times, it was agreed at Mr. Melody's suggestion, one day, as the quickest way of getting rid of him, that he should be allowed to come up. We conversed with the Indians, and assured them that there was not the slightest chance of harm, or witchcraft, or anything of the kind about it, and they agreed to let him come in. They had a hearty laugh when he came in, at Jim's wit, who said to him, though in Indian language that he didn't understand, "If you will shut the door now, you will be the ugliest-looking man in the whole room." This was not, of course, translated to the phrenologist, who proceeded with his examinations, and commenced on Jim's head first. Jim felt a little afraid, and considerably embarrassed also, being the first one called upon to undergo an operation which he knew so little about, or what was to be the result of. Stout, and warlike, and courageous as he was, he trembled at the thought of a thing that he could not yet in the least appreciate, and all were looking on and laughing at him for his embarrassment. The phrenologist proceeded, feeling for the bumps around his head, and, stopping once in a while to make his mental deductions, would then run his fingers along again. Jim's courage began to rally a little, seeing that there was to be nothing more than that sort of manipulation, and he relieved himself vastly by turning a little of his wit upon the operator, for a thing that looked to him so exceedingly ridiculous and absurd, by telling him "I don't think you'll find any in my head; we Indians shave a great part of our hair off, and we keep so much oil in the rest of it, that they won't live there: you will find much more in white men's heads, who don't oil their hair." This set the whole party and all of us in a roar, and Jim's head shook so as to embarrass the operator for a little time. When he got through, and entered his estimates in his book, Jim asked him "if he found anything in his head?" to which he replied in the affirmative. Placing his fingers on "*self-esteem*," he said there was great fulness there. "Well," said Jim, "I'm much obliged to you: I'll set my wife to look there by and by. And now," said Jim, "take the old Doctor here: his head is full of em." By this time Jim's jokes had got us all into a roar of laughter, and the Doctor was in the chair, and Jim looking on to see what he could discover. White Cloud thought Jim had cracked his jokes long enough, and as they had all laughed at them, he considered it most respectful now to let the man go through with it. So he finished with the Doctor and then with White Cloud and the War-chief, and when he came to the women they positively declined.

Jim, having been rebuked for laughing too much, had stopped suddenly, and, instantly resolving to try his jokes upon the poor man in another mood, assumed, as he easily could, the most treacherous and assassin look that the human face can put on, and asked the phrenologist if he was done, to which he replied "Yes." "Now," said Jim, "we have all waited upon you and given you a fair chance, and I now want you to sit down a minute and let me examine *your* head;" at the same time drawing his long scalping knife out from his belt, and wiping its blade as he laid it in a chair by the side of him. The phrenologist, having instantly consented, and just taking possession of the chair as he was drawing his knife out, could not well do otherwise than sit still for Jim's operations, though he was evidently in a greater trepidation than he had put Jim into by the first experiment that was made. Jim took the requisite time in his manipulations to crack a few jokes more among his fellow Indians upon the quackery of his patient, and then to let him up, telling him, for the amusement of those around, that "his face looked very pale" (which by the way was the case), "and that he found his head very full of them."

The phrenologist was a good-natured sort of man, and, only partially understanding their jokes, was delighted to get off with what he had learned, without losing his scalp-lock, which it would seem as if he had apprehended at one moment to have been in some danger. As he was leaving the room, Daniel came in, announcing that there were two Catholic clergymen in the room below, where they had been waiting half an hour to have some talk with the Indians. "Let them up," says Jim; "I will make a speech to them:" at which the old Doctor sprang up. "There," said he, "there's my robe; lay down quick." The Doctor's wit raised a great laugh, but, when a moment had blown it away, Mr. Melody asked the chief what was his wish, whether to see them or not. "Oh yes," said he (but rather painfully, and with a sigh); "yes, let them come in: we are in a strange country, and we don't wish to make any enemies: let them come up." They were then conducted up and spent half an hour in pleasant conversation with the chiefs, without questioning them about their religion, or urging their own religion upon them. This pleased the Indians very much, and, finding them such pleasant and social good-natured men, they felt almost reluctant to part company with them. Each of them left a handsome Bible as presents, and took affectionate leave.

After they had left, the Indians had much talk about them, and were then led to think of "the good people," the Friends, they had seen so many of in England and Ireland, and asked me if they should find any of them in Paris. I told them I thought they would not, at which they were evidently very much disappointed.

One of the next sight-seeing expeditions was to the *Jardin des Plantes*, to which our old friend M. Vattemare accompanied us. The animals here, from a difference of training, or other cause, were not quite so much alarmed as they were in the menagerie in London; but when the doctor breathed out the silvery notes of his howling *totem*, the wolf at once answered him in a remote part of the garden. Jim imitated the wild goose, and was answered in an instant by a cackling flock of them. The panthers hissed, and the hyænas were in great distress, and the monkeys also: the eagles chattered and bolted against the sides of their cages, and the parrots lost their voices by squalling, and many of their feathers by fluttering, when the Indians came within their sight. They pitied the poor old and jaded buffalo, as they did in London, he looked so broken-spirited and desolate; and also the deer and the elks; but the bears they said didn't seem to care much about it. They were far more delighted with the skins of animals, reptiles, and fishes in the museum of natural history; and I must say that *I* was also, considering it the finest collection I ever have seen.

The garden of plants was amusement enough for an hour or so, and then to the *Halle aux Vins* in the immediate neighbourhood. This grand magazine of *chickabobboo* has been described by many writers, and no doubt seen by many who read, but few have seen the expression of amazement upon the brows of a party of wild Indians from the forest of America, while their eyes were running over the vast and almost boundless lines of 800,000 casks of wine under one roof, and heard the piercing war-whoop echoing and vibrating through their long avenues, raised at the startling information that 20,000,000 of gallons of this are annually drawn out of this to be drunk in the city of Paris; and few of those who heard it knew whether it was raised to set the wine running, or as a note of exultation that they had found a greater fountain of *chickabobboo* than the brewery they were in, in London. However true the latter was, the first was supposed to have been the design, and it must needs have its effect. A few bottles, in kindness and hospitality cracked, cooled all parched and parching lips, and our faithful timepieces told us our engagement with the public was at hand, and we laid our course again for the *Salle Valentino*.

"Oh! what a glorious country," said Jim, as we were rolling along; "there's nothing like that in London: the *chickabobboo* is better here, and there's more of it too." Poor ignorant fellow! he was not aware that the brewery they saw in London was only one of some dozens, and that the wine in all those casks they had just seen was not quite as delicious as that with which his lips had just been moistened.

With their recollections dwelling on the scenes they had witnessed in London, they were naturally drawing comparisons as they were wending their way back; and they had in this mood taken it into their heads that there were no gin-shops in Paris, as they could see none, which was quite mysterious to them, until I explained to them the nature of the cafés, the splendid open shops they were every moment passing, glittering with gold and looking-glasses. They were surprised to learn that the delicious poison was dealt out in these neat "palaces," but which they had not known or suspected the meaning of. They admitted their surprise, and at once decided that "they liked the free, and open, and elegant appearance of them much better than those in London, where they are all shut up in front with great and gloomy doors, to prevent people from looking into them, as if they were ashamed."

The cemetery of Père la Chaise was next to be seen as soon as there should be a fine day: that day arrived, and half an hour's drive landed us at its entrance.

This wonderful place has been described by many travellers, and therefore needs but a passing notice here. This wilderness of tombs, of houses or boxes of the dead, thrown and jumbled together amidst its gloomy cypress groves and thickets, is perhaps one of the most extraordinary scenes of the kind in the world: beautiful in some respects, and absurd and ridiculous in others, it is still one of the wonders of Paris, and all who see the one must needs visit the other. The scene was one peculiarly calculated to excite and please the Indians. The wild and gloomy and almost endless labyrinths of the little mansions of the dead were pleasing contrasts to their imprisonment within the dry and heated walls of the city; the varied and endless designs that recorded the places and the deeds of the dead were themes of amusement to them, and the subject altogether one that filled their minds with awe, and with admiration of the people who treated their dead with so much respect.

We wandered for an hour through its intricate mazes of cypress, examining the tombs of the rich and the poor so closely and curiously grouped together—a type, even in the solitudes of death, of the great Babylon in which their days had been numbered and spent. Whilst we were strolling through the endless mazes of this *sub-rosa* city, we met an immense concourse of people, evidently bearing the body of some distinguished person to the grave. The pompous display of mourning feathers and fringes, &c., with hired mourners, was matter of some surprise to the Indians; but when a friend of the deceased stepped forward to pronounce an eulogium on his character, recounting his many virtues and heroic deeds, it reminded the Indians forcibly of the custom of their own country, and they all said they liked to see that.

We took them to the patched and vandalized tomb of Abelard and Eloisa; but as there was not time for so long a story, it lost its interest to them. They were evidently struck with amazement at the system and beauty of this place, and from that moment decided that they liked the French for the care they took of their old soldiers and the dead.

The poor fellows, the Indians, who were now proceeding daily and nightly with their exciting and "astonishing" exhibitions, were becoming so confounded and confused with the unaccountable sights and mysteries of Paris which they were daily visiting, that they began to believe there was no end to the curious and astonishing works of civilized man; and, instead of being any longer startled with excitement and wonder, decided that it would be better to look at everything else as simple and easy to be made by those that know how, and therefore divested of all further curiosity. This they told me they had altogether resolved upon: "they had no doubt there were yet many strange things for them to see in Paris, and they would like to follow me to see them all; but they would look with their eyes only half open, and not trouble us with their surprise and their questions."

With these views, and their eyes "half open," then, they still took their daily drives, and Mr. Melody or myself, in constant company, stopping to show them, and to see ourselves, what was yet new and wonderful to be seen. There was still much to be seen in Paris, and the poor Indians were a great way from a complete knowledge of all the tricks and arts of civilization.

A drive to the *School of Medicine* and the *Hôpital des Enfans Trouvés* was enough for one morning's recreation. The first, with *"Dupuytren's Room,"* was enough to open the old Doctor's eyes, and the latter, with its 6000 helpless and parentless infants added to it annually, sufficient to swell the orbs of Jim, and make him feel for his note-book. The School of Medicine, with Dupuytren's Room, forms one of the most surprising sights to be seen in Paris, and yet, save with the Doctor, there seemed to be but little interest excited by the sight. The Doctor's attitude was one of studied dignity and philosophic conceit as he stood before those wonderful preparations, not to be astonished, but to study as a critic, while he fanned himself with his eagle's tail. The expression of his face, which was the whole time unchanged, was one of a peculiar kind, and, as it was not sketched at the time, must be for ever lost.

The novel and pitiful sight of the thousands of innocent little creatures in the Foundling Hospital seemed to open the "half-closed eyes" and the hearts of the Indians, notwithstanding the resolutions they had made. When it was explained to them how these little creatures came into the world, and then into this most noble institution, and also that in the last year there had been born in the city of Paris 26,000 children, 9000 of whom were illegitimate, their eyes were surely open to the astounding facts of the vices of civilized society, and of the virtue of civilized governments in building and maintaining such noble institutions for the support of the fatherless and helpless in infancy, as well as for the veterans who have been maimed in the fields of glorious battle. When I told them that, of those thousands of little playful children, not one knew any other parent than the Government, they groaned in sympathy for them, and seemed at a loss to abhor or applaud the most, the sins of man that brought them into the world, or the kind and parental care that was taken of them by the Government of the country. Jim made a sure demand upon Daniel's kindness for the entry of these important facts, which he soon had in round and conspicuous numbers in his note-book, to teach to the *"cruel and relentless Indians."*

The sentimentalism and sympathy of the poor old Doctor were touched almost to melancholy by this scene; and in his long and serious cogitations on it he very gravely inquired why the thousands of women leading and petting little dogs in the streets could not be induced to discharge their dogs, and each one take a little child and be its mother? He said, if he were to take a Frenchwoman for his wife, he would rather take her with a little child, even if it were her own, than take her with a little dog.

The *guillotine*, which happened to be in our way, and which they had been promised a sight of, they thought was more like a *Mississippi saw-mill* than anything else they had seen. It drew a murmur or two when explained to them how the victim was placed, and his head rolled off when the knife fell, but seemed to have little further effect upon them except when the actual number was mentioned to them whose heads are there severed from their bodies annually, for their crimes committed in the streets and houses of Paris. Our stay before this awful and bloody machine was but short, and of course their remarks were few, until they got home, and their dinner was swallowed, and their *chickabobboo*, and, reclining on their buffalo robes, the pipe was passing around.

Their conversation was then with Daniel, who had been but the day before to see the very same things, and they gained much further information than we did, which he communicated to them. He entered in Jim's book, as he had desired, the numbers of the *illegitimates* and *foundlings* of Paris, which seemed to be a valuable addition to his estimates of the blessings of civilization; and also the number of annual victims whose heads roll from the side of the guillotine. His book was then closed, and a curious discussion arose between the Indians and Daniel, whether the gallows, which they had seen in the prisons in England and Ireland, was a preferable mode of execution to that of the guillotine, which they had just been to see. They had no doubt but both of them, or, at least, that one or the other of them was absolutely necessary in the civilized world; but the question was, which was the best. Daniel contended that the punishment which was most ignominious was best, and contended for the gallows, while the Indians thought the guillotine was the best. They thought that death was bad enough, without the Government trying to add to its pang by hanging people up by the neck with a rope, as the Indians hang dogs. From this grave subject, which they did not seem to settle, as there was no umpire, they got upon a somewhat parallel theme, and were quite as seriously engaged, when I was obliged to leave them, whether it would be preferable to be *swallowed whole* by a whale, or to be *chewed*. Daniel was referring to Scripture for some authority on this subject, by looking into one of Jim's Bibles, when Mr. Melody and I were apprised of an appointment, which prevented us from ever hearing the result.

The next promise we had to keep with them was the one that had been made to take them to see the fountain of all the pretty and ugly little dogs and huge mastiffs they saw carried and led through the streets of Paris—the "*Dog Market.*"

The *Dog Hospital*, being *en route*, was visited first; and though one could scarcely imagine what there could be there that was amusing or droll, still the old Doctor insisted on it that it must be very interesting, and all resolved to go. It was even so, and on that particular occasion was rendered very amusing, when the Doctor entered, with Jim and the rest following. The squalling of "There! there! there!" by the frightened parrots in Cross's Zoological Gardens bore little comparison to the barking and yelling of "les petits pauvres chiens," and the screams of the old ladies—"Ne les effrayez pas, Messieurs, s'il vous plaît! ils sont tous malades—tous malades: pauvres bêtes! pauvres bêtes!" It was soon perceived that the nerves of the poor little "malades," as well as those of the old women their doctors, were too much affected to stand the shock, and it was thought best to withdraw. The old Doctor, getting just a glance at the sick-wards, enough to convince him of the clean comforts these little patients had, and seeing that their physicians were females, and also that the wards were crowded with fashionable ladies looking and inquiring after the health of their little pets, he was quite reluctant to leave the establishment without going fairly in and making his profession known, which he had thought would, at least, command him some respect amongst female physicians. He had some notion for this purpose of going in alone, but sarcastic Jim said the whole fright of the poor dogs had been produced by his appearance; to which the Doctor replied that they only barked because Jim was coming behind him. However, our visit was necessarily thus short, and attention directed to the Dog Market, for which Jim was more eager, as he had a special object. This was a curiosity, to be sure, and well worth seeing; there was every sort of whelp and cur that could be found in Christendom, from the veriest minimum of dog to the stateliest mastiff and Newfoundland; and, at Jim and the Doctor's approach, hundreds of them barked and howled, many broke their strings, some laid upon their backs, and yelled (no doubt, if one could have understood their language) that they never saw before in their lives so ill-looking and frightful a couple, and so alarming a set as those who were following behind them. Jim wanted to buy, and, the business-meaning of his face being discovered, there were all sorts of offers made him, and every kind of pup protruded into his face;

but the barking of dogs was such that no one could be heard, and then many a poor dog was knocked flat with a broom, or whatever was handiest, and others were choked, to stop their noise. No one wanted to stand the din of this canine Bedlam longer than was necessary for Jim to make his choice, which the poor fellow was endeavouring to do with the greatest despatch possible. His mode was rather different from the ordinary mode of testing the qualities he was looking for, which was by feeling of the ribs; and having bargained for one that he thought would fit him, the lookers-on were somewhat amused at his choice. He made them understand by his signs that they were going to eat it, when the poor woman screamed out, "Diable! mange pas! mange pas!—venez, venez, ma pauvre bête!"

The crowd by this time was becoming so dense that it was thought advisable to be on the move, and off. The Doctor became exceedingly merry at Jim's expense, as he had come away without getting a dog for their Dog Feast, of which they had been for some time speaking.

On their return from this day's drive, they met, to their very great surprise, their old friend *Bobasheela*, who had left his business and crossed the Channel to see them once more before they should set sail for America. He said he could not keep away from them long at a time while they were in this country, because he loved them so much. They were all delighted to see him, and told him he was just in time to attend the Dog Feast, which they were going to have the next day. The Doctor told him of Jim's success in buying a dog, and poor Jim was teazed a great deal about his failure. *Bobasheela* told them all the news about England, and Jim and the Doctor had a long catalogue to give him of their visit to the King—of their medals—their visits to the great fountain of *chickabobboo* and the *Foundling Hospital*, all of which he told him he had got down in his book. All this delighted *Bobasheela*, until they very imprudently told him that they liked Paris much better than London. They told him that the people in Paris did not teaze them so much about religion; that there were fewer poor people in the streets; and that as yet they had kept all their money, for they had seen nobody poor enough to give it to. Their *chickabobboo* was very different, but it was about as good. The guillotine they were very well satisfied with, as they considered it much better to cut men's heads off than to hang them up, like dogs, by a rope around the neck. This, and keeping men in prison because they owe money, they considered were the two most cruel things they heard of amongst the English.

Bobasheela replied to them that he was delighted to hear of their success, and to learn that they had seen the King, an honour he should himself have been very proud of. He told them that he never had seen the King, but that, while travelling in Kentucky many years ago, he was close upon the heels of the King, and so near him that he slept on the same (not bed, but) floor in a cabin where the King had slept, with his feet to the fire, but a short time before. This was something quite new to the Indians, and, like most of *Bobasheela's* stories of the Far West, pleased them exceedingly.

Jim, who was a *matter-of-fact man*, more than one of fancy and imagination, rather sided with *Bobasheela*, and, turning to his round numbers last added to his book, of "9000 illegitimate children born in Paris in the last year," asked his friend if he could read it, to which he replied "Yes." "Well," said Jim, in broad English, "some *fish* there, I guess, ha? I no like em Frenchwomen—I no like em: no good! I no like em so many children, no fader!" We all saw by Jim's eye, and by the agitation commencing, that he had some ideas that were coming out, and at the instant he was turning over on to his back, and drawing up his knees, and evidently keeping his eyes fixed on some object on the ceiling of the room, not to lose the chain of his thoughts, and he continued (not in English, for he spoke more easily in his own language), "I do not like the Frenchwomen. I did not like them at first, when I saw them leading so many dogs. I thought then that they had more dogs than children, but I think otherwise now. We believe that those women, who we have seen leading their dogs around with strings, have put their children away to be raised in the great house of the Government, and they get these little dogs to fill their places, and to suck their breasts when they are full of milk."

"Hut—tut—tut!" said Melody, "you ill-mannerly fellow! what are you about? You will blow us all up here, Jim, if you utter such sentiments as those. I think the French ladies the finest in the world except the Americans, and if they heard such ideas as those, advanced by us, they would soon drive us out of Paris."

"Yes," said Jim (in English again), "yes, I know—I know you like em—may be very good, but you see I no like em!" In his decided dislike, Jim's excitement was too great for his ideas to flow smoothly any further, and Mr. Melody not disposed to push the argument, the subject was dropped, and preparations made for the day exhibition, the hour for which was at hand.

CHAPTER XXVII.

La Morgue—The Catacombs—The Doctor's dream—Their great alarm—Visit to the *Hippodrome*—Jim riding M. Franconi's horse—Indians in the Woods of Boulogne—Fright of the rabbits—Jim and the Doctor at the *Bal Mabille*, Champs Elysées—At the *Masquerade, Grand Opera*—Their opinions and criticisms on them—Frenchwomen at confession in St. Roch—Doctor's ideas of it—Jim's speech—*"Industrious fleas"*—Death of the wife of Little Wolf—Her baptism—Husband's distress—Her funeral in the Madeleine—Her burial in Montmartre—Council held—Indians resolve to return to America—Preparations to depart in a few days—*Bobasheela* goes to London to ship their boxes to New York—He returns, and accompanies the Indians to Havre—Indians take leave of *Chippehola* (the Author)—M. Vattemare accompanies them to Havre—Kindly treated by Mr. Winslow, an American gentleman, at Havre—A splendid dinner, and *(Queen's) Chickabobboo*—Indians embark—Taking leave of *Bobasheela*—Illness of the Author's lady—His alarm and distress—Her death—Obituary—Her remains embalmed and sent to New York.

After their exhibition was over, and they had taken their dinner and *chickabobboo* (at the former of which they had had the company of their old friend *Bobasheela*), their pipe was lit, and the conversation resumed about the French ladies, for whom Jim's dislike was daily increasing, and with his dislike, his slanderous propensity. He could not divest his mind of the 9000 illegitimate and abandoned little babies that he had seen, and the affection for dogs, which, instead of *exposing*, they secure with ribbons, and hold one end in their hands, or tie it to their apron-strings. This was a subject so glaring to Jim's imagination, that he was quite fluent upon it at a moment's warning, even when standing up or sitting, without the necessity of resorting to his usual and eccentric attitude. This facility caused him to be more lavish of his abuse, and at every interview in the rooms he seemed to be constantly frowning upon the ladies, and studying some new cause for abusing them, and drawing Mr. Melody and the Doctor into debates when they got back to their own apartments. Such was the nature of the debate he had just been waging, and which he had ended in his usual way, with the last word to himself, "I no care; me no like em."

The subject was here changed, however, by Mr. Melody's reminding them that this day was the time they had set to visit the *Morgue* and the *Catacombs*, for which an order had been procured. These had been the favourite themes for some days; and there had been the greatest impatience expressed to go and see the naked dead bodies of the murdered and *felo-de-ses* daily stretched out in the one, and the five millions of skulls and other human bones that are laid up like cobhouses under great part of the city. *Bobasheela* had described to them the wonders of this awful place, which he had been in on a former occasion, and Daniel had read descriptions from books while the Indians had smoked many a pipe; but when the subject was mentioned on this occasion, there were evident proofs instantly shown that some influence had produced a different effect upon their minds, and that they were no longer anxious to go. M. Vattemare, in speaking of the Catacombs a few days before, had said that about a year ago two young men from the West Indies came to Paris, and, getting an order to visit the Catacombs, entered them, and, leaving their guide, strolled so far away that they never got out, and never have been found, but their groans and cries are still often heard under different parts of the city. But the immediate difficulty with the Indians was a dream the Doctor had had the night before, and which he had been relating to them. He had not, he said, dreamed anything about the Catacombs, but he had seen *See-catch-e-wee-be*, the one-eyed wife of the *"fire-eater"* (a sorcerer of their tribe), who had followed his track all the way to the great village of the whites (London), and from that to Paris, where he saw her sitting on a bridge over the water; that she gave him a pair of new mocassins of moose-skin, and told him that the *Gitchee Manitou* (the Great Spirit) had been very kind in not allowing him and *Wash-ka-mon-ya* (Jim) to go under the ground in the Great Village of the Whites, in England, and their lives were thereby saved. She then went under an old woman's basket, who was selling apples, and disappeared. He could not understand why he should have such a vision as this the very night before they were to go underground to the Catacombs, unless it was to warn him of the catastrophe that might befall them if they were to make their visit there, as they had designed. They had smoked several pipes upon this information early in the morning, and the chiefs had closely questioned him and also consulted him as their oracle in all such cases, and had unanimously come to the conclusion that these were foreboding prognostications sufficient to decide it to be at least prudent to abandon their project, and thereby be sure to run no hazard.[40]

Mr. Melody and myself both agreed that their resolve placed them on the safe side at all events, and that we thought them wise in making it if they saw the least cause for apprehension. "They could easily run to the river, however, in their drive, and see the other place, the *Morgue*;" but that could not, on any account, be undertaken, as the two objects had been planned out for the same visit; and, from the Doctor's dream, it did not appear in the least certain in which of the places they were liable to incur the risk, and therefore they thought it best not to go to either. There was a great deal yet to see above ground, and quite as much as they should be able to see in the little time they had yet to remain there, and which would be much pleasanter to look at than white men's bones under ground.

Their minds were filled with amazement on this wonderful subject; but their curiosity to see it seemed quite stifled by the Doctor's dream, and the subject for the present was dropped, with a remark from Jim, "that he was not sure but that this accounted for the white people digging up all the Indians' graves on the frontiers, and that their bones were brought here and sold." The Catacombs were thus left for Daniel and myself to stroll through at our leisure, and the Indians were contented with the sketch I made, which, with Daniel's account, put them in possession of the principal features of that extraordinary and truly shocking place.

As their visit to the *Catacombs* and the *Morgue* was abandoned, we resolved to drive through the Champs Elysées and visit the woods of Boulogne, the favourite drive of the Parisians, and probably the most beautiful in the world. We had been solicited by M. Franconi, of the *Hippodrome*, to enter into an arrangement with him to have the Indians unite in his entertainments three days in the week, where their skill in riding and archery could be seen to great advantage, and for which he would be willing to offer liberal terms. He had invited us to bring the Indians down, at all events, to see the place; and we agreed to make the visit to M. Franconi on our way to the woods of Boulogne. The view was a private one, known only to a few of his friends, who were present, and his own operatic *troupe*. We were very civilly and politely received; and, all walking to the middle of his grand area, he proposed to make us the offer, on condition that the Indians were good riders, which I had already assured him was the case, and which seemed rather difficult for him to believe, as they had so little of civilization about them. As the best proof, however, he proposed to bring out a horse, and let one of them try and show what he could do. This we agreed to at once; and, having told the Indians before we started that we should make no arrangement for them there unless they were pleased with it and preferred it, they had decided, on entering the grounds, that the exercises would be too desperate and fatiguing to them and destructive to their clothes, and therefore not to engage with him. However, the horse was led into the area and placed upon the track for their chariot-races, which is nearly a quarter of a mile in circumference; and, the question being put, "Who will ride?" it was soon agreed that Jim should try it first. "Wal, me try em," said Jim; "me no ride good, but me try em little." He was already prepared, with his shield and quiver upon his back and his long and shining lance in his hand. The horse was held; though, with all its training, it was some time, with its two or three grooms about it, before they could get the frightened creature to stand steady enough for Jim to mount. In the first effort which they thought he was making to get on, they were surprised to find that he was ungirthing the saddle, which he flung upon the ground, and, throwing his buffalo robe across the animal's back and himself astride, the horse dashed off at his highest speed. Jim saw that the animal was used to the track, and, the course being clear, he leaned forward and brandished his lance, and, every time he came round and passed us, sounded a charge in the shrill notes of the war-whoop. The riding was pleasing and surprised M. Franconi exceedingly, and when he thought it was about time to stop he gave his signal for Jim to pull up, but, seeing no slack to the animal's pace, and Jim still brandishing his weapons in the air and sounding the war-whoop as he passed, he became all at once alarmed for the health of his horse. The Indians at this time were all in a roar of laughter, and the old gentleman was placing himself and his men upon the track as Jim came round, with uplifted arms, to try to stop the animal's speed, just finding at that time that Jim had rode in the true prairie style, without using the bridle, and which, by his neglect of it, had got out of his reach, when he would have used it to pull up with. Jim still dashed by them, brandishing his lance as they came in his way: when they retreated and ran to head him in another place, he there passed them also, and passed them and menaced them again and again as he came around. The alarm of the poor old gentleman for the life of his horse became very conspicuous, and, with additional efforts with his men, and a little pulling up by Jim, who had at length found the rein, the poor affrighted and half-dead animal was stopped, and Jim, leaping off, walked to the middle of the area, where we were in a group, laughing to the greatest excess at the fun. The poor horse was near done over, and led away by the grooms, M. Franconi came and merely bade us good-by, and was exceedingly obliged to us. Whether the poor animal died or not we never heard, but Jim was laid up for several days. On asking him why he ran the horse so hard, he said it was the horse's fault, that "it ran away with him the moment he was on its back—that the creature was frightened nearly to death; and he thought, if it preferred running, he resolved to give it running enough." The Doctor told him he acted imprudently in getting on, which had caused all the trouble. "In what way?" inquired Jim. "Why, by letting the animal see that ugly face of yours; if you had hid it till you were on, there would have been no trouble."

We were all obliged to laugh at the Doctor's wit; and having taken leave of the polite old gentleman, we were seated in our carriages again for a drive through the woods of Boulogne.

In the midst of these wild and truly beautiful grounds the Indians and all got down for a stroll. The native wildness of the forests and jungle seemed in a moment to inspire them with their wild feelings, which had, many of them, long slumbered whilst mingling amidst the crowds of civilization, and away they leapt and bounded among the trees in their wild and wonted amusements. Their shrill yells and the war-whoop were soon lost in the distant thickets which they penetrated, and an hour at least elapsed before they could all be gathered together and prepared to return. Their frightful yells had started up all the rabbits that were unburrowed in the forests; and whilst hundreds were bounding about, and many taking to the open fields for escape, they encompassed one, and with their united screams had scared it to death. This they assured us was the case, as they brought it in by the legs, without the mark of any weapon upon it.

Few scenes in Paris, if any, had pleased them more than this, and in their subsequent drives they repeatedly paid their visits to the "woods of Boulogne."

On their return home poor Jim lay down, complaining very much of lameness from his hard ride on Franconi's horse, which he knew would prevent him from dancing for some days, as he was getting very stiff, and afraid he would not be well enough to go and see the "Industrious Fleas" (as they were called), where he and the Doctor and Jeffrey had arranged to go with Daniel and several young American acquaintance, who had decided it to be one of the choicest little sights then to be seen in Paris, and which from all accounts is an exhibition of female nudities in living groups, ringing all the changes on attitude and action for the amusement of the lookers-on. There was a great deal of amusing conversation about this very popular exhibition, but in this poor Jim and the Doctor reluctantly submitted to disappointment when Mr. Melody very properly objected to their going to see it.

Jim had laid himself on his back at this time, and, not feeling in the best of humour, began in a tirade of abuse of the Frenchwomen, of whom he and the Doctor had seen more perhaps on the previous evening in the *Jardin Mabille* in the Champs Elysées, and the *masquerade* in the *Grand Opera House*, than they had seen since they entered Paris.

Their enterprise on that evening had taken place after their exhibition had closed, when Jim and the Doctor started with Jeffrey and Daniel and two or three friends who were pledged to take care of them. It was on Sunday evening, when the greatest crowds attend these places, and I have no other account of what they did and what they saw than that they gave me on their return home. They had first gone to the splendid *bal* in the popular garden, where they were told that the thousand elegant women they saw there dancing were all bad women, and that nearly all of them came to those places alone, as they had nothing to pay, but were all let in free, so as to make the men come who had to pay. This idea had tickled Jim and the Doctor very much, for, although they were from the wilderness, they could look a good way into a thing which was perfectly clear. It was a splendid sight for them, and, after strolling about a while, and seeing all that could be seen, they had turned their attention to the *"Bal Masqué"* in the *Grand Opera*. Here they had been overwhelmed with the splendour of the scene, and astonished at its novelty, and the modes of the women who, Jim said, "were all ashamed to show their faces," and whose strange manœuvres had added a vast deal to the fund of his objections to Frenchwomen, and which he said had constantly been accumulating ever since he first saw so many of them kissing the ends of little dogs' noses, and pretty little children on their foreheads. His mind here ran upon kissing, of which he had seen some the night before, and which he had often observed in the exhibition rooms and in the streets. He had laughed, he said, to see Frenchmen kiss each other on both cheeks; and he had observed that, when gentlemen kiss ladies, they kiss them on the forehead: he was not quite sure that they would do so in the dark, however. "In London always kiss em on the mouth; ladies kiss em Indians heap, and hug em too: in France ladies no kiss em—no like em—no good."

In speaking of the *bal* in the gardens, "he didn't see anything so very bad in that, but as for the masquerade, he looked upon it as a very immoral thing that so many thousands of ladies should come there and be ashamed to show their faces, and have the privilege of picking out just such men as they liked to go with them, and then take hold of their arms, as he said he repeatedly saw them, and lead them out." Amongst the Indians, he said, they had a custom much like that to be sure, but it was only given once a-year, and it was then only for the young married men to lend their wives to the old ones: this was only one night in the year, and it was a mark of respect that the young married men were willing to pay to the old warriors and chiefs, and the young married women were willing to agree to it because it pleased their husbands. On those occasions, he said, "none are admitted into the ring but old married men, and then the young married woman goes around and touches on the left shoulder the one who she wishes to follow her into the bushes, and she does it without being ashamed and obliged to cover her face."

The Doctor's prejudices against the Frenchwomen were nothing near as violent as those of Jim, and yet he said it made him feel very curious when he saw some thousands with their faces all hidden: he said it must be true that they had some object that was bad, or they wouldn't be ashamed and hide their faces. Mr. Melody told Jim and the Doctor, however, that he didn't consider there was so very much harm in it, for these very women had the handiest way in the world to get rid of all their sins. If they happened accidentally or otherwise during the week to do anything that was decidedly naughty or wicked, they went into their churches very early in the morning, where the priest was in a little box with his ear to the window, where the woman kneeled down and told in his ear all the sins she had committed during the week, and she then went away quite happy that, having confessed them to him, he would be sure to have them all forgiven by the Great Spirit. They had a great laugh at this, and all thought that Mr. Melody was quizzing them, until *Bobasheela* and *Daniel* both told them it was all true, and if they liked to go with them any morning they would take them into any of the

French churches or chapels, where they could see it; and would venture that they would see many of the same women confessing their sins whom they had seen at the *bal* and the masquerade, and in this way they could tell who had behaved the worst, for the most guilty of them would be sure to be there first. The Doctor seemed evidently to look upon this still with suspicion and doubt; and as the splendid church of *St. Roch* was nearly opposite to their rooms, and only across the street, it was proposed that the Doctor and Jim should accompany Daniel and their friend *Bobasheela* immediately there, where in five minutes they could see more or less women at confession, and at the same time a fine sight, one of the most splendid churches in Paris, and the place where the Queen goes on every Sunday to worship. This so excited the party, that they chiefly all arose and walked across the street to take a view of the church and the Frenchwomen confessing their sins into the ears of the priests. They happened to have a fair opportunity of seeing several upon their knees at confession; and the old Doctor had been curious to advance up so near to one, that he said he saw the priest's eyes shining through between the little slats, and then he was convinced, and not before. He said that still it didn't seem right to him, unless the Great Spirit had put those men there for that purpose. He thought it a very nice place for a young girl to tell the priest where she would meet him, and he had a very good chance to see whether she was pretty or not. Jim had by this time studied out an idea or two, and said, he thought that this way of confessing sins aided the *bals* and *masquerades* and the *industrious fleas* very much; and he believed that these were the principal causes of the great number of the poor little deserted and parentless babes they had seen in the hospital where they had been.

The hour for the exhibition arriving, the conversation about Paris morals and religion was broken suddenly off, and perhaps at a good time. There were great crowds now daily attending their amusements, and generally applauding enthusiastically, and making the Indians occasional presents. On this occasion the Doctor had made a tremendous boast in the part he was taking in the eagle-dance, for the spirit of which the audience, and particularly the ladies, gave him a great deal of applause, so much so that at the end of the dance his vanity called him out in an off-hand speech about the beauty of the city, &c., and, it being less energetic than the boasts he had just been strutting out, failed to draw forth the applause he was so confidently depending on. He tried sentence after sentence, and, stopping to listen, all were silent. This perplexed and disappointed the Doctor very much, and still he went on, and at length stopped and sat down, admired, but not applauded. His friend Jim was laughing at him as he took his seat, and telling him that if he had barked like a little dog the ladies would have been sure to applaud. To this the Doctor said, "You had better try yourself:" upon which the daring Jim, who professed never to refuse any challenge, sprang upon his feet, and, advancing to the edge of the platform, stood braced out with his brows knitting, and his eyes "in a frenzy rolling," for full two minutes before he began. He then thrust his lance forward in his right hand as far as he could dart it over the heads of the audience, and, coming back to his balance again, he commenced. Of his speech no report was made, but it was short and confined to three or four brief sentences, at the end of which he looked around with the most doleful expression to catch the applause, but there was none. The old Doctor was watching him close, and telling him he had better sit down.

In this dilemma he was still standing after all his good ideas had been spent, and each instant, as he continued to stand, making his case worse, he turned upon his heel, and as he was turning around he added, in an irritated manner, this amusing sentence: "You had better go and see the industrious fleas, and then you will applaud!" This made a great laugh amongst the Indians, but of course it was not translated to the audience. He then took his seat, looking exceedingly sober, and, with his pipe, was soon almost lost sight of in the columns of smoke that were rising around him.

About this time a very friendly invitation had been given them and us by Colonel Thorn, an American gentleman of great wealth residing in Paris, and all were anticipating much pleasure on the occasion when we were to dine at his house; but, unluckily for the happiness and enjoyment of the whole party, on the morning of the day of our invitation the wife of the Little Wolf suddenly and unexpectedly died. Our engagement to dine was of course broken, and our exhibition and amusements for some days delayed. This sad occurrence threw the party into great distress, but they met the kindness of many sympathising friends, who administered in many ways to their comfort, and joined in attending the poor woman's remains to the grave. Her disease was the consumption of the lungs, and her decline had been rapid, though her death at that time was unexpected. When it was discovered that her symptoms were alarming, a Catholic priest was called in, and she received the baptism a few moments before she breathed her last. Through the kindness of the excellent Curé of the *Madeleine church*, her remains were taken into that splendid temple, and the funeral rites performed over them according to the rules of that church, in the presence of some hundreds who were led there by sympathy and curiosity, and from thence her body was taken to the cemetery of Montmartre, and interred. The poor heartbroken noble fellow, the Little Wolf, shed the tears of bitterest sorrow to see her, from necessity, laid amongst the rows of the dead in a foreign land; and on every day that he afterwards spent in Paris he ordered a cab to take him to the grave, that he could cry over it, and talk to the departed spirit of his wife, as he was leaving some little offering he had brought with him. This was the second time we had seen him in grief; and we, who had been by him in all his misfortunes, admired the deep affection he showed for his little boy, and now for its mother, and at the same time the manly fortitude with which he met the fate that had been decreed to him. On this sad occasion their good friend M. Vattemare showed his kind sympathy for them, and took upon himself the whole arrangements of her funeral, and did all that was in his power to console and soothe the brokenhearted husband in the time of his affliction. He also proposed to have a suitable and appropriate monument erected over her grave, and for its accomplishment procured a considerable sum by subscription, with which, I presume, the monument has, ere this, been erected over her remains. The Little Wolf insisted on it that the exhibition should proceed, as the daily expenses were so very great, and in a few days, to give it all the interest it could have, resumed his part in the dance that he had taken before his misfortune.

Owing to letters received about this time from their tribe, and the misfortune that had happened, the Indians were now all getting anxious to start for their own country, and, holding a council on the subject, called Mr. Melody in, and informed him that they had resolved to sleep but six nights more in Paris, and that they should expect him to be ready to start with them after that time. This was a short notice for us, but was according to Indian modes, and there was no way but to conform to it. Mr. Melody had pledged his word to the Government to take care of these people, and to return to their country with them whenever the chiefs should desire it; and I was bound, from my deep interest for them, to assent to whatever regulations Mr. Melody and the chiefs should adopt as the best.

This notice came at a time when it was unexpected by me, and I think not anticipated by Mr. Melody, and was therefore unfortunate for us, and probably somewhat, though less so, to them. The very heavy outlays had all been made for their exhibitions, and their audiences were daily increasing. If their exhibitions could have been continued a month or two longer, the avails would have been considerable, and of great service to Mr. Melody, who had the heavy responsibility on his shoulders of taking these people back to their country at his own expense.

The closing of their amusements, and positive time of their departure, was now announced, and immense crowds came in within the remaining few days to get the last possible glance at the faces and the curious modes of *"les Peaux Rouges."* The poor fellows enjoyed their interviews with the public to the last, and also their roast beef and beef-steaks and *chickabobboo*.

They had much to say in the few days that were left; they quitted their daily drives and sight-seeing, and devoted their time to the pipe and conversation, in a sort of recapitulation of what they had seen and said and done on this side of the Atlantic, and of friends and affairs in their own humble villages, where their thoughts were now roaming. They were counting their cash also, packing away all their things they were to carry, and looking out for the little presents they wished to purchase, to take home to their friends. In all of these occupations they had the constant attention of their old and faithful friends *Bobasheela* and *Daniel*.

In one of their conversations after the funeral of the poor woman, the Doctor and Jim had much to say of the honours paid to her remains by the French people, which the whole party would recollect as long as they lived. They were pleased with and astonished at the beauty and magnificence of the Madeleine church, and wished to get some account of it to carry home to show their people, and thus, besides several engravings of it, Jim's book carried the following entry by my own hand:—"*La Madeleine*, the most splendid temple of worship in Paris, or perhaps in the world; surrounded with 52 Corinthian columns, 60 feet high; south pediment, a bas-relief, representing the Day of Judgment, with the figure of Magdalene at the feet of Christ."

As the party were to embark at Havre on their homeward voyage, it became a question how they were to get their numerous trunks and boxes they had left in London, filled with clothes and other articles that they had purchased or received as presents while in England. To relieve them of this difficulty, their friend *Bobasheela* volunteered to go to London and take all their boxes to Liverpool, and ship them to New York, and was soon on the way. This was a noble and kind act on the part of *Bobasheela*, and it was done with despatch, and he was back in Paris just in time to accompany his friends to Havre. M. Vattemare was in readiness to attend them also; and all their transactions in Paris being brought to a close, and they having taken leave of *Chippehola* and other friends, started for their native land, with my highest admiration for the sober and respectful manner in which they had conducted themselves while under my direction, and with my most ardent desire for their future success and happiness.[41]

Here was about the period at which my dear wife and I had contemplated our return, with our little children, to our native land, where we should have returned in the enjoyment of all the happiness we had anticipated or could have wished, but for the misfortune that had been for some time awaiting me, but not until then duly appreciated, in my own house. Those of my readers who were not familiar with the completeness of my domestic happiness prior to this period of my life, will scarcely know how to sympathize with me, or perhaps to excuse me for adverting to it here. My dear Clara, whom I have introduced to the reader before, who shared with me many of the toils and pleasures of the prairies of the "Far West," and was now meeting with me the mutual enjoyments of the refined and splendid world, had, a few weeks before, in company with a couple of English ladies of her acquaintance, paid a visit to the Mint, from which they all returned indisposed, having taken severe colds by a sudden change from the heated rooms into the chilly atmosphere of the streets. With my dear wife, who was obliged to retire to her room, the disease was discovered in a few days to have attached to her lungs; and although for several weeks she had been suffering very much, and confined to her bed, no serious apprehensions were entertained until about the time that the Indians left, when my whole thoughts and attentions were turned to her, but to discover in a few days that our plans for further mutual happiness in this world were at an end—that her days were nearly numbered, and that her four dear little children were to be committed to my sole care.

To those who have felt pangs like mine which followed, I need but merely mention them; and to those who have not felt them, it would be in vain to describe. Her feeble form wasted away; and in her dying moments, with a Christian's hope, she was in the midst of happiness, blessing her dear little children as she committed them to my care and protection.

The following obituary notice, penned by a lady of her intimate acquaintance, the reader will excuse me for inserting here, as it is the only record of her, except those engraven on the hearts of those who knew and loved her:—

> DIED—On the 28th inst., No. 11 *bis*, Avenue Lord Byron, Paris, Mrs. Clara B. Catlin, the wife of the eminent traveller so distinguished for his researches into Indian history and antiquities of America, and so universally known and respected in Europe and his native country, Geo. Catlin, Esq., from the United States of America. The devoted friends who watched the last moments of this most amiable, interesting woman with intense anxiety, still clung to a faint hope, deceived by a moral energy never surpassed, and the most unruffled serenity of temper, that (had it been the will of Heaven) they might have been permitted to rescue a life so precious—but, alas! this gentle, affectionate, intellectual being was destined never more to revisit the land of her birth, and all that was earthly of so much worth and loveliness has passed away, whilst the immortal spirit has ascended to its kindred skies!

"None knew her, but to love her;

None named her, but to praise."

Galignani's Messenger, 30th July, 1845.

The reader can imagine something of the gloom that was cast over my house and little family, thus suddenly closed for ever from the smiles and cheer of an affectionate wife and a devoted mother, whose remains were sent back to her native land—not to greet and bring joy to her kindred and anxious friends, from whom she had been five years absent, but to afford them the last glance at her loved features, then to take their place amongst the ranks of the peaceful dead.

CHAPTER XXVIII.

Eleven Ojibbeway Indians arrive from London—Their exhibitions in the Author's Collection—Portraits and description of—Their amusements—Their pledge to sobriety—*Chickabobboo* explained to them—Birth of a *Pappoose*—M. Gudin—Indians and the Author dine with him—His kind lady—The Author breakfasts with the Royal Family in the palace at St. Cloud—Two Kings and two Queens at the table—The Author presented to the King and Queen of the Belgians by Louis Philippe, in the salon—Count de Paris—Duc de Brabant—Recollects the Indian pipe and mocassins presented to him by the Author in the Egyptian Hall—Duchess of Orleans—The Princess Adelaide—The King relates anecdotes of his life in America—Washington's farewell address—Losing his dog in the Seneca village—Crossing Buffalo Creek—Descending the Tioga and Susquehana rivers in an Indian canoe, to Wyoming, the Author's native valley—The King desires the Author to arrange his whole Collection in the Louvre for the private views of the Royal Family—He also appoints a day to see the Ojibbeways in the Park, at St. Cloud—Great rejoicing of the Indians—A *dog-feast*—The Indians and the Author dine a second time at M. Gudin's.

In the midst of my grief, with my little family around me, with my collection still open, and my lease for the Salle Valentino not yet expired, there suddenly arrived from London a party of eleven *Ojibbeway Indians*, from the region of Lake Huron, in Upper Canada, who had been brought to England by a Canadian, but had since been under the management of a young man from the city of London. They had heard of the great success of the Ioways in Paris, and also of their sudden departure, and were easily prevailed upon to make a visit there. On their arrival, I entered into the same arrangement with them that I had with the two former parties, agreeing with the young man who had charge of them to receive them into my collection, sharing the expenses and receipts as I had done before; he being obligated to pay the Indians a certain sum per month, and bound to return them to London, from whence they came, at his own expense. As my collection was all arranged and prepared, I thought such an arrangement calculated to promote their interest and my own, and in a few days their arrival and exhibitions were announced, they having been quartered in the same apartments which had been occupied by the Ioways before them.

No. 18.

The following are the names of the party, with their respective ages given (see *Plate No. 18*):—

		Age.
1.	*Maun-gua-daus* (a Great Hero)—Chief	41
2.	*Say-say-gon* (the Hail-Storm)	31
3.	*Ke-che-us-sin* (the Strong Rock)	27
4.	*Mush-she-mong* (the King of the Loons)	25
5.	*Au-nim-muck-kwah-um* (the Tempest Bird)	20
6.	*A-wun-ne-wa-be* (the Bird of Thunder)	19
7.	*Wau-bud-dick* (the Elk)	18
8.	*U-je-jock* (the Pelican)	10
9.	*Noo-din-no-kay* (the Furious Storm)	4
10.	*Min-nis-sin-noo* (a Brave Warrior)	3
11.	*Uh-wus-sig-gee-zigh-gook-kway* (Woman of the Upper World)—wife of Chief	38
12.	*Pappoose*—born in the Salle Valentino.	

- 205 -

The chief of this party, *Maun-gua-daus*, was a remarkably fine man, both in his personal appearance and intellectual faculties. He was a half-caste, and, speaking the English language tolerably well, acted as chief and interpreter of the party.

The War-chief, *Say-say-gon*, was also a fine and intelligent Indian, full-blooded, and spoke no English. The several younger men were generally good-looking, and exceedingly supple and active, giving great life and excitement to their dances. In personal appearance the party, taken all together, was less interesting than that of the Ioways, yet, at the same time, their dances and other amusements were equally, if not more spirited and beautiful than those of their predecessors.

Thus, in the midst of my sorrow, I was commencing anxieties again, and advertised the arrival of the new party, and the commencement of their exhibitions. They began with more limited but respectable audiences, and seemed to please and surprise all who came, by the excitement of their dances and their skill in shooting with the bow and arrows, in the last of which they far surpassed the Ioways. It was impossible, however, by all the advertising that could be done, to move the crowds again that had been excited to see the Ioways; the public seeming to have taken the idea that these were merely an imitation got up to take advantage of their sudden departure. It happened quite curious, that, although the party consisted of eleven when they arrived, about the time of the commencement of their exhibitions the wife of the chief was delivered of a *pappoose*, which was born in the same room where the poor wife of the Little Wolf had died. This occurrence enabled us to announce the party as *twelve*—the same number as the Ioways; which, with the name somewhat similar, furnished very strong grounds for many of the Parisians to believe that they were paying their francs to see their own countrymen aping the Indians of America.

It seemed strange that it was so difficult to do away this impression, which operated against them the whole time they were in Paris, though all who saw them but a moment were satisfied and pleased. Their amusements were much like those of the Ioways, but with national differences in the modes of giving them, which were, to the curious, subjects of great interest.

The same hours were adopted for their exhibitions—the same vehicles were contracted for, for their daily exercise and sight-seeing—and their guardian, with Daniel, took charge of all their movements on these occasions. Their daily routine therefore was in most respects the same as that of the Ioways, and it would be waste of valuable time here for me to follow them through all.

We held the council, as we had done in the other cases, before our arrangements were entered upon, and all was placed upon the condition that they were to conduct themselves soberly, and to drink no spirituous liquors. The temperance pledge was therefore given, after I had explained to them that, with the two other parties, ale in England, and *vin ordinaire* in France, when taken to a moderate degree, were not included in the term "*spirituous liquors*," and that they would of course, as the other parties had been indulged, have their regular glass at their dinners, and also after their suppers, and before going to bed; and that they would call it, as the others had done, *chickabobboo*. This indulgence seemed to please them very much, and, being at a loss to know the meaning of *chickabobboo*, I took an occasion to give them the history of the word, which they would see was of Ojibbeway origin, and, laughing excessively at the ingenuity of their predecessors, they all resolved to keep up their word, and to be sure at the same time not to drop their custom, of taking the licensed glasses of *chickabobboo*.

Amongst the kind friends whom this party made in Paris, one of the best was M. Gudin, the celebrated marine painter, in the employment of the King. This most excellent gentleman and his kind lady were frequent visitors to their exhibitions, and several times invited the whole party and myself to dine at their table, and spend the day in the beautiful grounds around his noble mansion (the "Chateau Beaujon"), and, in its present improved condition, little less than a palace.

Not only will the Indians feel bound for life to acknowledge their gratitude to this kind lady and gentleman, but the writer of these notes will feel equally and more so for the kind and unmerited attentions they paid to him during his stay in Paris. It was through the friendly agency of M. Gudin that the King invited my collection to the Louvre, and myself, in company with him, to the royal breakfast-table in the palace at St. Cloud. I take no little satisfaction in recording here these facts, not only for myself, but injustice to one of the most distinguished painters (and one of the best fellows) of the age. On this occasion, the proudest one of my wild and erratic life, we were conducted through several rooms of the palace to the one in which the Royal Family, chiefly all assembled, with their numerous guests, were standing and ready to be seated around a circular table of 15 or 18 feet in diameter, at which, our seats being indicated to us, and the bow of recognition (so far as we were able to recognise acquaintances) having been made, all were seated. This extraordinary occasion of my life was rendered peculiarly memorable and gratifying to me, from the fact that there were two Kings and two Queens at the table, and nearly every member of the Royal Family. The King and Queen of the Belgians, who were at that time on a visit to Paris, with his Royal Highness the little Duc de Brabant, were the unusual Royal guests at the table on the occasion. The number of persons at the table, consisting of the two Royal Families, the King's aides-de-camp, and orderly officers of the palace, with the invited guests, amounted to about 30 in all; and as Kings and

Queens and royal families eat exactly like other people, I see nothing further that need be noticed until their Majesties arose and retired to the salon or drawing-room, into which we all followed. I was there met as I entered, in the most gracious and cordial manner by His Majesty, who presented me to the King of the Belgians, who did me the honour to address me in these words:—"I am very happy, Mr. Catlin, to meet a gentleman whose name is familiar to us all, and who has done so much for science, and also for the poor Indians. You know that the Queen, and myself, and the Duc de Brabant were all subscribers to your valuable work, and we have taken great interest in reading it."

The two heirs-apparent, the little Count de Paris and His Royal Highness the Duc de Brabant, came to me, and, recognising me, inquired about the Indians. The conversation with her Majesty, and also with the Princess Adelaide, and the Duchess of Orleans, was about the Indians, who they had heard had gone home, and in whom they all seemed to have taken a deep interest.

The little Duc de Brabant recollected the small pipe and mocassins I had presented him when he visited my collection in the Egyptian Hall, under the protection of the Hon. Mr. Murray.

I had a few minutes' conversation with the King of the Belgians, and also with the graceful and pensive Duchess of Orleans, and our ears were then all turned to the recitals of his Majesty, around whom we had gathered, whilst he was relating several scenes of his early life in America, in company with his two brothers, the Duc de Montpensier and the Count Beaujolais, which it seemed my advent with the Indians had brought up with unusual freshness in his mind.

He commented in the most eloquent terms upon the greatness and goodness of General Washington, and told us that he and his brothers were lucky enough to have been present and heard his farewell address in Philadelphia, which he had been in the habit of reflecting upon as one of the most pleasurable and satisfactory incidents of his life.

He gave us an amusing account of his horse getting mired in crossing Buffalo Creek, and of his paying a visit to the tribe of Seneca Indians, near to the town of Buffalo, on Lake Erie:—

> "Being conducted," said he, "to the village and to the chief's wigwam, I shook hands with the chief, who came and stood by my horse's head, and while some hundreds of men, women, and children were gathering around, I told the chief that I had come to make him a visit of a day or two, to which he replied that he was very glad to see me, and I should be made quite welcome, and treated to the best that he had. He said there

would be one condition, however, which was, that he should require me to give him everything I had; he should demand my horse, from which I would dismount, and having given him the bridle, he said, 'I now want your gun, your watch, and all your money; these are indispensable.'

"I then, for the first time in my life, began to think that I was completely robbed and plundered; but at the moment when he had got all, and before I had time for more than an instant thought of my awkward condition, he released me from all further alarm by continuing, 'If you have anything else which you wish to be sure to get again, I wish you to let me have it; for whatever you deliver into my hands now you will be sure to find safe when you are about to leave; otherwise I would not be willing to vouch for their safety; for there are some of my people whom we cannot trust to.'

"From this moment I felt quite easy, and spent a day or two in their village very pleasantly, and with much amusement. When I was about to leave, my horse was brought to the chief's door and saddled, and all the property I had left in his hands safely restored.

"I then mounted my horse, and, having taken leave, and proceeded a short distance on my route, I discovered that I had left my favourite dog, which I had been too much excited and amused to think of, and did not recollect to have seen after I entered their village.

"I turned my horse and rode back to the door of the chief's wigwam, and made inquiries for it. The chief said, 'But you did not intrust your dog to my care, did you?' 'No, I did not think of my poor dog at the time.' 'Well then,' said he, 'I can't answer for it. If you had done as I told you, your dog would have been safe. However,' said he, 'we will inquire for it.' At which moment one of his little sons was ordered to run and open a rude pen or cage by the corner of the wigwam, and out leaped my dog, and sprang upon my leg as I was sitting on my horse. I offered the honest chief a reward for his kindness; but he refused to accept it, wishing me to recollect, whenever I was amongst Indians again, to repose confidence in an Indian's word, and feel assured that all the property intrusted to an Indian's care I would be sure to find safe whenever I wanted it again."

After reciting this amusing incident, his Majesty described to me the route which he and his brothers took from Buffalo to the falls of Niagara, and thence on horseback to Geneva, a small town at the foot of the Seneca Lake, where they sold their horses, and, having purchased a small boat, rowed it 90 miles to Ithaca, at the head of the lake. From thence they travelled on foot, with their luggage carried on their backs, 30 miles to Tioga, on the banks of the Susquehana, where they purchased a canoe from the Indians, and descended in it that romantic and beautiful river, to a small town called Wilkesbarre, in the valley of Wyoming.

From thence, with their knapsacks on their backs, they crossed the Wilkesbarre and Pokono mountains to Easton, and from thence were conveyed in a coach to Philadelphia.

I here surprised his Majesty a little, and his listeners, and seemed to add a fresh interest to his narrative, by informing him that I was a native of Wilkesbarre, in the valley of Wyoming, and that while his Majesty was there I was an infant in my mother's arms, only a few months old.

He related a number of pleasing recollections of his visit to my native valley, and then gave us an account of an Indian *ball-play* amongst the Cherokees and Choctaws, where he saw 500 or 600 engaged, during the whole day, before the game was decided; and he pronounced it one of the most exciting and beautiful scenes he had ever beheld.

After an hour or so spent in amusing us with the pleasing reminiscences of his wild life in America, he expressed a wish to see my collection, and requested me to place it in a large hall in the Louvre, for the private views of the Royal Family; and also appointed a day and an hour when he would be glad to see the Ojibbeway Indians at St. Cloud, and desired me to accompany them.

From the Palace, my friend M. Gudin, at the request of the King, proceeded with me to Paris and to the Louvre, with his Majesty's command to M. de Caillaux, director of the Louvre, to prepare the Salle de Séance for the reception of my collection, which was ordered to be arranged in it. My return from thence to the Indians, with the information that they were to visit the King, created a pleasing excitement amongst them, and, as the reader can easily imagine, great joy and rejoicing.

This was an excitement and a piece of good news to the poor fellows that could not be passed over without some signal and unusual notice, and the result was, that a *dog-feast* was to be the ceremony for the next day. Consequently a dog was procured at an early hour, and, according to the custom of their country, was roasted whole, and, when ready, was partaken of with a due observance of all the forms used in their own country on such occasions, it being strictly a religious ceremony.

The same indulgence in seeing the sights of Paris, and of exercise in the open air, was shown to them as to the other party; and the same carriages contracted for, to give them their daily drives; in all of which they were accompanied by their guardian, to whom the sights of Paris were also new and equally entertaining, and they all made the best use of their time in these amusements.

Their good friend M. Gudin appointed another day for the whole party to dine at his house, and having a number of distinguished guests at his table, the scene was a very brilliant and merry one. The orator of the party was the chief *Maun-gua-daus*, though on this occasion the War-chief, whose name was *Say-say-gon* (the Hail-storm), arose at the table and addressed M. Gudin and his lady in a very affectionate manner; thanking them for their kindness to them, who were strangers in Paris and a great way from their homes, and at the same time proposing to give to his friend M. Gudin a new name, saying that, whenever the Indians made a new friend whom they loved very much, they liked to call him by a name that had some meaning to it, and he should hereafter call him by the name of *Ken-ne-wab-a-min* (the Sun that guides us through the Wilderness).

There were several gentlemen of high rank and titles present, and all seemed much entertained with the appearance and conduct of the Indians.

CHAPTER XXIX.

Indians' visit to the Palace of St. Cloud—The Park—Artificial lake—Royal Family—Prince de Joinville—Recollected seeing the Author and Collection in Washington—King and Queen of Belgians—The *regatta*—The birch-bark canoe and the Prince de Joinville's "Whitehaller"—War-dance—Ball-play—Archery—Dinner prepared for the Indians—M. Gudin and the Author join them—Indians' return—Gossip at night—Their ideas of the King and Royal Family—Messenger from the King, with gold and silver medals and money, to the Indians—The War-chief cures a cancer—Author's Collection in the *Salle de Séance*, in the Louvre—The Indians and the Author dine with M. Passy, Member of Deputies—Kind treatment by himself and lady—King visits the Collection in the Louvre—The Author explains his pictures—Persons present—An hour's visit—The King retires—Second visit of the King and Royal Family to the Collection—The Author's four little children presented to the King—His Majesty relates the anecdote of bleeding himself in America, and his visit to General Washington at Mount Vernon—His descent of the Ohio and Mississippi rivers, in a small boat, to New Orleans—Orders the Author to paint fifteen pictures for Versailles.

The day, which had arrived, for our visit to the King at St. Cloud, was a pleasant one, and, all the party being ready, we went off in good spirits; and on our arrival our carriages were driven into the Royal Park, and conducted to a lovely spot on the bank of an artificial lake, where there were a considerable number of persons attached to the Court already assembled to see the Indians; and in the lake, at their feet, a beautiful birch-bark canoe from their own tribe, belonging to the Duchess of Orleans, and by the side of it an elegant regatta-boat, belonging to the Prince de Joinville, with "*White Hall,*" in large letters, on her sides, showing that she was a native of New York.

The Indians had been told that they were to paddle one of their own canoes for the amusement of the Royal Family, but had not as yet dreamed that they were to contend for speed with a full-manned "*White-Haller,*" in a trial for speed, before two kings and two queens and all of the Royal Family.

Just learning this fact, and seeing the complement of men in blue jackets and tarpaulin hats, in readiness for the contest, they felt somewhat alarmed. However, I encouraged them on, and the appearance of the Royal Family and the King and Queen of the Belgians, in their carriages, at the next moment, changed the subject, and their alarms were apparently forgotten.

Their Majesties, and all of the two Royal Families, descended from their carriages, and, gathering around the Indians in a group, listened to each one's name as they were in turn presented. (*Plate No. 19.*)

Louis Phillipe, and also the King of the Belgians, conversed for some time with the chiefs, while her Majesty and the other ladies seemed more amused with the women, and the little pappoose, in its beautifully embroidered cradle, slung on its mother's back.

After this conversation and an examination of their costumes, weapons, &c., the targets were placed, and an exhibition of their skill in archery ensued. And after that, taking up their ball-sticks, "the ball was tossed," and they soon illustrated the surprising mode of catching and throwing the ball with their rackets or "ball-sticks."

This illustration being finished, they sounded the war-whoop, and brandished their shields and tomahawks and war-clubs in the war-dance, which their Majesties had expressed a desire to see. (*Plate No. 20.*)

Every member of the two Royal Families happened to be present, I was told, on this occasion—a very unusual occurrence; and all had descended from their carriages, and grouped in a beautiful lawn, to witness the wild sports of these sons of the forest. I was called upon at that moment to explain the meaning of the war-dance, war-song, war-whoop, &c., for doing which I received the thanks of all the party, which gave me peculiar satisfaction.

Nº. 19.

Nº· 20.

The King at this time announced to the chief that he wished to see how they paddled the birch canoe, that he had two American canoes, which they had put into the water; one was a canoe, he said, made of birch-bark by their own tribe, the Ojibbeways, and had belonged to his son, the Duke of Orleans; and the other, now belonging to the Prince de Joinville, was made in the city of New York; and he was anxious to be able to decide which could make the best canoe, the white men or the Indians.

The whole party now assembled on the shore, and the sailors and the Indians took their seats in their respective boats, with oars and paddles in hand, and the race soon took place. (*Plate No. 21.*) It was a very exciting scene, but it seemed to be regretted by all that the Indians were beaten, but which I think might not have been the case if they had put two in their canoe instead of four, sinking it so deep as to impede its progress; or if they had put two squaws into it instead of the men, as they are in the Indian country much superior to the men in paddling canoes.

N°. 21.

I had much conversation on this occasion with H.R.H. the Prince de Joinville relative to the Indian modes and his travels in America, when he recollected to have seen me and my collection in Washington city.

Whilst these amusements were thus going on, my friend M. Gudin had prepared his canvas and easel near the ground, where he was busily engaged in painting the group, and of which he made a charming picture for the King.

These curious and amusing scenes altogether lasted about two hours, after which their Majesties and all took leave, the King, the Queen, and the Duchess of Orleans successively thanking me for the interesting treat I had afforded them. Their carriages were then ordered to drive back empty, and all the royal party were seen strolling amidst the forest towards the Palace.

The Indians and ourselves were soon seated in our carriages, and, being driven to a wing of the palace, were informed that a feast was prepared for us, to which we were conducted, and soon found our good friend M. Gudin by our side, who took a seat and joined us in it. The healths of the King and the Queen and the little Count de Paris were drunk in the best of *chickabobboo*, and from that we returned, and all in good glee, to our quarters in the city.

The reader by this time knows that this interview afforded the Indians a rich subject for weeks of gossip in their leisure hours, and charged their minds with a burthen of impatience to know what communications there might yet be from the King, as they had heard that gold and silver medals and presents of other descriptions were sent to the Ioways after their interview.

They proceeded with their exhibitions, as usual, however, and on the second day after the interview there came a messenger from the King with medals of gold for the two chiefs, and silver ones for each of the others of the party, and also 500 francs in money, which was handed to the head chief, and, as in the former instances, equally divided amongst them.

This completed all their anxieties, and finished the grandest epoch of the poor fellows' lives, and of which they will be sure to make their boasts as long as they live, and give me some credit for bringing it about—their presentation to the Kings and Queens of France and Belgium.

A curious occurrence took place a few days after this, as I learned on inquiring the object for which two ladies and a gentleman were in daily attendance on the Indians, and occasionally taking the War-chief away for an hour or two in their carriage and bringing him back again. Daniel told me that the young lady, who was one of the party, had dreamed that *Say-say-gon* could cure a cancer on the face of her father, which had baffled all the skill of the medical faculty and was likely to terminate his life; and in consequence of her dream, the relatives and herself were calling on him to induce him to make the attempt, which he had engaged in, and in their daily drives with him they were taking him to the Garden of Plants and to various parts of the country, where he was searching for a particular kind of herb or root, with which he felt confident he could cure it.

These visits were continued for some weeks, and I was informed by Daniel and by the Indians that he succeeded in effecting the cure, and that they handsomely rewarded him for it.

About this time, my lease expiring, I closed my exhibition, removing my collection to the *Salle de Séance*, in the Louvre, where Daniel and I soon arranged it for the inspection of the King and Royal Family; and it being ready, I met his Majesty in it by appointment to explain its contents to him.

The King entered at the hour appointed, with four or five of his orderly officers about him, and, on casting his eyes around the room, his first exclamation was that of surprise at its unexpected extent and picturesque effect.

My friend M. Vattemare, and also another friend, Maj. Poore, from the United States, were by my side, and greatly amused and pleased with the remarks made by the King during the interview, relative to my paintings, and also to incidents of his life amongst the Indians of America during his exile. His Majesty soon recognised the picture of an Indian ball-play, and several other scenes he had witnessed on the American frontier, and repeatedly remarked that my paintings all had the strong impress of nature in them, and were executed with much spirit and effect. He seemed pleased and amused with the various Indian manufactures, and particularly with the beautiful Crow wigwam from the Rocky Mountains standing in the middle of the room, the door of which I opened for his Majesty to pass under.

After his visit of half an hour he retired, appointing another interview, telling me that the Queen must see the collection with him, and also commanding the director of the Louvre to admit my little children to his presence, having heard of their misfortune of losing their mother, for which he felt much sympathy.

At the time appointed, a few days after, I met his Majesty again, with a number of his illustrious friends, in my collection; and after he had taken them around the room awhile to describe familiar scenes which he had met there on his former visit, I continued to explain other paintings and Indian manufactures in the collection. (*Plate No. 22.*)

In the midst of our tour around the hall his Majesty met something that again reminded him of scenes he had witnessed in his rambling life in the backwoods of America, and he held us still for half an hour during his recitals of them. He described the mode in which he and his two brothers descended the Ohio and Mississippi rivers in an old Mackinaw boat which they purchased at Pittsburg, and in which they made their way amongst snags and sawyers and sandbars to the mouth of the Ohio, six hundred miles, and from that down the still more wild and dangerous current of the Mississippi, one thousand miles, to New Orleans, fifty-two years ago, when nearly the whole shores of these rivers, with their heavy forests, were in their native state, inhabited only by Indians and wild beasts. They lived upon the game and fish they could kill or purchase from the various tribes of Indians they visited along the banks, and slept sometimes in their leaking and rickety boat, or amongst the canebrake, and mosquitos, and alligators, and rattlesnakes on the shores.

I took the liberty to ask his Majesty on this occasion whether the story that has been current in the American prints "of an Indian bleeding him" was correct; to which he replied, "No, not exactly; it had been misunderstood. He had bled himself on one occasion in presence of some Indians and a number of country people, when he had been thrown out of his waggon, and carried, much injured, to a country inn; and the people around him, seeing the ease and success with which he did it, supposed him, of course, to be a physician; and when he had sufficiently recovered from his fall to be able to start on his tour again, the neighbours assembled around him and proposed that he should abandon his plan of going farther west; that if he would remain amongst them they would show him much better land than he would find by proceeding on, and they would also elect him county physician, which they stood much in need of, and in which capacity he would meet no opposition. He thanked them for their kindness, assuring them that he was not a physician, and also that he was not in search of lands, and, taking leave, drove off."

N⁰. 22.

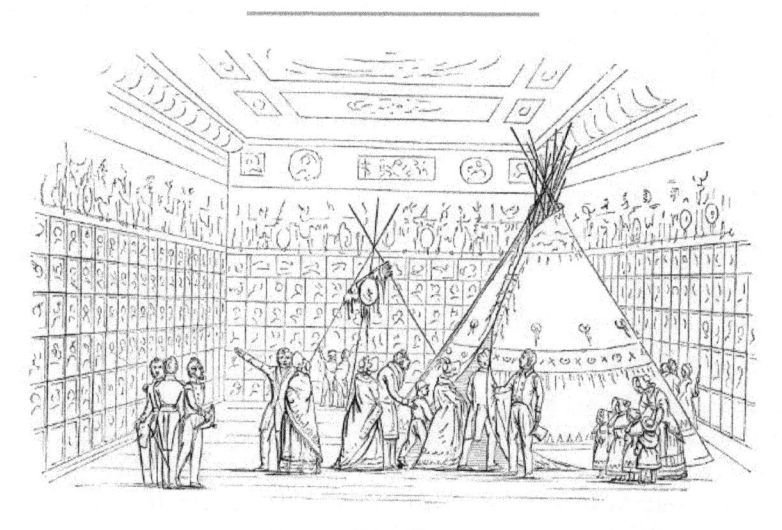

He also gave an account of their visit to General Washington at Mount Vernon, where they remained several days. General Washington gave them directions about the route to follow in the journey they were about to make across the Alleghany Mountains on horseback, and gave them also several letters of introduction to be made use of on their way.

While we were thus listening to the narrations of his Majesty, my kind and faithful nurse was approaching from the other end of the room and leading up my little children (*Plate No. 22*), whom he immediately recognised as my little family, and in the most kind and condescending manner took them by their hands and chatted with them in language and sentences suited to their age.

His next object was to designate the paintings he wished me to copy and somewhat enlarge, and soon pointed out the number of fifteen, which I was commanded to paint for the palace at Versailles.

During the time that my collection was thus remaining in the Louvre many distinguished persons about the Court had access to it, and amongst the number an excellent and kind lady, Madame Passy, the wife of one of the distinguished members of the House of Deputies. This charming lady sought an acquaintance with the Indians also, and, taking a deep interest in their character and situation, invited them all to dine at her house, where they were treated with genuine kindness and liberality, which they will never forget.

CHAPTER XXX.

The Author leaves his Collection in the Louvre, and arrives with the Indians in Bruxelles—Indians at the soirée of the American Minister in Bruxelles—Author's reception by the King in the Palace—Small-pox among the Indians—Indians unable to visit the Palace—Exhibition closes—Seven sick with small-pox—Death of one of them—His will—A second dies—His will—The rest recover—Faithful attentions of Daniel—The Author accompanies them to Antwerp, and pays their expenses to London on a steamer—Death of the War-chief in London—His will—The Author raises money by subscription and sends to them—Letter from the survivors, in England, to the Author—Drawings by the War-chief—The Author stopped in the streets of London and invited to see the skeleton of the War-chief!—His indignation—Subsequent deaths of four others of this party in England—The three parties of Indians in Europe—Their objects—Their success—Their conduct—Their reception and treatment—Things which they saw and learned—Estimates and statistics of civilized life which they have carried home—Their mode of reasoning from such premises—And the probable results.

During the time that my collection was exposed to the exclusive views of the Royal Family and their guests, the Indians were lying still, at my expense, which was by no means a trifling item. The young man whom I said they were under a contract with to pay them so much per month had performed his agreement with them for the two first months, and when the third month's wages became due he declared to them and to me that he could not pay them, nor pay their expenses back to London, as he was obligated to do. These duties then devolved on me, or at least, the Indians having been so long under my control and direction, I assumed them, and told the chiefs I would pay their expenses to London, and probably make something for them on the way, after my exhibition in the Louvre was finished.

They were thus lying idle at this time, waiting for me to be at liberty to go with them, and, as I have said, living at my expense. I told them that I designed going by the way of Belgium, and making their exhibitions in Bruxelles, Antwerp, and Ghent for a few weeks, the whole receipts of which, over the expenses, they should have, and I fully believed it would be sufficient to pay their expenses quite home to their own country; and that I would also, as I had promised, pay all their expenses from Paris to London myself.

With this design and with these views, leaving my collection in the Louvre, I started with the Indians for Bruxelles, where we arrived the next evening.

We were all delighted with the appearance of Bruxelles, and the Indians in fine glee, in the fresh recollections of the honours just paid them in Paris, and the golden prospect which they considered now lay before them. But little did they dream, poor fellows! of the different fate that there awaited them. While resting a few days, preparing for the commencement of their exhibitions, they were kindly invited, with the author, to attend the *soirée* of the American Minister, Mr. Clemson, where they were ushered into a brilliant and numerous crowd of distinguished and fashionable people, and seemed to be the lions of the evening, admired and complimented by all, and their way was thus paved for the commencement of their exhibitions. I had in the mean time made all the preparations and the necessary outlays for their operations, which they merely began upon, when it became necessary to suspend their exhibitions, owing to one of the number having been taken sick with the small-pox.

I had at this time an audience appointed with the King, at the Palace, where I went and was most kindly received and amused in half an hour's conversation with His Majesty about the condition and modes of the American Indians. He expressed the deepest sympathy for them and solicitude for their welfare and protection, and, a few days after my audience, transmitted to me, through one of his ministers, a beautiful gold medal, with an appropriate inscription on it.

The nature of the sickness that had now appeared amongst the Indians prevented the contemplated interview at the Palace, and also all communication with the public. It was still hoped by the physicians that a few days would remove all difficulty, but it was destined to be otherwise, for in a few days two others were attacked, and in a day or two more another and another, and at last they were in that pitiable and alarming state that seven of them were on their backs with that awful and (to them) most fatal of all diseases.

My position then, as the reader will perceive, was one of a most distressing and painful kind, with my natural sympathy for their race, and now with the whole responsibility for the expenses, lives, and welfare of these poor people on my shoulders, their only friend and protector in a foreign country, as their conductor had left them and returned to London, and my own life in imminent danger whilst I was attending on them.

One of these poor fellows died in the course of a few days in their rooms, another died in one of the hospitals to which he was removed, and a third died a few days after they reached London, though he was in good health when he travelled across the Channel.

Such were the melancholy results of this awful catastrophe, which the reader will easily see broke up all their plans of exhibitions in Belgium, and ended in the death of three of the finest men of the party.

Their sickness in Bruxelles detained me there near two months before the survivors were well enough to travel, during which gloomy time I had opportunity enough to test the fidelity of my man Daniel and his attachment to the Indians, who stayed by them night and day, fearless of his own danger, as he lifted them about in his arms in their loathsome condition both when dead and alive.

When the party were well enough to travel I went to Antwerp with them, and placed them on a steamer for London, having paid their fare and given them a little money to cover their first expenses when they should arrive there. I then took leave of them, and returned to my little family in Paris, having been absent near three months, with an expenditure of 350*l*.

With the poor fellows who died there seemed to be a presentiment with each, the moment he was broken out with the disease, that he was to die, and a very curious circumstance attended this conviction in each case.

The first one, when he found the disease was well identified on him, sat down upon the floor with the next one, his faithful and confiding friend, and, having very deliberately told him he was going to die, unlocked his little trunk, and spreading all his trinkets, money, &c., upon the floor, bequeathed them to his friends, making the other the sole executor of his will, intrusting them all to him, directing him to take them to his country and deliver them with his own hand. As he was intrusting these precious gifts, with his commands, to an Indian, he was certain, poor fellow! that they would be sacredly preserved and delivered, and he then locked his little trunk, and, having given to his friend the key, he turned to his bed, where he seemed composed and ready to die, because, he said, it was the will of the Great Spirit, and he didn't think that the Great Spirit would have selected him unless it was to better his condition in some way.

About the time of the death of this young man his confiding and faithful friend was discovered to be breaking out with the disease also, and, seeming to be under a similar conviction, he called *Say-say-gon* (the War-chief) to him, and, like the other, unlocked *his* little trunk, and, taking out his medal from the King, and other presents and money, he designated a similar distribution of them amongst his relatives; and trusting to the War-chief to execute his will, he locked his trunk, having taken the last look at his little hard-earned treasures, and, unlocking that of his deceased companion, and designating, as well as he could, the manner in which the verbal instructions had been left with him, gave the key to the War-chief, and begged of him to take charge of the trunk and the presents, and to see them bestowed according to the will of the testator. After this he turned away from his little worldly treasures, and suddenly lost all knowledge of them in the distress of the awful disease that soon terminated his existence.

The War-chief was one who escaped the disease in Bruxelles, and, being amongst those whom I took to Antwerp and sent by steamer to London, was at that time in good health and spirits; but letters which I received a few days after their arrival in London informed me that he was there attacked with the same disease, and, most singular to relate, as soon as he discovered the disease breaking out upon his skin, he said that he should die, and, calling the chief *Maun-gua-daus* to him, he, like the others, opened *his* trunk, and, willing his gold medal from the hand of Louis Philippe, to his little son, and his other trinkets and money to his wife and other relatives, intrusted the whole to the chief to execute. He then unlocked the trunks of his two friends who were dead, and, as well as he could recollect them, communicated to *Maun-gua-daus* the nature of the two bequests that had been intrusted to him, and died, leaving the chief to be the bearer of all the little effects they had earned, and sole executor of their three wills.

It is a fact which may be of interest to be made known, that all of this party had been vaccinated in their own country, and supposed themselves protected from the disease; and also that the only three full-blooded men of the party died. The other four who had the disease had it in a modified form, and, in all probability, with the three who died, the vaccine matter had not been properly communicated, or, what is more probable, and often the case in the exposed lives they lead, it had in some way been prevented from taking its usual effect.

After their misfortunes in Belgium and in London the excellent lady of the American Ambassador in Bruxelles raised, by a subscription, several hundred francs and sent to me in Paris, to which I got other additions in that city, and forwarded to them in England, to assist in paying their expenses back to their own country; and shortly after, and before they embarked for America, I received the following letter from them, which I feel it my duty to myself to insert here, lest any one should be led to believe that I did less than my duty to these unfortunate people:—

"To Geo. Catlin, Esq., now in Paris.

"*London, Jan. 27, 1846.*

"Our dear Friend,

"We send you our words on paper to let you know that we are thankful for your kindness to us. You have done everything to make us happy while with you in Paris and Belgium; and as all our people know in America that you are indeed their best friend, they will be glad to hear that you have taken us into your kind care whilst we were in a foreign land, and that while you were in a deep affliction with your own family.

MAUN-GUA-DAUS,
KE-CHE-US-SIN,
A-WUN-NE-WA-BE,
WAU-BUD-DICK,
UH-WUS-SIG-GEE-ZIGH-GOOK-KWAY."

The above letter was spontaneous on their part, and written in the hand of *Maun-gua-daus*, the chief, who spoke and wrote the English language very correctly.

I was much shocked and distressed to hear of the death of *Say-say-gon*, the War-chief, for he was a remarkably fine Indian, and had become much attached to me. His life, as a warrior and a hunter, had been one of an extraordinary nature, and the principal incidents of it, particularly in the hunting department, he had been for some weeks engaged, just before their disastrous sickness, in illustrating by a series of designs in his rude way, presenting me a portfolio of them, with the story of each, which I wrote down from his own lips as he narrated them.

This most amusing and original keepsake, which I shall treasure up as long as I live, and which I regret that the dimensions of this work did not allow me the space to insert, can at all times be seen by the curious of my friends who desire to see it.

For the amusement of the reader, however, I have made room for a couple of his drawings, which will convey some idea of their general character, and of the decided cleverness of this good fellow at story-telling and design. The woodcuts are traced from the originals, and are therefore as near fac-similes as I could make them. *Plate No. 23* represents *Pane-way-ee-tung*, the brother-in-law of *Say-say-gon*, crossing the river Thomas in a bark canoe, who had the following curious and amusing encounter with a bear which he met swimming in the middle of the river. Though the Indian had no other weapon than a paddle, he pursued the bear, and, overtaking it, struck it a blow, upon which it made an effort to climb into the canoe, by which the canoe was upset and the Indian sank under it. He arose to the surface, however, just behind the canoe, which in its progress had passed over him, and, being bottom upwards, the bear had climbed upon it, as seen in the sketch, and, having seen the man sink under it, was feeling under the canoe with his paws in hopes of getting hold of him. The bear, having made no calculation for the progress of the canoe, had not thought of looking behind it for his enemy, but balanced himself with difficulty without being able to look back; and whilst he was thus engaged feeling for his enemy under the canoe the Indian silently swam behind it, and, cautiously pushing it forward with his hand, succeeded in moving it near the shore, where he discovered his friend *Say-say-gon* hunting with his rifle, who was in waiting for it, and when near enough shot it in the head.

Plate No. 24 is his illustration of the first interview between white men and the Ojibbeway Indians; his description of it is as follows:—

> "*Gitch-ee-gaw-ga-osh* (the point that remains for ever), who died many snows since, and who was so old that he had smoked with three generations, said that his grandfather, *On-daig*, met the first white man who ever entered an Ojibbeway's wigwam. That white man was a great chief, who wore a red coat. He had many warriors with him, who all came in sight of the village of *On-daig* (the crow), and, leaving his warriors behind, he walked towards the wigwam of *On-daig*, who came out, with his pipe of peace in one hand, and his war-club in the other. *On-daig* offered his pipe to the white chief to smoke, who put his sword behind him in one hand, and raised his hat with the other. *On-daig* never had seen a white man's hat before, and, thinking the white chief was going to strike him with it, drew his war-club. They soon, however, understood each other, and smoked the pipe together."

Nº. 23.

N°. 24.

But a few months after the death of this fine Indian I was on a visit to London, and while walking in Piccadilly was accosted by an old acquaintance, who in our conversation informed me that the skeleton of my old friend the War-chief had been preserved, and he seemed to think it might be an interesting thing for me to see. The struggle between the ebullition of indignation and the quiescence of disgust rendered me for the moment almost unfit for a reply; and I withheld it for a moment, until the poor Indian's ideas of hyænas before described had time to run through my mind, and some other similar reflections, when I calmly replied, "I have no doubt but the skeleton is a subject of interest, but I shall not have time to see it."

My friend and I parted here, and I went on through Piccadilly, and I know not where, meditating on the virtues of scientific and mercenary man. I thought of the heroic *Osceola*, who was captured when he was disarmed and was bearing a white flag in his hand; who died a prisoner of war, and whose head was a few months afterwards offered for sale in the city of New York! I thought also of the thousands of Indian graves I had seen on the frontier thrown open by sacrilegious hands for the skulls and trinkets they enclosed, to which the retiring relatives were lurking back to take the last glance of, and to mingle their last tears over, with the horror of seeing the bones of their fathers and children strewed over the ground by hands too averse to labour and too ruthless to cover them again.

I was here forcibly struck with the fitness of Jim's remarks about the hyænas, of "their resemblance to *Chemokimons* or pale-faces," when I told him that they lived by digging up and devouring bodies that had been consigned to the grave.

I thought also of the distress of mind of the Little Wolf when he lost his child at Dundee—of his objections to bury it in a foreign land; and also of the double pang with which the fine fellow suffered when dire necessity compelled him to leave the body of his affectionate wife amidst the graves of the thousands whose limbs and bones were no curiosity. And I could thus appreciate the earnestness with which, in his last embrace of me in Paris, he desired me to drive every day in a cab, as he had been in the habit of doing, to the cemetery of Montmartre, to see that no one disturbed the grave of her whom he had loved, but was then to leave; and that I should urge his kind friend M. Vattemare to hasten the completion of the beautiful monument he was getting made, that it might be sure to be erected over her grave before she might be dug up.

With regard to the remainder of the party of Ojibbeways whom I have said I had advised to return as soon as possible to their own country, I am grieved to inform the reader that, from letters from several friends in England, I have learned that the chief has persisted in travelling through various parts of the kingdom, making his exhibitions of Indian life during the last year, and has had the singular and lamentable misfortune of burying three of his children and his wife! These, being facts, show a loss of seven out of twelve of that party, affording a shocking argument against the propriety of persons bringing Indians to Europe with a view to making their exhibitions a just or profitable speculation.

Three of the former party died while under my direction, as I have described in the foregoing pages; and a noble fine Indian, by the name of *Jock-o-sot*, of the Sac tribe, brought to England by a Mr. Wallace about the same time, was dying, and died on his way home, from causes he met in this country; making the melancholy list of eleven who lost their lives in the space of eighteen months.

These are facts which bring the reader's mind, as well as that of the author, to inquire what were the objects of these parties in England—how they came here—and what their success, as well as what will be the results that will probably flow from them. Each of these speculations has undoubtedly been projected by the white men who brought the Indians over, having conceived a plan of employing and taking to Europe such parties, who would be great curiosities in a foreign country, and by their exhibitions enabled to realise a great deal of money.

These parties, in each case, have been employed, and induced to come on condition of a certain sum of money to be paid them per month, or so much per year, to be given them on their return to their own country, with the additional advantage of having all their expenses borne, and themselves entitled to all the numerous presents they would receive during their travels.

As I have been with each of these parties the greater part of the time while they were making their exhibitions, I feel quite sure that this last condition of their engagements has been strictly kept with them, and that by it the Indians profited to a considerable amount from the kind and charitable hands of people whom they were amusing. But how far they have been benefited by the other conditions of their engagements, after they have returned to their homes, I am unable to tell.

As for their reception by the public generally where they have travelled, and their conduct whilst amongst and dealing with the world, it gives me great pleasure, as a living witness, to tender to that public my grateful acknowledgments for the kindness and friendship with which they received those unsophisticated people; and in justice to the Indians, as well as for the satisfaction of those who knew them, to acknowledge the perfect propriety of their conduct and dignity of deportment whilst they were abroad.

There were of the three parties thirty-five in all, and I am proud, for the character of the abused race which I am yet advocating, that, for the year and a half that I was daily and hourly in familiarity with them in Europe, I never discovered either of them intoxicated, or in a passion with one another, or with the world. They met the people, and all the wondrous and unaccountable works which their eyes were daily opened to in the enlightened world, with an evenness of temper and apparent ease and familiarity which surprised all who saw them.

Their conduct was uniformly decent and respectful, and through their whole tour, whilst abroad, they furnished a striking corroboration of two of the leading traits of their national character, which I have advanced in my former work, of their strict adherance to promises they make, and of their never-ending garrulity and anecdote when, in their little fireside circles, they are out of the embarrassing gaze of the enlightened world, who are wiser than themselves.

For these nightly gossips, which generally took place in their private apartments after the labours of the day were done and the pipe was lit, the excitements of the day, and the droll and marvellous things they had seen in their exhibition-room and in the streets of London and Paris, afforded them the endless themes; and of these little sittings I was almost an inseparable member, as will have been seen by many anecdotes entered in the pages which the reader has already passed over.

It will be pleasing therefore to the reader, at least to those who felt an interest in those poor people, to learn, that, though they might have been objects of concern and pity whilst making a show of themselves in this country, they were, nevertheless, happy, and in the height of amusements, philosophically enjoying life as they went along; and to those who know me, and feel any anxiety for my welfare, that, although I was aiding them in a mode of living to which I was always opposed, I was happy in their society, and also in the belief that I was rendering them an essential service, although my labours were much less successful as regarded my own pecuniary interest.

One of the leading inducements for Indians to enter into such enterprises, and the one which gains the consent of their friends and relations around them, and more particularly is advanced to the world as the plausible motive for taking Indians abroad, is that of enlightening them—of opening their eyes to the length and breadth of civilization, and all the inventions and improvements of enlightened society. These three parties (having met their old friend and advocate abroad, who has introduced them to the highest society of the world—has led them into three palaces, and from those down through every grade of society, and into almost every institution and factory of the continent—whose eyes and whose ears have been opened to most of the information and improvements of this enlightened age, and who have gone back to relate and to apply, in their own country, the knowledge they have gained) will furnish the best argument on record, for or against the propriety of bringing American Indians abroad, as the means of enlightening them and making them suitable teachers of civilization when they go back to the wilderness. And though the pages of this book cannot sum up the results of these visits, which can only be looked up ultimately in the respective tribes to which they have returned, yet a few words more upon the materials with which they have returned, and the author's opinion (in his familiar knowledge of the Indians' mode of reasoning) of their probable results, may not be obtrusive, as a sort of recapitulation of scenes and estimates, with their tendencies, made in the foregoing pages.

It is natural, or at least habitual, to suppose that, for the ignorant to learn is always to improve; and that what a savage people can learn amongst civilized society *must be* for their benefit. But in this view of the case, which would generally be correct, there arises a very fair question how far, for the benefit of the unenlightened parts of the world, it is judicious to acquaint them at a glance, with the whole glare of the lights and shades of civilized life, by opening the eyes of such parties to so many virtues and so many luxuries and refinements so far beyond the possibility of their acquiring, and at the same time to so many vices, to so much poverty and beggary not known in their simple modes of life, to teach to their people and to descant on when they get home; themselves as well as those whom they are teaching, despairing of ever attaining to what they have seen to admire and covet, and unwilling to descend to the degrading vices and poverty which they have seen mixed up in the mysterious and money-making medley of civilization.

If I startle the readers, let them reflect for a moment upon what perhaps some of them have never yet exactly appreciated—that a man, to know how his own house looks, must see how the houses of others appear. To know how his own city and country actually look, and how his countrymen act and live, he should see how cities and countries look, and how people act, in other parts of the world. If he will do this, and then leave all civilized countries a while, and the din and clatter, and the struggles for wealth amidst the rags and vices of the community he has lived in, and taste for a time the simple, silent life of the wilderness, he will find, on returning to his home, that he has been raised amongst a variety of vices and follies which he never before had duly appreciated, and will then realise, to a certain degree, the view which the savages take of the scenes in civilized life when they look into the strange medley of human existence in our great towns and cities, where all the contrasts are before their eyes, of rich and poor, equally struggling for wealth or the means of existence.

With such eyes were those wild people here to look; and without the cares and hourly and momentary concerns which lead the scrambling, busy world through and across the streets, blinded to what is about them, the poor but entirely independent Indians were daily and hourly scanning from the top of their buss, or the platform of their exhibition-rooms, the scenes, and manners, and expressions that were about them; and though they looked with unenlightened eyes, they saw and correctly appreciated many things in London and Paris which the eyes of Londoners and Parisians scarcely see. They saw their sights and got their estimates and statistics, and in the leisure of their inquisitive and abstracted minds drew deductions which few of the business world have leisure or inclination to make; and with all of these they have gone back to be the illustrators and teachers of civilization in the wilderness.

Each one will be a verbal chronicler, as long as he lives, of the events and scenes he witnessed while abroad, and *Wash-ka-mon-ya* (or Jim), with his smattering of civilization, and his book of entries, which he will find enough to read and translate, will furnish abundance of written evidence for them to comment upon to their nation, who will be looking to them for information of the secret of civilization.

The bazaar of toys and trinkets presented to them, with the money and medals which they will open to view in the wilderness, will glitter in the eyes of their people, and, it is to be feared, may be an inducement to others to follow their example. œ Their *Bibles* had increased in their various boxes since the last census to more than a hundred and fifty; their *religious tracts*, which they could not read, to some thousands; their *dolls*, in all, to fifty; and other useless toys, to a great number. Then came their *medals*, their *grosses of buttons*, their *beads, ribbons, brooches, fans, knives, daggers, combs, pistols, shawls, blankets, handkerchiefs, canes, umbrellas, beaver hats, caps, coats, bracelets, pins, eye-glasses,* &c. &c.; and then their prints—views of countries they had seen, of *churches, cathedrals*, *maps of London and Paris*, *views of bridges*, of *factories*, of *coal-pits*, of *catacombs*, of *Morgues*, &c. &c., to an almost countless number, all to be opened and commented upon, and then scattered, as the first indications of civilization, in the wilderness. These are but mere toys, however, but gewgaws that will be met as matters of course, and soon used up and lost sight of. But Jim's book of the statistics of London, of Paris, and New York, will stand the *Magna Charta* of his nation, and around it will assemble the wiseacres of the tribe, descanting on and seeking for a solution of the blessings of civilization, as the passing pipe sends off its curling fumes, to future ages, over its astounding and marvellous estimates of civilized *nations*, of *cities*, of *churches*, of *courts of justice*, and *gaols*—of the tens of thousands of civilized people who are in it recorded (to their amazement) as *blind*, as *deaf and dumb*, and *insane*; of *gallows* and *guillotines*, of *massacres* and *robberies*, the number of *grog-shops* and *breweries*, of *coal-pits*, of *tread-mills* and *foundling hospitals*, of *poorhouses* and *paupers*, of *beggars* and *starvation*, of *brothels*, of *prisons for debtors*, of *rapes*, of *bigamy*, of *taxation*, of *game-laws*, of *Christianity*, of *drunkenness*, of *national debt* and *repudiation*.

The estimates of all these subjects have gone to the wilderness, with what the eyes of the Indians saw of the poverty and distress of the civilized world, to be taught to the untaught, and hereafter to be arrayed, if they choose, against the teachings of civilization and Christianity in the Indian communities: a table of the enormous numbers in the civilized world who by their own folly or wickedness drag through lives of pain and misery, leaving their Indian critics, in the richness of their imaginations, to judge of the immense proportion of the enlightened world who, in just retribution, must perish for their crimes and their follies; and in their ignorance, and the violence of their prejudices, to imagine what proportion of them are actually indulged in the comforts of this life, or destined to enjoy the happiness of the world to come.

Teaching, I have always thought, should be gradual, and but one thing (or at most but few things) taught at a time. By all who know me and my views, I am known to be, as I am, an advocate of civilization; but of civilization, as it has generally been taught amongst the American Indians, I have a poor opinion; and of the plan I am now treating of, of sending parties to foreign countries to see all that can be seen and learned in civilized life, I have a still poorer opinion, being fully convinced that they learn too much for useful teachers in their own country. The strides that they thus take are too great and too sudden for the slow and gradual steps that can alone bring man from a savage to a civilized state. They require absolutely the reverse of what they will learn from such teachers. They should, with all their natural prejudices against civilized man, be held in ignorance of the actual crime, dissipation, and poverty that belong to the enlightened world, until the honest pioneer, in his simple life, with his plough and his hoe, can wile them into the mode of raising the necessaries of life, which are the first steps from savage to civil, and which they will only take when their prejudices against white men are broken down, which is most effectually done by teaching them the modes of raising their food and acquiring property. I therefore am constrained to give judgment here against the propriety of parties of Indians visiting foreign countries with a view to enlightening their people when they go back; and here also to register my opinion, for which I am daily asked, as to the effects which these visits to Europe will have upon the parties who have been abroad, and what impressions they will make amongst their people when they return.

I am sure they saw many things which pleased them and gained their highest admiration, and which they might be benefited by seeing; and also that they saw many others which it would have been decidedly better they had never seen. They have witnessed and appreciated the virtues and blessings, and at the same time the vices and miseries and degradations of civilized life, the latter of which will doubtless have made the deepest impressions upon their minds, and which (not unlike some *more distinguished travellers than themselves*) they will comment and enlarge upon, and about in equal justice to the nation they represent and are endeavouring to instruct.

Their tour of a year or two abroad, amidst the mazes and mysteries of civilized life, will rest in their minds like a romantic dream, not to be forgotten, nor to be dreamed over again; their lives too short to aspire to what they have seen to approve, and their own humble sphere in their native wilds so decidedly preferable to the parts of civilized life which they did not admire, that they will probably convert the little money they have made, and their medals and trinkets, into whisky and rum, and drown out, if possible, the puzzling enigma, which, with arguments, the poor fellows have found it more difficult to solve.

With this chapter I take leave of my Indian friends; and as the main subject of this work ends with their mission to Europe, the reader finds himself near the end of his task.

In taking leave of my red friends, I will be pardoned for repeating what I have before said, that on this side of the Atlantic they invariably did the best they could do; and that, loving them still as I have done, I shall continue to do for them and their race, all the justice that shall be in the power of my future strength to do.

CHAPTER XXXI.

The Author returns to his little children in Paris—His loss of time and money—The three Indian speculations—His efforts to promote the interests of the Indians, and the persons who brought them to Europe—His advice to other persons wishing to engage in similar enterprises—The Author retires to his atelier, and paints the fifteen pictures for the King—The pleasure of quiet and retirement with his four little children around him—He offers his Indian Collection to the American Government—And sends his memorial to Congress—Bill reported in favour of the purchase—The Author has an interview with the King in the Tuileries—Delivers the fifteen pictures—Subjects of the pictures painted—Conversations with the King—Reflections upon his extraordinary life—The Author's thoughts, while at his easel, upon scenes of his life gone by—And those that were about him, as he strolled, with his little children, through the streets and society of Paris—Distressing and alarming illness of the Author's four little children—Kindness of sympathizing friends—Death of "little George"—His remains sent to New York, and laid by the side of his mother—A father's tears and loneliness—The Author returns with his Collection to London.

The commencement of this chapter finds me at my easel, in a comfortable *atelier* in my own apartments in Paris, where I had retired, with my little children about me, to paint the fifteen pictures for the King, and others for which I had some standing orders.

My collection was at this time placed in a magazine in the vicinity of my dwelling, and my faithful man Daniel still continued his charge over it, keeping it in repair, and plying between it and my painting-room when I required models from my collection to work from.

The true measure of ordinary happiness I have long believed to be the amount of distress or anxiety we have escaped from; and in this instance I felt, retired from the constant anxieties I had lived under for the last six or seven years, demanding all my time, and holding my hand from my easel, as if I could be happy, even in my grief, with my four dear little children around me, whom their kind mother had but a few months before, in her dying breath, committed to my sole keeping and protection.

My house, though there was a gloom about it, had a melancholy charm from its associations, whilst its halls were enlivened by the notes of my little innocents, who were just old enough for my amusement, and too young fully to appreciate the loss they had sustained, and whose little arms were now concentrated about my neck, as the only one to whom they claimed kindred and looked for protection.

My dear little namesake, George, and my only boy, then three years and a half old, was my youngest, and, being the only one of my little flock to perpetuate my name, had adopted my painting-room as his constant playhouse, and, cronies as we had become there, our mutual enjoyment was as complete as my happiness was, in the dependence I was placing on him for the society of my future days. His first passion, like that of most children, had been for the drum, with which, slung upon his back, with drumsticks in hand, he made my *atelier* and apartments ring, and never was happier or more proud than when we addressed him as "Tambour Major," by which name he familiarly went, and to which he as promptly answered.

Besides the company of this dear little fellow, I had the sweet society of my three little girls, of ten, eight, and six years old, and with all, and the pleasures at my easel, I counted myself in the enjoyments of life that I would have been unwilling for any consideration to part with. I thus painted on, dividing my time between my easel, my little children, and the few friends I had in Paris, resolving and re-resolving to devote the remainder of my life to my art, being in possession of the fullest studies from nature to enable me to illustrate the early history of my country in its various dealings with the Indian tribes of America; and in these labours I also with pleasure resolved to continue my efforts to do justice to their character and their memory.

The American Congress was at that time in session, with a surplus revenue in the treasury of more than 12,000,000 of dollars; and, deeming it an auspicious time, I proposed the sale of my collection by my Memorial, to that body, believing there was sympathy enough for the poor Indians in my country, and disposition to preserve all the records of this dying race, to induce the Congress to purchase the collection as connected with the history of the country.

I had been stimulated, the whole time whilst making the collection, with the hope that it would be perpetuated on the soil where these ill-fated people have lived and perished; and was constantly encouraged in my labours with the belief that such would be the case.

On my Memorial, a Bill was reported by the Joint Committee on the Library, complimenting me in the strongest terms, and recommending its purchase; but, owing to the sudden commencement of the Mexican war at that time, no action was had upon it, and it now remains to be seen whether the Government will take it up again, or whether the collection will be left, because more highly appreciated, in a foreign land. My unavoidable belief still is, that some measure will be adopted for its preservation in my native country, a monument to those people who have bequeathed to the United States all her dominions, and who are rapidly wasting away; though I have fears that the call for it may be too late, either to gratify my ambition to see it perpetuated amongst the records of my country, or to enable me to feel the reward for my hard labour.

The Bill reported in the Congress I have taken the liberty to insert here, for the very high compliment it conveys, as well as for the benefit it may in some way afford me by the value therein set upon my works.

BILL reported in the AMERICAN CONGRESS, 1846, for the Purchase of CATLIN'S INDIAN GALLERY, July 24th, 1846. Read and laid upon the table. Mr. W. W. CAMPBELL, from the Joint Committee on the Library, made the following REPORT:—

The Joint Committee on the Library, to whom was referred the Memorial of Mr. Catlin for the purchase of his Gallery of Indian Collections and Paintings; and also the Memorial of American artists abroad, and of American citizens resident in London, respectfully report—

That of Mr. Catlin, who desires to place, on certain conditions, his extensive collection of Indian portraits, costumes, and other objects of interest connected with Indian life, in the possession of the Government, it is hardly necessary to speak, since his reputation is established throughout this country and Europe. A native of the state of Pennsylvania, his early studies were directed to the law, which, under an impulse of enthusiasm that often marks original genius, he soon abandoned for the pencil, stimulated by desire to give to his country exact and spirited representations of the persons, costumes, ceremonies, and homes of the aboriginal inhabitants of this continent, now retreating and gradually vanishing away before the power of civilization. Nor did he devote himself to his enterprises merely to gratify curiosity and preserve memorials of a bold, independent, and remarkable race of men, but to direct attention to certain lofty traits of their character, and excite, generally, friendly sentiments and efforts for their benefit. In making this collection, he expended eight entire years of his life and 20,000 dollars, and visited, often at great hazard of his personal safety, more than forty different (and most of them remote) tribes. Unaided by public or private patronage, he pursued and effected his object, sustained, as he observes, by the ambition of procuring a full and complete pictorial history of a numerous and interesting race of human beings rapidly sinking into oblivion, and encouraged by the belief that the collection would finally be appropriated and protected by the Government of his own country, as a monument to a race once sole proprietors of this country, but who will soon have yielded it up, and with it probably their existence also, to civilized man.

On Mr. Catlin's return from the western prairies, the attention of Congress was, in 1837 and 1838, turned towards his collection, and a resolution for its purchase was moved in the House, and referred to the

Committee on Indian Affairs, who, it is understood, expressed in their report an unanimous opinion in favour of the purchase, though the near approach of the close of the session prevented its being submitted for consideration.

In transferring his collection to Europe, Mr. Catlin had no intention of alienating it, or changing its nationality and destination; but, by its exhibition, sought to secure support for his family, and obtain means of bringing out his great and expensive work on the Indians—a work which has thrown much light upon their character and customs, and been received with distinguished favour on both sides of the Atlantic.

The judgment of our citizens, and that of eminent foreigners, is concurrent in regard to the value of this collection for the illustration of our history, and as a work of art. By desire of the King of France, it now occupies a gallery in the Louvre, and has been highly eulogized by the most distinguished artists and men of science in Paris. A large gold medal has been presented to Mr. Catlin by the King of the Belgians, with a letter expressing a high opinion of his productions.

The American artists now in Paris, in a memorial addressed to Congress, urging the importance of securing this collection to our country, say, "Having made ourselves acquainted with the extent and interest of this unique collection, and of its peculiar interest to our country; and also aware of the encouraging offers now made to its proprietor for its permanent establishment in England, as well as the desire generally manifested here to have it added to the historical gallery of Versailles, we have ventured to unite in the joint expression of our anxiety that the members of the present Congress may pass some resolution that may be the means of restoring so valuable a collection to our country, and fixing it among its records. Interesting to our countrymen generally, it is absolutely necessary to American artists. The Italian who wishes to portray the history of Rome finds remnants of her sons in the Vatican; the French artist can study the ancient Gauls in the museums of the Louvre; and the Tower of London is rich in the armour and weapons of the Saxon race.

"Your memorialists, therefore, most respectfully trust that Mr. Catlin's collection may be purchased and cherished by the Federal Government, as a nucleus for a national museum, where American artists may freely study that bold race who once held possession of our country, and who are so fast disappearing before the tide of civilization. Without such a collection, few of the glorious pages of our early history can be illustrated, while the use made of it here by French artists, in recording upon canvas the American discoveries of their countrymen in the last century, shows its importance."

Your Committee feel the justice of these sentiments of American artists, and also the importance, as suggested in their memorial, of securing, by the purchase of his collection, the future efforts of Mr. Catlin for its enlargement. Let the Government appropriate his collection, and the chief ambition of its author's life will be realized, and he will be enabled, in a few years, to double it in value and extent.

The bill which has recently passed the House for the establishment of the Smithsonian Institution provides that there shall belong to it a "gallery of art;" and of course it must be intended that such gallery shall be occupied by works of art. That such works should be principally American, is the obvious dictate of patriotism. No productions, your Committee believe, at present exist, more appropriate to this gallery than those of Mr. Catlin, or of equal importance. Should Congress fail to act on this subject, or decide unfavourably to Mr. Catlin's proposal, he may, notwithstanding his reluctance, be compelled to accept the positive and advantageous offers now made to him in England.

The love of art, and respect for those who have cultivated it with success, especially for those who have illustrated, by their productions, the history of their country, have ever been cherished by the most civilized nations. It has been justly observed, that "among the Greeks the arts were not so much objects to promote gratification as of public interest; they were employed as the most powerful stimulants of piety and patriotism, commissioned to confer distinction upon those who were conspicuous for valour, for wisdom, and for virtue. A statue or picture gave celebrity to a city or a state, and a great artist was considered a national ornament— a public benefactor, whom all were bound to honour and reward."

Your Committee believe the price of his collection, as named by Mr. Catlin, is moderate, and that a failure to obtain it would occasion deep regret to all the friends of art, and to all Americans who reasonably and justly desire to preserve memorials of the Indian race, or the means by which our future artists and historians may illustrate the great and most interesting events in the early periods and progress of our country.

The Committee, therefore, recommend that the bill for the establishment of the Smithsonian Institute be so amended as that provision shall be made therein for the purchase of Mr. Catlin's gallery at the price mentioned by him—namely, sixty-five thousand dollars—payable in annual instalments of ten thousand dollars.

New York Journal of Commerce, Nov. 12th.

When I had completed the pictures ordered by the King, his Majesty graciously granted me an audience in the Palace of the Tuileries to deliver them, on which occasion he met me with great cheerfulness, and, having received from me a verbal description of each picture, he complimented me on the spirit of their execution, and expressed the highest satisfaction with them, and desired me to attach to the back of each a full written description. The dimensions of these paintings were 30 by 36 inches, and the subjects as follow:—

No. 1.	An Indian ball-play.
2.	A Sioux Council of War.
3.	Buffalo-hunt on snow-shoes.
4.	*Mah-to-toh-pa* (the Four Bears), a Mandan chief, full length.
5.	A Buffalo-hunt, Sioux.
6.	Eagle-dance, and view of Ioway village.
7.	*Mah-to-he-ha* (the Old Bear), a medicine-man of the Mandans.
8.	*Wan-ee-ton*, one of the most distinguished chiefs of the Sioux.
9.	*Ee-ah-sa-pa* (the Black Rock), a Sioux chief, full length.
10.	*Mu-hu-shee-kaw* (the White Cloud), Ioway chief.
11.	*Shon-ta-ye-ee-ga* (the Little Wolf), an Ioway warrior.
12.	*Wa-tah-we-buck-a-nah* (the Commanding General), an Ioway boy.
13.	*Maun-gua-daus*, an Ojibbeway chief.
14.	*Say-say-gon* (the Hail Storm), an Ojibbeway warrior.
15.	*Ah-wun-ne-wa-be* (the Thunder-bird), Ojibbeway warrior.

His Majesty had on several occasions, in former interviews, spoken of the great interest of the scenes of the early history of the French colonies of America, and French explorations and discoveries in those regions, and the subject was now resumed again, as one of peculiar interest, affording some of the finest scenes for the pencil of the artist, which he thought I was peculiarly qualified to illustrate. Additional anecdotes of his rambling life in America were very humorously related; and after the interview I returned to my painting-room, and continued happily engaged at my other pictures, with my familiar sweet smiles and caresses about me.

As a painter often works at his easel with a double thought, one upon the subject he is creating upon the canvas, and the other upon the world that is about him, I kept constantly at work, and pleasantly divided my extra thoughts upon the amusing little tricks that were being played around me, and the contemplation of scenes and events of my life gone by. I ran over its table of contents in this way: "My native valley of Wyoming—the days and recollections of my earliest boyhood in it—my ten years in the valley of the *Oc-qua-go*, where I held alternately the plough, my rifle, and fishing-tackle—my five years at the classics—my siege with Blackstone and Coke upon Littleton—my three years' practice of the law in the Courts of Pennsylvania—the five years' practice of my art of portrait-painting in Philadelphia—my eight years spent amongst the Indian tribes of the prairies and Rocky Mountains—and, since that, my eight years spent in the light of the refined and civilized world, where I have been admitted to Palaces, and into the society of Kings, Queens, and Princes—and *now* at my easel, in my studio, with my dear little babes around me, thanking Him who has blessed me with them, and courage and health, through all the vicissitudes of my chequered life, and now with strength to stand by and support and protect them."

I thought also of the King, the wonderful man, with whose benignant and cheerful face I had been so often conversing; whose extraordinary life had been so much more chequered than my own; many of whose early days had been spent on the broad rivers and amongst the dense and gloomy forests of my own country; who, driven by political commotions from his native land, sought an asylum in the United States of America, and there, in the youthful energy of his native character, 52 years ago, crossed and re-crossed the Alleghany Mountains, descended the Ohio river 600 miles in his simple and rickety pirogue, and from the mouth of the Ohio to New Orleans, 1000 miles on the muddy waves of the Mississippi, amidst its dangerous snags and sand-bars, when the banks of those two mighty rivers were inhabited only by savages, whose humble wigwams he entered, and shared their hospitality; who afterwards visited the shores of Lake Erie, and also the Falls of Niagara, before the axe of sacrilegious man had shorn it of its wild and native beauties; who visited the little commencement of the town of Buffalo and the village of the Seneca Indians; who paddled his canoe 90 miles through the Seneca Lake to Ithaca, and from thence travelled by an Indian's path, with his knapsack on his back, to the Susquehana river, which he descended in an Indian canoe to Wyoming, my native valley; and then on foot, with his knapsack again upon his back, crossed the Wilkesbarre and Pokono Mountains to Easton and Philadelphia; and who consequently thus knew, 52 years ago, more of the great western regions of America, and of the modes of its people, than one of a thousand Americans do at the present day.

I contemplated the character of this extraordinary man, reared in the luxuries of Palaces, thrown thus into the midst of the vast and dreary forests of the Mississippi, launching his fragile boat and staking his life upon its dangerous waves, and laying his wearied limbs upon its damp and foggy banks at night, amidst the howling wolves and rattlesnakes and mosquitoes; and after that, and all these adventures, called, in the commotions of his country, to mount the throne and wield the sceptre over one of the greatest and most enlightened nations of the earth. I beheld this great man in these strange vicissitudes of life, and France, whose helm he took in the midst of a tempest, now raised to the zenith of her national wealth and glory, after 17 years of uninterrupted peace and prosperity. I contemplated the present wealth and health of that nation and her institutions, her grand internal improvements, and cultivation of science and the arts; and I reflected also, with equal pleasure and surprise, on what I had seen with my own eyes, the *greatness of soul* of that monarch as he was taking the poor Indians of the forest by the hand in his Palace, and expressing to them the gratitude he never yet had lost sight of, that he bore them for the kindness with which their tribes everywhere treated him when he entered their wigwams, hungry, on the banks of the Mississippi and the great lakes in America. He had the frankness and truthfulness to tell them that "he loved them," for the reasons he had given, and the kindness of heart to convince them of his sincerity in the way that carries the most satisfactory conviction to the mind of an Indian as well as it often does to that of a white man.

These contemplations were rapid and often repeated, and there were many more; and they never passed through my mind without compelling me to admire and revere the man whose energy of character and skill have enabled him, with like success, to steer his pirogue amidst the snags of the Mississippi, and at the helm of his nation, to guide her out of the tempest of a revolution, and onward, through a reign of peace and industry, to wealth and power, to which she never before has attained.

In the midst of such reflections I often strolled alone in a contemplative mood through the wilderness throngs of the Boulevards—the great central avenue and crossing-place—the *aorta* of all the circulating world—to gaze upon the endless throng of human beings sweeping by me, bent upon their peculiar avocations of business or of pleasure—of virtue or of vice; contrasting the glittering views about me with the quiet and humble scenes I had witnessed in various parts of my roaming life.

In the midst of this sweeping throng, knowing none and unknown, I found I could almost imagine myself in the desert wilderness, with as little to disturb the current of contemplative thoughts as if I were floating down the gliding current of the Missouri in my bark canoe, in silent contemplation of the rocks and forests on its banks.

In a different mood, also, I as often left my easel and mingled with the throng, with my little chattering children by my side, forgetting to think, and with eyes like theirs, scanned the thousands and tens of thousands of pretty things displayed in the shops, and whiled away in perfect bliss, as others do, an hour upon the pavements of the Boulevards.

The reader has learned, from various books, the features of this splendid scene, with all its life and din and glittering toys, and of Paris, with its endless mysteries, and beauties, and luxuries, and vices, which it is not the province of this work to describe; but from all that he has read he may not yet know how completely he may be lost sight of in the crowds of the Boulevards, and what positive retirement he may find and enjoy, unknowing and unknown, if he wishes to do so, in his apartments in the centre of Paris, where his neighbours are certainly the nearest and most numerous in the world.

In London and New York one often thinks it strange that he knows not his neighbours by the side of him; but in Paris, those on the *sides* are seldom taken into consideration as such, and so little do people know of, or care for, each other's business, that few have any acquaintance with their neighbours ABOVE and BELOW them.

The circumscribed limits of the city, and the density of its population, enable the Parisians to make a glittering display in the streets, in the brilliancy and taste of which they no doubt outdo any other people in the world. The close vicinity of its inhabitants, and the facility with which they get into the streets, and the tens of thousands of inducements that tempt them there, tend to the concentration of fashion and gaiety in the principal avenues and arcades, which, in the pleasant evenings of spring and summer, seem converted into splendid and brilliant salons, with the appearance of continuous and elegant soirées. To these scenes all Parisians and all foreigners are alike admitted, to see and enjoy the myriads of sights to be seen in the shop-windows, as well as to most of the splendid collections of works of literature and the arts, which, being under the Government control, are free to the inspection of all who wish to see them. Amidst most of these I have been, like thousands of others, a visitor and admirer for two years, seeking for information and amusement—for study and contemplation—alone; or enjoying them in company with my little children, or travelling friends, for whose aid and amusement I have as often given my time.

The reader will here see that I have before me the materials for another book, but as the object of this work is attained, and its limits approached, with my known aversion to travel over frequented ground, I must refer him to other pens than mine for what I might have written had I the room for it, and had it not been written twenty times before.

The little bit of my life thus spent in the capital of France, though filled with anxieties and grief, has had its pleasant parts, having seen much to instruct and amuse me, and having also met with, as in London, many warm friends, to whom I shall feel attached as long as I live. In the English society in Paris

I met a number of my London friends, where the acquaintance was renewed, with great kindness on their parts, and with much pleasure to myself.

I met also many American families residing in Paris; and, added to their numbers, the constant throng of Americans who are passing to and from the classic ground of the East, or making their way across the Atlantic to the French metropolis, and swelling their occasional overflowing and cheerful soirées. At these I saw many of the élite and fashionable of the French, and noticed also, and much to my regret, as well as surprise, that, in the various intercourse I had in different classes, the Americans generally mixed less with the English than the French society.

This is probably attributable in a great degree to the passion which English and Americans have, in their flying visits to the city of all novelties, to see and study something new, instead of spending their valuable time with people of their own family and language, whom and whose modes they can see at home. This I deem a pity; and though among the passing travellers the cause is easily applied, and the excuse as easily accepted, yet among the resident English and Americans, of whom there are a great many and fashionable families, there seems a mutual unsocial and studied reserve, which stands in the way of much enjoyment, that I believe lies at the doors of kindred people in a foreign land.

My time, however, was so much engrossed with anxieties and grief and my application to my art, that I shared but moderately in the pleasures of any society; and the few observations I have been able to make I have consequently drawn from less intercourse than has been had by many others, who have more fully described than I could do had this book been written for the purpose.

My interviews with society in this part of the world, as far as they have been held, have been general, and my observations, I believe, have been unbiassed. And as I mingled with society to see and enjoy, but not to describe, my remarks in this place, on the society and manners of Parisians and people in Paris, must end here, and necessarily be thus brief, to come within the bounds of my intentions in commencing this work.

The society which fascinated me most and called for all my idle hours was that of my four dear little children, whose arms, having been for ever torn from the embrace of an affectionate mother, were ready to cling to my neck whenever I quitted the toils of my painting-room. There was a charm in that little circle of society which all the fascinations of the fashionable world could never afford me, and I preferred the simple happiness that was thus sweetly spread around me to the amusements and arts of matured and fashionable life.

The days and nights and weeks and months of my life were passing on whilst my house rang with the constant notes of my little girls and my dear little "Tambour Major," producing a glow of happiness in my life, as its hours were thus carolled away, which I never before had attained to.

My happiness was here too complete to last long, and, as the sequel will show, like most precious gifts, was too confidently counted on to continue. A sudden change came over this pleasing dream of life; the cheering notes of my little companions were suddenly changed into groans, and my occupations at my easel were at an end. The chirping and chattering in the giddy maze of their little dances were finished, and, having taken to their beds, my occupation was changed to their bedsides, where they were all together writhing in the agonies of disease, and that of so serious a nature as to require all my attention by night and by day, and at length anxieties of the most painful kind, and alarm—of grief, and a broken heart! To those of my readers who have ever set their whole heart upon and identified their existence with that of a darling little boy, and wept for him, it is unnecessary—and to those who have never been blessed with such a gift it would be useless—for me to name the pangs that broke my heart for the fate of my little "Tambour Major," who, in that unlucky hour, thoughtlessly relinquishing all his little toys, laid down with his three little sisters, to run the chances with them, and then to be singled out as he was by the hand of death.

In kindness the reader will pardon these few words that flow in tears from the broken and burning heart of a fond father; they take but a line or two, and are the only monument that will be raised to the memory of my dear little George, who lived, in the sweetness of his innocence, to gladden and then to break the heart of his doating parent, the only one while he was living, to appreciate his loveliness, and now the only one to mourn for him. The remains of this dear little fellow were sent to New York, as a lovely flower to be planted by the grave of his mother, and thus were my pleasures and peace in Paris ended. Two idols of my heart had thus vanished from me there, leaving my breast with a *healing* and a *fresh wound*, to be opened and bleeding together. My *atelier* had lost all its charms; the *escalier* also was dreary, for its wonted echoing and enlivening notes had ceased; and the beautiful pavement of the Place Madeleine, which was under my windows, and the daily resort, with his hoop and his drum, of my little "Tambour Major."

The Boulevards also, and the Champs Elysées, and the garden of the Tuileries, the scenes of our daily enjoyment, were overcast with a gloom, and I left them all.

At the time of writing this my heart flies back and daily hovers about the scenes of so many endearing associations, while my hand is at work seeking amusement and forgetfulness at my easel. I have before said that the practice of my art is to be the principal ambition of the rest of my life; and as the beginning of this chapter found me in my *atelier* in Paris, the end of it leaves me in my *studio* at *No. 6, Waterloo Place*, in London, with my collection, my thousands of studies, and my little children about me where I shall be hereafter steadily seeking the rational pleasures and benefits I can draw from them; and where my friends and the world who value me or my works may find me without ceremony, and will be greeted, amongst the numerous and curious works in my collection, enumerated in the catalogue which I have given, for the amusement and benefit of the reader, at the end of my first volume.

APPENDIX. (A.)

The two following Letters, written from the Ioway Mission on the Upper Missouri, with several others more recently received by Mrs. A. Richardson, of Newcastle-on-Tyne, bear conclusive proof of the sincerity of the Society of Friends, and of the benefit that promises to flow from their well-directed and charitable exertions.

IOWAY INDIANS.

EXTRACT OF A LETTER FROM S. M. IRVIN.

Ioway and Sac Mission, May 24th, 1847.

Having a leisure morning, I most cheerfully give a few minutes to my dear friend in England. I have just been thinking, before I took my pen, how very mysterious are the workings of God's providence! Near four years ago, a party of our Ioway Indians started out on what appeared to us to be a wrong and uncalled-for expedition. We dreaded the result, and, so far as our opinion was consulted, it was given against the design, advising rather that they should stay at home, go to labour and economy, and not go to be shown as wild animals. In these notions we thought we were sustained by reason and Scripture, and were at least sincere in our views. We, however, made but little resistance, and when it was determined that they should go we submitted, did what we could for their comfort and success, gave them the parting hand, and commended them to the care of a merciful Providence. They started, spent the winter in St. Louis and New Orleans, associated with bad company, were exceedingly intemperate, and seemed to have grown much worse, which tended to confirm us in the belief of the error and impropriety of such a measure, and our hearts mourned over them. In the spring they went to the eastern part of the United States, and from thence to England. From the latter place we heard of the death of one and another, and of a probability of their going to France, and becoming enchained with the externals of the Catholic religion. Here we thought our opinions were fully confirmed. How can any good result from this? How much harm must ensue to these poor people, and probably through them to their nation!

But at this point a ray of light seemed to break forth, and we could see through the dark vista a possibility of good resulting from it. Hitherto we could only trust in the government of God, knowing that He would bring good out of evil, but we could not see by what process it could be accomplished. But we now began to learn that the people of England, particularly the Society of Friends, were taking a warm interest in their welfare, stimulating their minds in favour of industry, economy, and Christianity, and especially guarding them against the pernicious effects of ardent spirits. There the foundation of hope, on rational and tangible principles, commenced. Perhaps the friends of God and his cause in England were to be the honoured instruments of making an indelible impression on the minds of these poor wanderers, and, if so, how well will they be repaid for their pilgrimage, and how happily shall we be disappointed! Next came an affectionate letter from your own hand. This was the second development of the unseen but operating hand of God in carrying on his own work. A young man of ardent piety and devotion to the cause of God was next recommended as a suitable person to come and labour among the Indians as missionary from England. I may say that the whole mystery was now plain. We could now say to each other, God has taken them over to England to send a suitable missionary, whose labours will be, doubtless, blessed to their conversion, and thus we could see how easily God, our *covenant-keeping God*, can foil the designs of Satan. How our hearts did burn within us when we thought of the goodness of God in these things! The original design we could not but look upon as a work of the enemy, got up for the purpose of selfishness and speculation, but now we could see the scale turn, and the pleasing prospect of hailing our young brother as a fellow-helper in this cause more than reconciled us to the hitherto mysterious movement. He came, and, though it was found best under the circumstances to assign him for a time to a different field of labour, still it is the same common cause, whether among the Otoes or Ioways.

Very important pecuniary aid, both in money and clothing, was also subsequently received, from which our cause has, in no small degree, been aided and encouraged. Next a helpmate is proposed for our young friend, who is here alone, and toiling against the trials of a new and strange society and manners, and the prejudices of the Indians. God, through suitable instrumentality, conducts the negotiation to a favourable issue; the solitary individual is strengthened to part from her friends and country, is conducted by the hand of God across the dangerous deep, is brought more than 2000 miles, and, by a great variety of hazardous conveyances, almost to the centre of a great continent, and is now safely landed within the walls of this house. Truly may we exclaim, What hath God wrought! But the wonders and cause for gratitude stop not here. Our kind friend, Miss G., is not only here, but already is she engaged, twice or thrice a-day, in instructing the poor little daughters of the forest in needlework and such other instruction as may be suitable, and as yet I see nothing in the way but that she may very soon be able to give every moment of time that she can spare to these little ones. How pleasing will this be! How cheerfully and happily will the hours pass away, and how largely will she be rewarded for all her toil! I have skipped, as you will see, with more than eagle flight, over this narrative, for it furnishes materials enough for an interesting volume. I should like much to dwell upon it, but your mind can carry out the details, and see, as clearly as any other, the lineaments of God's goodness.

Miss G. will have so much to say to you, that I am sure she will not know where to commence, and I think she will be about as much puzzled to describe many things so that you can understand.

Mr. Bloohm has not yet arrived from the Otoe mission, but we look for him daily. So soon as I heard of Miss G.'s approach, I advised him of it, but he, being about fifty miles from the post-office, may not have received the letter. That you may better understand our relative situations, I will subjoin a rude outline of them with the pen.

Miss G. remained some time in St. Louis for Mr. Lowrie, and was afterwards instructed by him to come on to this place, he being prevented, by low water, from calling for her at St. Louis. Last Friday he passed up the Missouri river to the Otoe and Omahaw mission, leaving word that he would be back, at the farthest, by the end of this week. If Mr. Bloohm be able, he will come down with Mr. L., if not before him. As soon as they arrive, we hope to be able to make full arrangements about all our affairs, and you may expect to be informed of all that will interest you in due time.

EXTRACT OF A LETTER FROM JANE M. BLOOHM.

Ioway and Sac Mission, May 28th, 1847.

[After giving several interesting particulars of her journey from St. Louis, and arrival at the station, the writer proceeds:—]

I feel assured, my dear friend, you would be pleased with this institution. The boarding-house is a most excellent building, three stories high. On the ground floor are the dining-room, kitchen, pantry, milk-house, and two sleeping-rooms. On the second story, the chapel in the centre, from back to front, and on one side the boys' school in front, with two small rooms behind, which Mr. Hamilton occupies. On the other side of the chapel is the girls' school, with two small rooms behind it for Mr. Irvin. The third story has the girls' bedroom, back and front, with a small one off it parted with deals, where I sleep. The boys' on the other side is the same; in the middle is a spare bedroom and Mr. Irvin's study.

We rise at five o'clock, and at half-past assemble in the chapel for worship. While there, breakfast is placed on the table, and the bell rings again, when we go down. There are four tables, but not all full at present, as some of the children have left. Mr. Irvin sits at one table with the boys, Mr. Hamilton and his lady (when able) with the girls. Our table is called the family table; there are Mrs. Irvin, their father and mother, Mrs. I.'s two children, Mrs. H.'s eldest girl, the two men, and myself, as also any other strangers. Mr. Irvin's father and mother are two very old people; they intend leaving as soon as Mr. Lowrie comes, old Mr. I. not being able to manage the farm now. At breakfast each child has a pewter plate, with a tin pot turned upside down upon it, a knife and fork, and spoon. As soon as a blessing is asked, they each turn over their tin pot, and those who sit with them at table fill it with milk, and give them corn bread, boiled corn, batten cake (which is much like our pancake), a piece of bacon, and treacle. Of this they all eat as much as they like. Each table is served the same, with the exception that we have coffee for breakfast, and tea for supper. At dinner there is sometimes a little boiled rice, greens, &c., but no other kind of meat than bacon. We dine at half-past twelve, and sup at seven. After supper we all remain, and have worship in the dining-room; sometimes Mr. Hamilton prays and sings in Indian; and, oh! my beloved friend, could you only hear the sweet voices of those dear heathen children, you would be astonished, they sing so well. I do most sincerely hope that the day is not far distant when they shall not only worship Him with the voice, but with the understanding, and in truth.

Mr. H. teaches all the children from nine till twelve. After breakfast I take the girls up to make their beds; two and two sleep together; they did it so neatly this morning. When done, they go with me to school to sew or knit till nine, then again after dinner till two, and after five till supper-time, when I assist to wash their hands and faces, and put them to bed. Some of them are very fine children, but I am surprised I am able to go so near them, for they are very dirty; but they seem very fond of me. You will laugh when I say that two or three of them often come running to me, and clasp me round the waist. They wish to teach me to speak their language; they can say a good many English words; they call their teachers father and mother. A few of them are very little. After I put on their nightcaps, and lift them into bed, they all repeat a prayer. You will be surprised when I say I do feel such an interest in them; I do wish these feelings may not only continue, but increase. I feel quite happy, and have never had the least feeling of regret at my coming out, and I trust I never shall.

Both Mr. and Mrs. Irvin are most desirous for us to remain here, but that will rest with Mr. Lowrie and P. B. I am willing to go wherever I am of most use. It is a most arduous and responsible office we each hold, from the little I have seen (and it is but little to what I shall see if the Lord spare me). We need the prayers of our dear friends. Oh! forget us not, you, our far distant and beloved friends; entreat our Heavenly Father to give us much of his Spirit, and to us help along. Your old friend *Little Wolf* came to see me. He said I might give his and his family's love to you. A few more came to welcome me; they are constantly coming about the house. I am just sent for to assist in the ironing, and have had to write this while the irons were heating. There is no mangle here. The children's clothes are washed and repaired every week.

May 31st.—Just as I finished the above on Friday afternoon, the arrival of two gentlemen was announced. They were Mr. Lowrie and my dear P. B. The latter is looking thin, but upon the whole is much better, as also much better than I expected to find him; as for colour, an Indian: but setting aside his Indian complexion, I was glad to see a known face, and to meet a beloved friend; and now, my dear friend, I can call him my beloved husband. The marriage took place on Saturday the 29th, at eight o'clock in the evening, by Mr. Hamilton, in Mr. Irvin's room. Old Mr. and Mrs. Irvin were there, Mr. and Mrs. Irvin junior, Mr. Lowrie, Mr. Melody (who had come to the mission on a visit), and one of the men, who had expressed a wish to be present. Mrs. H. was not strong enough to join us, which I did regret. Mr. Lowrie has settled for us to remain here, at least for some time; P. B. to assist Mr. H. with the boys and other labour, while I take the full charge of the girls. Oh! that we may each have strength to perform these our arduous duties. The old people leave in a few days, when we shall have their room, which is on the ground floor, close by the dining-room. We shall have to sit at table with the children, and should Mr. H. be from home or sick, at any time, we shall have the full charge. We have, one and all, made up our minds to assist each other when it is needful, and I do most sincerely pray that we may be enabled to labour together in the same spirit which was in Christ Jesus. It is His work, it is His cause; and we all, I trust, esteem our privilege great, that we, unworthy as we are, should be permitted to take part in this glorious work. Mr. Lowrie, I believe, intends leaving to-morrow; it will be three weeks before he can reach New York. Mr. Melody left this morning; he speaks highly of the kindness he received while in England, and, I believe, would very well like to pay a second visit. * * * * And now, dear friend, I think I have given you all the intelligence that it is in my power to send at the present time. It is likely that my dear husband may send a note, but he is much occupied, and, I believe, going to St. Joseph with Mr. Lowrie. He joins with me in kindest love to you and Mr. ———, not forgetting all our dear friends, to whom you will be so kind as to present it, and ever believe me to remain

Your most affectionate friend,
J. M. BLOOHM.

APPENDIX. (B.)

HORSE-TAMING:

Being an Account of the successful application, in two recent Experiments made in England, of the expeditious method of Taming Horses, as practised by the Red Indians of North America.—Communicated by ALEXANDER JOHN ELLIS, B.A., *of Trinity College, Cambridge, in 1842.*

EXTRACT.

The object of the following pages is two-fold: first, to extract the account of the North American Indian method of Horse-taming, as given by Mr. Catlin in his new work, entitled 'Letters and Notes on the Manners, Customs, and Condition of the North American Indians,' and to detail certain experiments which have been tried by the direction and in the presence of the Communicator; and, second, to urge gentlemen, farmers, stable-keepers, horse-trainers, horse-breakers, and all others who may be interested in the taming of horses, to try for themselves experiments similar to those here detailed, experiments which are exceedingly easy of trial, and will be found exceedingly important in result.

The following is a detail of the experiments witnessed and directed by the Communicator:—

During a visit in the North Riding of Yorkshire, the volumes of Mr. Catlin first fell under the Communicator's observation, and among other passages those just quoted struck him forcibly. Although he scarcely hesitated to comprehend the circumstances there detailed, under a well-known though much-disputed class of phenomena, he was nevertheless anxious to verify them by actual experiment before he attempted to theorize upon them. And he now prefers to give the naked facts to the public, and leave his readers to account for them after their own fashion. It so happened that, while staying with his brother-in-law, F. M., of M—— Park, the Communicator had the pleasure of meeting W. F. W., of B——, a great amateur in all matters relating to horses. In the course of conversation the Communicator mentioned what he had read about horse-taming, and the detail seemed to amuse them, although they evidently discredited the fact. The Communicator begged them to put the matter to the test of experiment, and M., who had in his stables a filly, not yet a year old, who had never been taken out since she had been removed from her dam, in the preceding November, agreed that he would try the experiment upon this filly. The Communicator made a note of the experiments on the very days on which they were tried, and he here gives the substance of what he then wrote down.

Experiment the First.

SUBJECT—*A Filly, not yet a year old, who had never been taken out of the stable since she had been removed from her dam in the preceding November.*

Friday, Feb. 11, 1842.—In the morning W. and M. brought the filly from the stable to the front of M.'s house. The filly was quite wild, and on being first taken out of the stable she bolted, and dragged W., who only held her by a short halter, through a heap of manure. W. changed the halter for a long training halter, which gave him such power over her that he was easily able to bring the little scared thing up to the front of the house. Both M. and W. seemed much amused, and laughingly asked E. (the Communicator) to instruct them in Catlin's method of taming horses. E. did so as well as he could, quoting only from memory. The experiment was not tried very satisfactorily, but rather under disadvantages. The filly was in the open air, many strangers about her, and both the experimenters were seeking rather amusement from the failure than knowledge from the success of their experiment. W. kept hold of the halter, and M., with considerable difficulty, for the filly was very restive and frightened, managed to cover her eyes. He had been smoking just before, and the smoke must have had some effect on his breath. When he covered her eyes, he *blew* into the nostrils, but afterwards, at E.'s request, he *breathed*; and, as he immediately told E., directly that he began to breathe, the filly, who had very much resisted having her eyes covered and had been very restive, "*stood perfectly still and trembled.*" From that time she became very tractable. W. also breathed into her nostrils, and she evidently enjoyed it, and kept putting up her nose to receive the breath. She was exceedingly tractable and well behaved, and very loth to start, however much provoked. The waving of a red handkerchief, and the presenting of a hat to her eyes, while the presenter made a noise inside it, hardly seemed to startle her at all.

Saturday, Feb. 12, 1842.—This morning the filly was again led out to show its behaviour, which was so good as to call forth both astonishment and praise. It was exceedingly tractable, and followed W. about with a loose halter. Attempts were made to frighten it. M. put on a long scarlet Italian cap, and E. flapped a large Spanish cloak during a violent wind before its eyes, and any well broken-in horse would have started much more than did this yearling.

Experiment the Second.

SUBJECT—*A Filly, three years old, coming four, and very obstinate; quite unbroken-in.*

Saturday, Feb. 12, 1842.—While the last experiments were being tried on the yearling, W. espied B., a farmer and tenant of M., with several men, at the distance of some fields, trying, most ineffectually, on the old system, to break-in a horse. W. proposed to go down and show him what effect had been produced on the yearling. The rest agreed, and W., M., and E. proceeded towards B., W. leading the yearling. On their way they had to lead her over a brook, which she passed after a little persuasion, *without force*. One of the fields through which she had to pass contained four horses, three of which trotted up and surrounded her, but she did not become in the least degree restive, or desirous of getting loose. When the party arrived at the spot, they found that B. and his men had tied their filly short up to a tree in the corner of a field, one side of which was walled, and the other hedged in. W. now delivered the yearling up to M., and proposed to B. to tame his horse after the new method, or (to use his own phrase) to "puff" it. B., who was aware of the character of his horse, anxiously warned W. not to approach it, cautioning him especially against the fore-feet, asserting that the horse would rear and strike him with the fore-feet, as it had "lamed" his own (B.'s) thigh just before they had come up. W. therefore proceeded very cautiously. He climbed the wall, and came at the horse through the tree, to the trunk of which he clung for some time, that he might secure a retreat in case of need. Immediately upon his touching the halter, the horse pranced about, and finally pulled away with a dogged and stubborn expression, which seemed to bid W. defiance. Taking advantage of this, W. leaned over as far as he could, clinging all the time to the tree with his right hand, and succeeded in breathing into one nostril, without, however, being able to blind the eyes. From that moment all became easy. W., who is very skilful in the management of a horse, coaxed it, and rubbed its face, and breathed from time to time into the nostrils, while the horse offered no resistance. In about ten minutes W. declared his conviction that the horse was subdued; and he then unfastened it, and, to the great and evident astonishment of B. (who had been trying all the morning in vain to gain a mastery over it), led it quietly away with a loose halter. Stopping in the middle of the field, with no one else near, W. quietly walked up to the horse, placed his arm over one eye and his hand over the other, and breathed into the nostrils. It was pleasing to observe how agreeable this operation appeared to the horse, who put up its nose continually to receive the "puff." In this manner W. led the horse through all the fields, in one of which were the four horses already mentioned, who had formerly been the companions of the one just tamed, and who surrounded it, without, however, making it in the least degree restive. At length W. and the horse reached the stable-yard, where they were joined by C. W. C. C., of S—— Hall, and J. B. son of B. the farmer. In the presence of these, M., and E., W. first examined the fore-feet, and then the hind-feet of the horse, who offered no resistance, but, while W. was examining the hind-feet, leant its neck round, and kept nosing W.'s back. He next buckled on a surcingle, and then a saddle, and finally bitted the horse with a rope. During the whole of these operations the horse did not offer the slightest resistance, nor did it flinch in the least degree. All who witnessed the transaction were astonished at the result obtained. The Communicator regrets only that he is not at liberty to publish the names at length. This experiment of bitting was the last that W. tried, since the nature of the country about M—— Park did not admit of ridings being tried with any prospect of safety. The whole experiment lasted about an hour. It should be mentioned that when J. B., to whom W. delivered up the horse, attempted to lead it away, it resisted; whereupon E. recommended J. B. to breathe into its nostrils. He did so, and the horse followed him easily. The next day, B., who is severe and obstinate, began at this horse in the old method, and belaboured it dreadfully, whereupon the horse very sensibly broke away. This result is important, since it shows that the spirit is subdued, not broken.

These are all the experiments which the Communicator has as yet had the opportunity of either witnessing or hearing the results of, but they are to him perfectly satisfactory; the more so, that Mr. W., who made the experiments, was himself perfectly ignorant of any process of the kind until informed of it at the actual time of making the experiment. It may be considered overhasty to publish these experiments in their present crude state, but the Communicator does so with a view to investigation. He will have no opportunity himself of making any experiments, as he is unacquainted with the treatment of horses, and neither owns any nor is likely to be thrown in the way of any unbroken colts. But the experiment is easy for any horse-owner, and would be best made in the stable, where the horse might easily be haltered down so as to offer no resistance. The method would, no doubt, be found efficacious for the subjugation and taming of vicious horses. The readers will, of course, have heard of the celebrated Irish horse-charmers. They never would communicate the secret, nor allow any one to be with them while they were in the stable taming the horse. It is agreed, however, that they approached the head. The Communicator feels sure that the method they employed was analogous to that contained in these pages. Persons have paid high prices for having their horses charmed; they have now an opportunity of charming horses themselves, at a very small expense of time and labour. Half an hour will suffice to subdue the most fiery steed— the wild horse of the prairies of North America.

The Communicator has no object but that of benefiting the public in the above communication. The method is not his own, nor has he the merit of having first published it; but he thinks that he is the first who has caused the experiment to be made in England, and the entire success of that experiment induces him to make the present communication, in the hope that he may benefit not only his countrymen by the publication of a simple, easy, and rapid method of performing what was formerly a long, tedious, and difficult process, but also the "puir beasties" themselves, by saving them from the pains and tortures of what is very aptly termed *"breaking*-in." Mr. Catlin, indeed, speaks of the horse's struggles being severe, but they were the struggles of a wild horse, just caught on a prairie, and not of the domestic animal quietly haltered in a stable. The process as now presented is one of great humanity to the horse, as well as ease and economy to the horse-owner. The only objections to it are its novelty and simplicity. Those who have strength of mind to act for themselves, and not to despise any means, however simple or apparently childish, will have cause to rejoice over the great results at which they will arrive. But the great watchword which the Communicator would impress upon his readers is, "Experiment!"

Magna est veritas et prævalebit.

A. J. E.

Note.—*The above experiments, which the Author has supposed might be interesting to some of his readers, have been even more successful than he would have anticipated, having always believed that to bring about the surprising compromise he has so often witnessed by exchanging breath, the animal should be a wild one, and in the last extremity of fear and exhaustion.*—THE AUTHOR.

THE END.

Footnotes

[1] Some allowance will be made for the freedom with which the Ioways occasionally speak of their predecessors, the Ojibbeways, as these two tribes have lived in a state of constant warfare from time immemorial.

[2] *Names of the Indians.*

1. Mew-hew-she-kaw (the white cloud), first chief of the nation.
2. Neu-mon-ya (the walking rain), war-chief.
3. Se-non-ti-yah (the blistered feet), the medicine man (or Doctor).
4. Wash-ka-mon-ya (the fast dancer).
5. Shon-ta-yi-ga (the little wolf).
6. No-ho-mun-ya (one who gives no attention), or Roman Nose.
7. Wa-ton-ye (the foremost man).
8. Wa-ta-we-buck-a-na (commanding general).

Women.

9. Ru-ton-ye-wee-ma (strutting pigeon), wife of White Cloud.
10. Ru-ton-wee-me (pigeon on the wing).
11. O-kee-wee-me (female bear that walks on the back of another).
12. Koon-za-ya-me (female war-eagle sailing).
13. Ta-pa-ta-me (wisdom), girl.
14. Corsair (pap-poose).

[3] KNOW ALL MEN BY THESE PRESENTS, That Shon-ta-yi-ga or the *Little Wolf*, an Ioway brave, is well entitled to be called a brave, from the fact of his having been engaged in many expeditions against the enemies of his tribe: in all such excursions he has, I am informed, universally behaved bravely. But especially is he entitled to the love and confidence of all men, whether white or red, on account of his humanity and daring conduct in arresting from the cruel nation of which he is a member, a party of *Omahaws*. On last Sabbath day he saved from the tomahawk and scalping-knife ten unoffending Omahaws: one of the party was decoyed out of sight and murdered; the other ten consisting of the well-known and much-loved chiefs Big Elk, Big Eyes, and Washkamonia, one squaw and six young men. This party was on a visit of friendship, by special invitation from the Ioways. When they arrived within ten miles of this post, they were seen and conversed with by the son in law of Neu-mon-ya, a chief of the Ioways, who undertook to bring the *tobacco* and *sticks* to the Ioway chiefs, as is a custom of Indians when on a begging expedition. This young man proved treacherous, and failed to deliver his message to his chiefs, and gave information of the approach of the Omahaws to a man who was preparing to go on a war party. He and two-thirds of the nation started out to murder

their visitors, and were only prevented by the timely assistance and interference of the Little Wolf, or Shon-ta-yi-ga, and one other Ioway, whose name is the Roman Nose.

This man (the Little Wolf) interfered, as he says, and doubtless he tells the truth, because he considered it treacherous and cowardly to strike a brother, after having invited them to visit their nation. Such treachery is rare indeed among the wildest North-American Indians, and never occurred with the Ioways before. I met him and Jeffrey, the Ioway interpreter, together with two other Ioways, guarding the Big Elk and his party on to my agency, in a short time after this occurrence took place.

I cannot close this communication without expressing my sincere thanks to the Little Wolf and his comrade for their good conduct; and I most respectfully beg leave to recommend them to the kind attention of their great father, the President of the United States, and all gentlemen to whom this paper may be shown.

W. P. RICHARDSON.

Great Nemahaw Sub-Agency, Oct. 23, 1843.

Office of Indian Affairs, St. Louis, Missouri, April 10, 1844.

SIR,

Permit me to introduce to you the bearer, No-ho-mun-ya (Roman Nose), an Ioway brave. Roman Nose, in company with Shon-ta-yi-ga, or Little Wolf, in October last defended and rescued from impending death by a party of his own nation, ten Omahaw Indians, consisting of four respected chiefs, braves, and squaws, under circumstances highly flattering to their bravery and humanity.

I would recommend that a medal be presented to No-ho-mun-ya (Roman Nose) as a testimonial of his meritorious conduct on the occasion referred to. Medals from the Government are highly esteemed by the Indians; and if bravery and humanity are merits in the Indian, then I think Roman Nose richly merits one. His character in every respect is good.

A notice by the Government of meritorious acts by the Indians has a happy tendency in making a favourable impression in reference to the act that may be the cause of the notice.

I have presented Little Wolf with a medal that was in the office. On receiving it, he very delicately replied, that "he deserved no credit for what he had done—that he had only done his duty, but was gratified that his conduct had merited the approbation of his nation and his father."

I have the honour to be, very respectfully, Sir,
Your obedient servant,
W. H. HARVEY, Sup. Ind. Aff.

To his Excellency John Tyler, President of the United States, Washington City.

I concur with Mr. Harvey in thinking this Indian Chief entitled for his bravery and humanity to a medal.

June 8, 1844.

J. TYLER, Presid. U. States, Washington City.

Medal delivered accordingly to Mr. Geo. H. C. Melody, for the Chief.

June 8, 1844.

J. HARTLEY CRAWFORD.

[4] The railway tunnel at Liverpool.

[5] The red willow, from the inner bark of which the Indians make their substitute for tobacco.

[6] A medicinal herb, the roots of which the Indians use as a cathartic medicine.

[7] The frightful war-whoop is sounded at the instant when Indians are rushing into battle, as the signal of attack. It is a shrill sounded note, on a high key, given out with a gradual swell, and shaken by a rapid vibration of the four fingers of the right hand over the mouth. This note is not allowed to be given in the Indian countries unless in battle, or in the war or other dances, where they are privileged to give it.

[8] The Approaching Dance is a spirited part of the *War Dance*, in which the dancers are by their gestures exhibiting the mode of advancing upon an enemy, by hunting out and following up the track, discovering the enemy, and preparing for the attack, &c., and the song for this dance runs thus:—

O-ta-pa!

I am creeping on your track,

Keep on your guard, O-ta-pa!

Or I will hop on your back,

I will hop on you, I will hop on you.

Stand back, my friends, I see them;

The enemies are here, I see them!

They are in a good place,

Don't move, I see them!

&c. &c. &c.

[9] WOLF SONG.—This amusing song, which I have since learned more of, and which I believe to be peculiar to the Ioways, seems to come strictly under the province of the *medicine* or *mystery* man. I will venture to say, that this ingenious adaptation will excite a smile, if not some degree of real amusement, as well as applause, whenever it is fairly heard and understood by an English audience. The occasion that calls for this song in the Ioway country is, when a party of young men who are preparing to start on a war excursion against their enemy (after having fatigued the whole village for several days with the war dance, making their boasts how they are going to slay their enemies, &c.) have retired to rest, at a late hour in the night, to start the next morning, at break of day, on their intended expedition. In the dead of that night, and after the vaunting war party have got into a sound sleep, the serenading party, to sing this song, made up of a number of young fellows who care at that time much less about taking scalps than they do for a little good fun, appear back of the wig-wams of these "*men of war*" and commence serenading them with this curious song, which they have ingeniously taken from the howling of a gang of wolves, and so admirably adapted it to music as to form it into a most amusing duet, quartet, or whatever it may be better termed; and with this song, with its barking and howling chorus, they are sure to annoy the party until they get up, light the fire, get out their tobacco, and other little luxuries they may have prepared for their excursion, which they will smoke and partake with them until daylight, if they last so long, when they will take leave of their morning friends who are for the "death," thanking them for their liberality and kindness in starting, wishing them a good night's sleep (when night comes again) and a successful campaign against their enemies.

[10] This peculiar dance is given to a stranger, or strangers, whom they are decided to welcome in their village; and out of respect to the person or persons to whom they are expressing this welcome, the musicians and all the spectators rise upon their feet while it is being danced.

The song is at first a lament for some friend, or friends, who are dead or gone away, and ends in a gay and lively and cheerful step, whilst they are announcing that the friend to whom they are addressing it is received into the place which has been left.

[11] This barbarous and exciting scene is the Indian mode of celebrating a victory, and is given fifteen nights in succession, when a war party returns from battle, having taken scalps from the heads of their enemies. Taking the scalp is practised by all the American tribes, and by them all very much in the same way, by cutting off a patch of the skin from a victim's head when killed in battle; and this piece of skin, with the hair on it, is the scalp, which is taken and preserved solely for a trophy, as the proof positive that its possessor has killed an enemy in battle, and this because they have no books of history or public records to refer to for the account of the battles of military men. The scalp dance is generally danced by torch light, at a late hour in the night; and, in all tribes, the women take a conspicuous part in it, by dancing in the circle with the men, holding up the scalps just brought from battle, attached to the top of a pole, or the handle of a lance.

A scalp, to be a genuine one, must have been taken from the head of an *enemy*, and that enemy *dead*. The living are sometimes scalped, but whenever it occurs, it is on a field of battle, amongst the wounded, and supposed to be dead, who sometimes survive, but with the signal disgrace of having lost a patch of the skin and hair from the top of their heads.

[12] The *Pipe of Peace* (or calumet) is a sacred pipe, so held by all the American tribes, and kept in possession of the chiefs, to be smoked only at times of peace-making. When the terms of a treaty have been agreed upon, this sacred pipe, the stem of which is ornamented with eagle's quills, is brought forward, and the solemn pledge to keep the peace is passed through the sacred stem by each chief and warrior drawing the smoke once through it. After this ceremony is over, the warriors of the two tribes unite in the dance, with the pipe of peace held in the left hand, and a she-she-quoi (or rattle) in the right.

[13] Geo. Catlin.

[14] Being a silent listener to these conversations, I took out my note book and wrote down the remarks here given, as they were translated by Jeffrey.

[15] Clergymen.

[16] The author.

[17] Though the old War-chief, who was their speaking oracle on the subject of religion, remained sad and contemplative, there was daily much conversation and levity amongst the rest of the party on the subject of the "six religions of white men," which they had discovered; and either Jim or the little "commanding general" (son of the War-chief), both of whom were busy with their pencils, left on the table for my portfolio the subjoined curious, but significant illustration of their ideas of white man's paradise, and the six different modes of getting to it. *Plate No.* 11 is a *fac simile* of this curious document, which the reader will appreciate on examination.

[18] This is, undoubtedly, the favourite and most manly and exciting game of the North American Indians, and often played by three or four hundred on a side, who venture their horses, robes, weapons, and even the very clothes upon their backs, on the issue of the game. For this beautiful game two byes or goals are established, at three or four hundred yards from each other, by erecting two poles in the ground for each, four or five feet apart, between which it is the strife of either party to force the ball (it having been thrown up at a point half-way between) by catching it in a little hoop, or racket, at the end of a stick, three feet in length, held in both hands as they run, throwing the ball an immense distance when they get it in the stick. This game is always played over an extensive prairie or meadow, and the confusion and laughable scrambles for the ball when it is falling, and often sought for by two or three hundred gathered to a focus, are curious and amusing beyond the reach of any description or painting.

[19] The polite Doctor often spoke of his admiration of this excellent lady and of her beautiful park, and expressed his regrets also that the day they spent there was so short; for while hunting for the ball which they had lost, it seemed he had strolled alone into her beautiful *Conservatoire*, where he said, "in just casting his eyes around, he thought there were roots that they had not yet been able to find in this country, and which they stood much in need of." He said "he believed from what he had seen when he was looking for the ball, though nobody had ever told him, that this lady was a great root-doctor."

[20] No Indian language in America affords the power of swearing, not being sufficiently rich and refined.

[21] The reverend gentleman.

[22] Mr. Catlin.

[23] One of the most violent causes of the Indian's hatred of white men is, that nearly every Indian grave is opened by them on the frontier for their skulls or for the weapons and trinkets buried with them.

[24] This unfortunate "friend of mine" called the next day, with a handkerchief tied over one eye, and one arm in a sling; and while we *happened* to be talking of their intended visit to some of the "hells," he took occasion to exclaim at once, "My good fellows, let me advise you, go and see everything else in London, but take especial care you don't go into any of those infernal regions, and get served as I have been, or ten times worse, for I was lucky that I didn't lose my life." "Then you have seen them?" said I. "Seen them? yes, I *saw*, till I was knocked down three or four times, and my pockets picked, after I paid out to those infernal demons fifteen pounds; so I lost about thirty pounds altogether, and have not been able to see since.

Nat B—n of New York was with me, and he got off much worse than I did; he was carried home for dead and hasn't been out of his room since. When I get a little better, my good fellows, I will give you a long account of what we saw, and I'll venture you never will want to risk your heads there." My friend here left us, and Jim and the Doctor had evidently changed their minds about going to see the "Hells of London."

[25] St Louis.

[26] The Royal Arms (the Lion and the Unicorn).

[27] It is worthy of remark, and due to these kind-hearted people, that I should here explain that this was by no means a solitary instance of their benevolence in Birmingham. Whenever they could get out upon the portico to look into the streets, they threw their pence to the poor; and during the time they were residing in London, we ascertained to a certainty that they gave away to poor Lascars and others in the streets, from their omnibus, many pounds sterling.

[28] *Bennett's Hill, near Birmingham, Nov. 1st, 1844.*

My dear Mr. Catlin,—I have seen the nobility of England at a birth-night ball in St. James's palace. I have seen the King and Queen move around the circle, stopping to speak to every individual, and I have wondered what they could have to say. I have seen the Prince of Wales (afterwards George the Fourth) open the ball with a minuet, and afterwards dance down a country dance; and I thought him a handsome young man, and a fine dancer. This was in the year 1780.

Yesterday, as you well know, for you brought them to visit me, I saw the fourteen Ioway Indians. I shook hands with each, and told them, through the interpreter, that red men were my friends. I looked at them, as they were seated in a half-circle in my drawing-room, immoveable as statues, and magnificently dressed in their own costume, with astonishment. I had never seen a spectacle so imposing. At my request, you presented them to me separately—first the men, and then the women and children—and I gave each a small present, for which they were so thankful. At parting, the War-chief stood before me and made a speech, thanking me for my kindness to them, which they should long recollect, and saying, "that, although we should meet no more in this world, yet he hoped the Great Spirit would make us meet in the next." The action of the chief was free and natural, and most graceful; far superior to anything I ever saw. Indeed, these people are the nobility of nature.

I am, my dear Sir, your very obliged and very respectful
CATHERINE HUTTON.

[29] Miss E. Fothergill.

[30] The Author.

[31] See in Appendix (A) to this volume Correspondence, &c., relative to Ioway Mission.

[32] The Tower.

[33] The reader is referred to the fervent breathing pages of a little periodical, entitled the 'Olive Branch,' for a most feeling and impressive account of the reception of this little child's remains, and its burial in their beautiful cemetery, by the Friends in Newcastle-on-Tyne.

[34] See English experiments in breaking horses by the Indian mode. Appendix B.

[35] Only to be appreciated by those who have seen the Dublin "cars."

[36] The Author.

[37] White man.

[38] An ingenious whistle made to imitate the chattering of the soaring eagle, and used in the eagle dance.

[39] See critical notices of the French Press, Appendix to vol. i. p. 239.

[40] The place they had escaped in the great village of the whites they had been told was a Hell. It had been explained to them, however, that there were several of those places in London, and that they were only *imitations* of hell, but they seemed to believe that these catacombs (as there were so many millions of the bones of Frenchmen gone into them) might be the real hell of the pale-faces, and it was best to run no risk.

[41] I learned from M. Vattemare, on his return, that the party were treated with great friendship by an American gentleman in Havre, Mr. Winslow, who invited them to dine at his house, and bestowed on them liberal presents. They embraced their old friend Bobasheela in their arms on the deck of their vessel, and he sailed for London as their vessel was under weigh for America. The rest of their history is for other historians, and my narrative will continue a little further on events in Paris.